Compendium of crochet techniques

300 tips, techniques and trade secrets

Jan Eaton

SEARCH PRESS

A QUARTO BOOK

First published in 2007 by Search Press Ltd
Paperback edition published in 2008 by
Search Press Ltd
Wellwood
North Farm Road
Tunbridge Wells
Kent TN2 3DR
United Kingdom

Reprinted 2009

ISBN: 978-1-84448-401-0

A catalogue record for this book is available from the British Library

Conceived, designed and produced by
Quarto Publishing plc
The Old Brewery
6 Blundell Street
London N7 9BH

QUAR: CRT

Project Editor: Anna Amari-Parker
Art Editor: Julie Joubinaux
Editor: Anna Amari-Parker
Designer: Jon Wainwright
Assistant Art Director: Caroline Guest
Illustrators: Emma Brownjohn and Kuo Kang Chen
Photographer: Phil Wilkins
Proofreader: Susan Niner Janes
Indexer: Diana LeCore

Art Director: Moira Clinch
Publisher: Paul Carslake

Manufactured by Modern Age Repro House Ltd, Hong Kong
Printed in China by 1010 Printing International Limited

10 9 8 7 6 5 4 3 2

Compendium of
crochet techniques

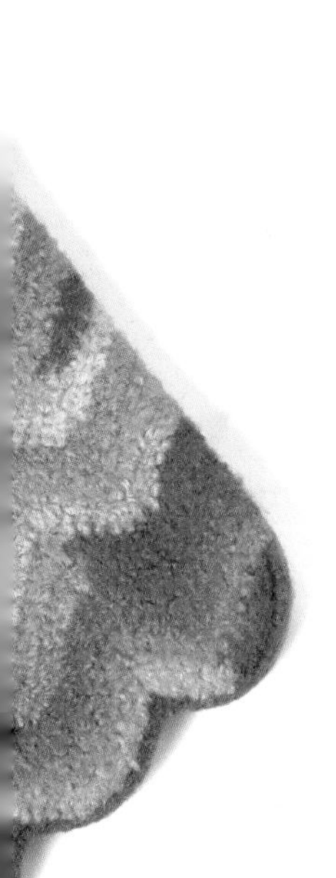

Contents

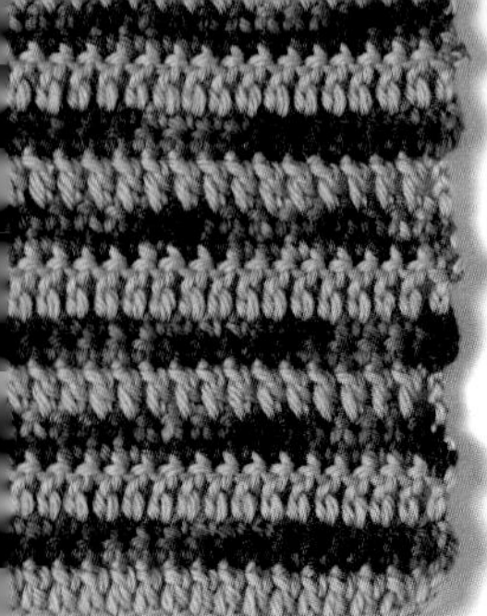

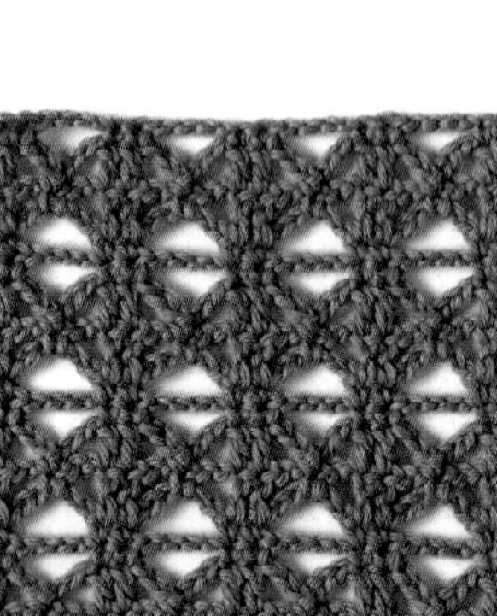
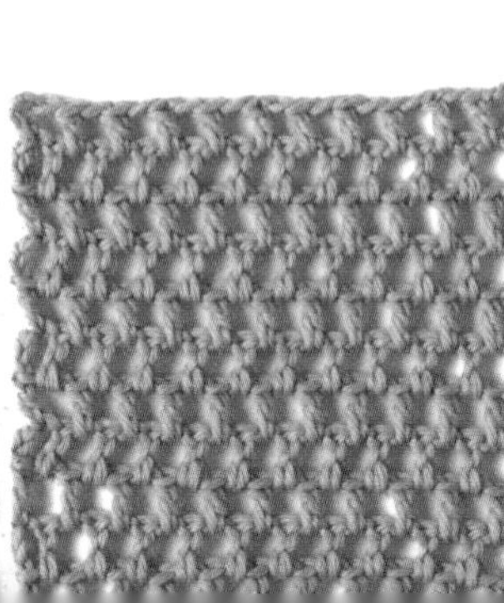

About this book

Aimed at all levels, this book shares over 300 expert fixes, tips and insider secrets that will enable any crafter to achieve great results every time. The information is organized by topic and divided into seven chapters.

Hooks, Tools and Yarns (pages 10–21)

This presents a complete overview on equipment, from the kinds of crochet hooks to the types of yarn available today. From classic to novelty yarns, it will show you how to substitute yarns and estimate the amounts required when working garments and accessories.

Patterns and Charts (pages 22–31)

Helps you to understand written patterns, symbol charts, mix-and-match stitch patterns, colourwork and filet crochet charts.

Design (pages 32–45)

Be guided through the process of creating your own garments, from working the first swatch and choosing a shape that is flattering for your body, to drawing up a schematic of the finished item.

Crochet Techniques (pages 46–105)

This part includes both basic and advanced crochet techniques – making a foundation chain, working complex and textured stitches, shaping crochet and working professional garment details such as pockets, neckbands, edgings, fastenings and trims.

Working in the Round (pages 106–25)

Learn how to produce flat crochet pieces in a variety of shapes, plus spirals, tubes, cylinders and socks and mittens.

Fun with Colour (pages 126–41)

Explore the world of colour, from making a yarn colour palette to adding stripes, colourwork patterns and embellishments to your work.

Assembling and Finishing (pages 142–151)

Find out about the practicalities of pressing, blocking and joining your pieces of crochet for a professional finish.

Resources (pages 152–157)

This contains size conversion charts for men, women and children, plus essential information on terminology, deciphering crochet abbreviations and symbols, as well as aftercare instructions.

Fix it panels: these regular companion features contain handy suggestions for repairing your work and avoiding common crochet pitfalls

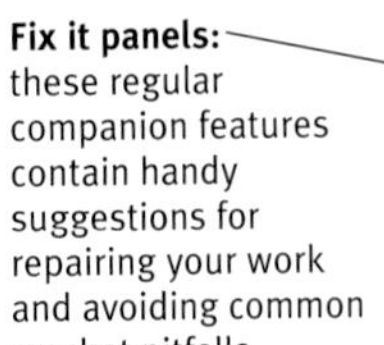

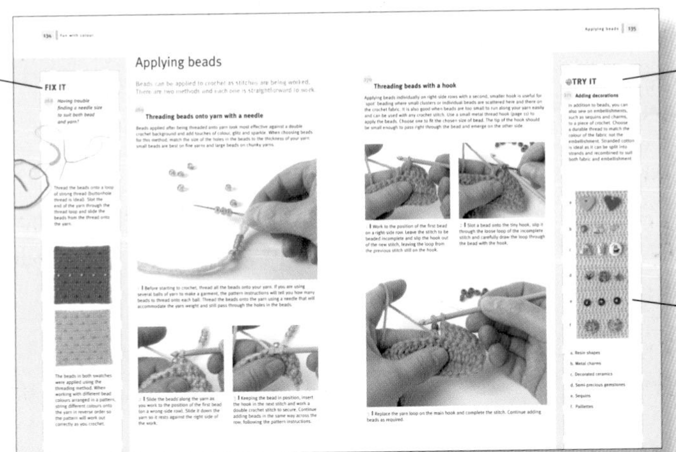

Try it panels: these regular companion features contain great ideas for experimenting with methods and materials, plus exciting projects for practising and developing new skills and techniques

Design ideas: dozens of suggestions for embellishments, from necklines and edgings to pockets and buttons

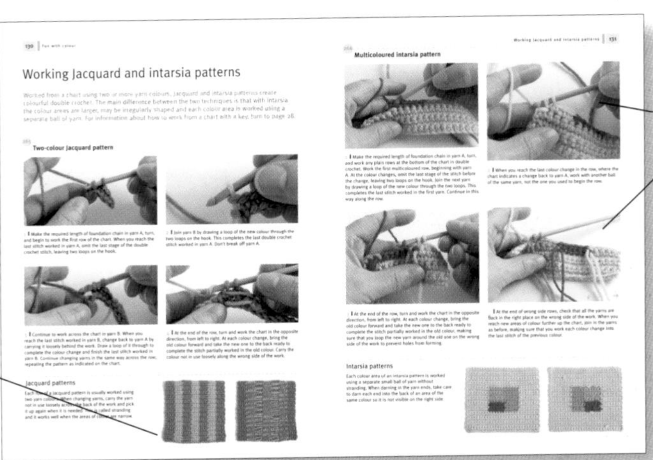

Step-by-step sequences: presented in logical order by the number of stages needed to work a given piece of crochet, these help you learn new skills and brush up on old ones

Completed swatch: a fully worked swatch shows you what the finished item will look like

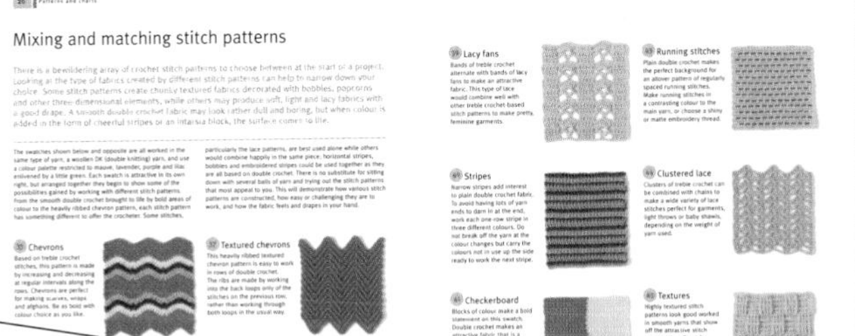

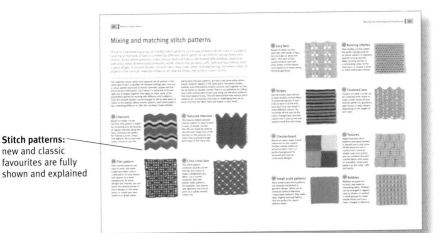

Stitch patterns: new and classic favourites are fully shown and explained

Resources: turn to this useful section for information about body measurements, garment sizes, crochet abbreviations, symbols, yarn information and aftercare instructions.

Fold-out flap: this interactive feature can be folded out and used to clarify the abbreviations used in the stitch patterns.

HOOKS, TOOLS AND YARNS

All you need to begin crochet is a hook and a ball of yarn. Hooks and yarns come in a huge range of sizes, weights and materials so it is a good idea to experiment with as many as you can until you find the ones you are most comfortable using. You will also need a few essential supplies such as large-headed pins, needles and scissors.

Choosing and holding a hook

The most important things to consider when choosing a hook are how the hook feels in your hand and the ease with which it works with your chosen yarn. Once you have discovered the perfect brand of hook, it is useful to buy a few different sizes so they are always on hand. You may need to buy hooks made from different materials to work with different types of yarn.

1

Basic hooks

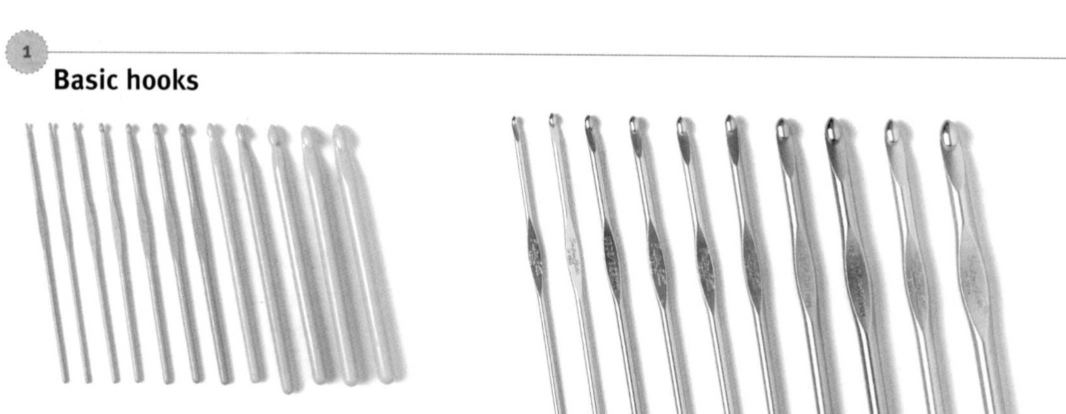

The most common type of hook is made from aluminium and comes in a wide range of sizes to suit different yarn weights. Larger sizes of basic hooks are often made out of plastic. Hooks come with either a rounded or cut-in throat and usually have a flattened grip or thumb rest. Many crocheters find a basic hook is the easiest type to use.

2

Anatomy of the hook

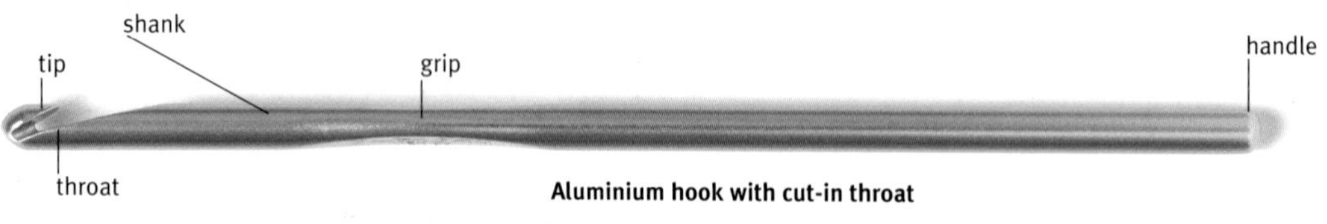

Aluminium hook with cut-in throat

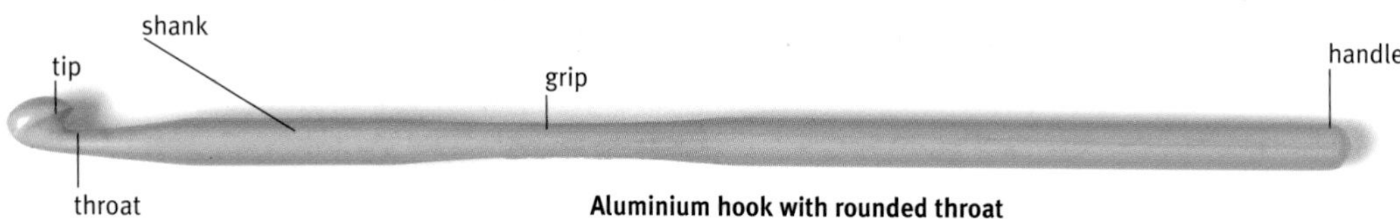

Aluminium hook with rounded throat

3 Plastic hooks

As well as being attractively coloured, hooks made from plastic are easy to use. They are slightly flexible and feel warm to the touch. Available with rounded or cut-in throats, depending on the brand, they come in a range of opaque or transparent colours, often with different colours denoting different sizes.

4 Wooden and bamboo hooks

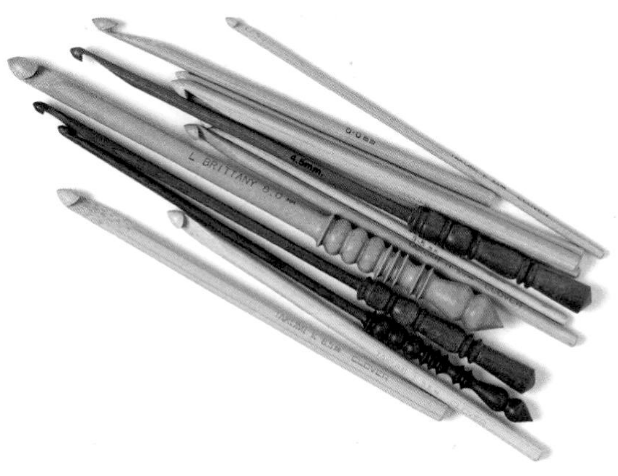

Bamboo hooks are made from fine-grained bamboo and are very light to hold. They are available in a restricted range of sizes, from 3.5 mm (size E) to 6 mm (K). Wooden hooks are handcrafted from a variety of different hardwoods and usually have decorative finials. They range upward from 3.5 mm (size E).

5 Steel hooks

Small-sized steel hooks are made for working crochet with fine cotton yarns (this type of fine work is often called thread crochet). They often have plastic handles to give a better grip, as the shanks are so narrow. Steel hooks are also useful for working bead crochet (page 134).

6 Japanese hooks

Japanese hooks are gold-coloured and slightly shorter than either American or European hooks. They are comfortable to use if you have small hands and come in a range of sizes, from 2.5 mm (C) to 6 mm (K). The same hooks are available with cushioned, wide plastic handles and an inset grip made from softer plastic. This type of handle makes the hook very easy to hold, especially for those with complaints such as arthritis. Japanese hooks can be bought individually or in a case containing a full set of sizes.

FIX IT

7 *Hook too long to fit comfortably in your hand?*

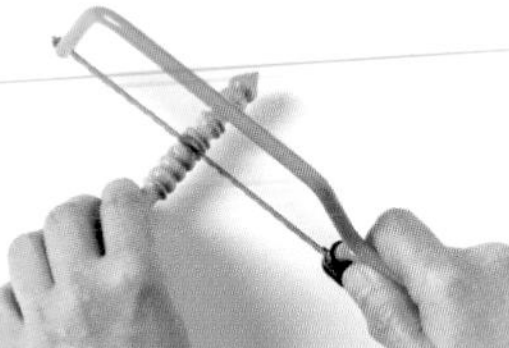

If it is made from wood or bamboo, shorten it with a hacksaw. Smooth off the edges of the cut with fine sandpaper.

8 *Hook too small to grip?*

To get a better grip on a small hook, wrap masking tape or duct tape around the handle to make it thicker. To make a really chunky grip, wrap a strip of foam around the handle, then the tape.

9 *Cannot use metal hooks?*

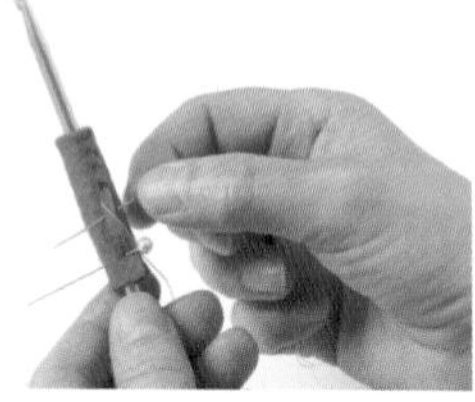

Metal hooks are hard, cold, and can be a problem on lengthy projects. To make a cushioned grip, wrap a strip of thick felt around the handle and secure with a row of oversewing.

Note for left-handed stitchers

10 When following the step-by-step photographs, hold a mirror up to the side of each picture, or read the book with a large mirror at the side. The photographs reflected in the mirror will show how to work left-handed.

11 Double-ended hooks

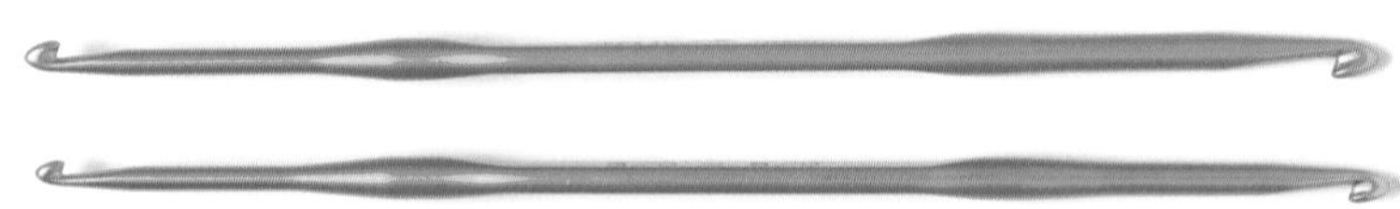

Double-ended hooks with a different size of hook at each end are useful additions to a hook collection, as are special hooks with easy-to-hold handles (previous page).

12 Holding a hook

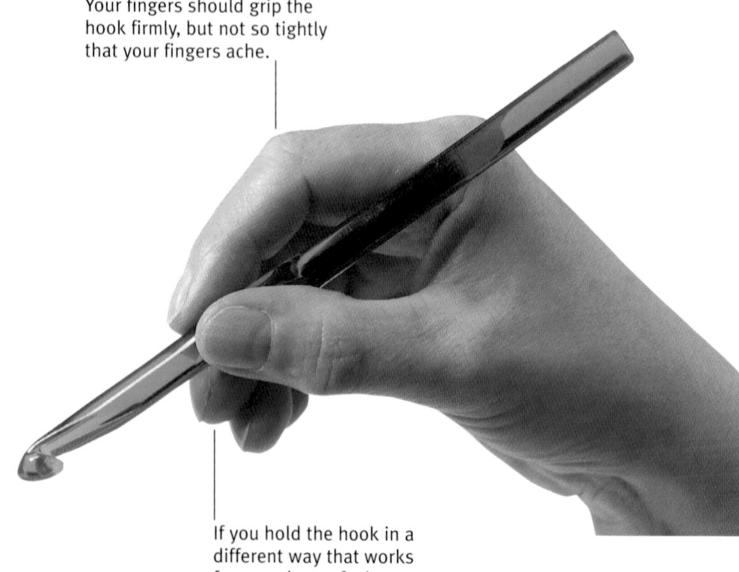

Your fingers should grip the hook firmly, but not so tightly that your fingers ache.
If you hold the hook in a different way that works for you, do not feel you have to change.

Most crocheters hold the hook as if it were a pen. Centre the tips of your right thumb and index finger over the grip (the flat section of the hook). When using a hook without a grip, hold it by the handle, gripping it a comfortable distance from the tip.

13 Hook sizes

Hooks made by different manufacturers or hooks made from different materials can vary in shape and size. To make matters more confusing, they may all be branded with the same letter or number system to indicate their size. The only way to be sure of a hook's size is to follow the millimetre measurements. When using a needle gauge to determine a hook's size, take care to measure the shank, not the tip or throat.

Although the hook sizes quoted in pattern instructions are a useful guide, you may find that you need to use a smaller or larger hook than suggested, depending on the brand of the hook used, to achieve the correct gauge for a particular pattern. Some brands offer a narrower range of hooks than others, so you may decide to use two or more brands of hook in the same project to get the size range you need.

Some hook sizes have no exact metric equivalent. Where this occurs, the nearest match in size is given.

Metric size	US size
2 mm	B
2.5 mm	C
3 mm	D
3.5 mm	E
4 mm	F
4.5 mm	G
5 mm	H
-	I
6 mm	K
7 mm	-
8 mm	L
9 mm	M
10 mm	N

2 mm/B

2.5 mm/C

3 mm/D

3.5 mm/E

4 mm/F

4.5 mm/G

5 mm/H

6 mm/K

7 mm

8 mm/L

9 mm/M

10 mm/N

Essential tool kit

As well as hooks, you will need a range of essential tools and equipment including pins, needles and scissors. A divided plastic box with snap-on lid keeps your tool kit organized and always to hand. A notebook and pencil are handy for jotting down measurements and pattern changes. While travelling, you may prefer to carry the equipment you need in a small, sturdy zipped pouch.

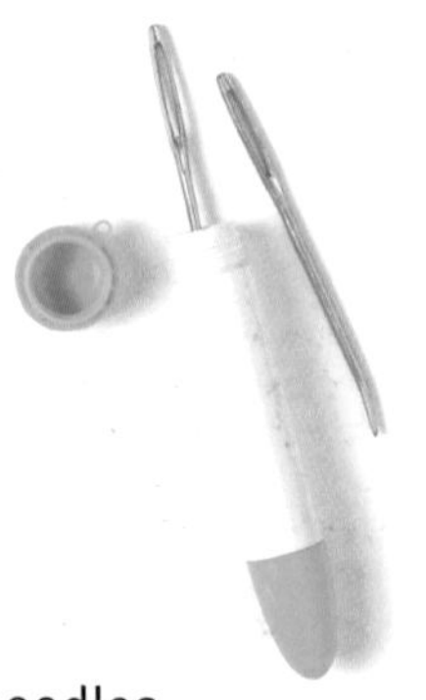

Yarn needles

Yarn needles have blunt points that may be straight or bent, and long eyes for easy threading. They come in a range of sizes and are used for darning in yarn ends and sewing pieces of crochet together.

Quilter's needle box

A flat box fitted with a magnetic sheet in the base is useful for holding an assortment of needles securely in place. They are available in different sizes; choose one large enough to hold chunky yarn needles.

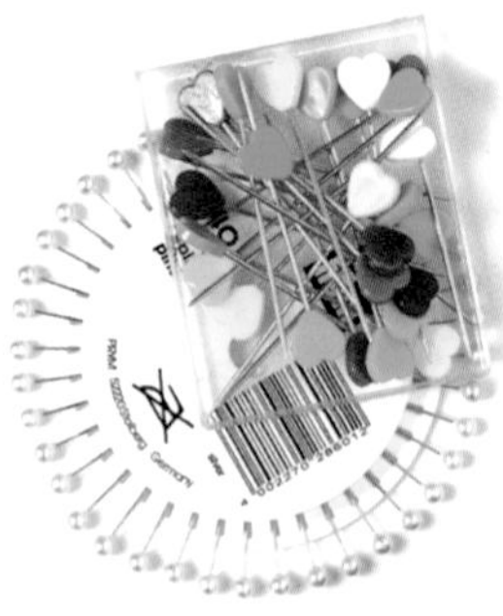

Knitter's plastic-headed pins

Pins with large plastic heads are good for pinning pieces of crochet together as the heads are easy to see and will not slip through the crochet fabric. Avoid this kind of pin when blocking as the plastic may melt.

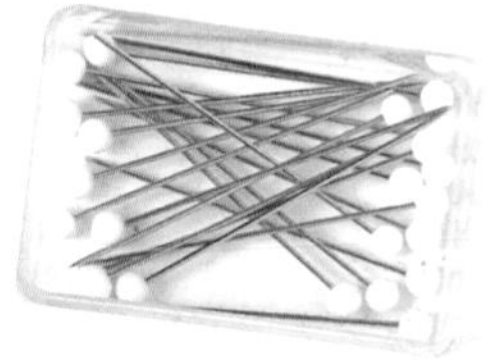

Glass-headed pins

Pins with round heads made out of glass are essential for blocking crochet as the heads will withstand the heat of your iron. Choose large pins with chunky heads in preference to the smaller type used in dressmaking.

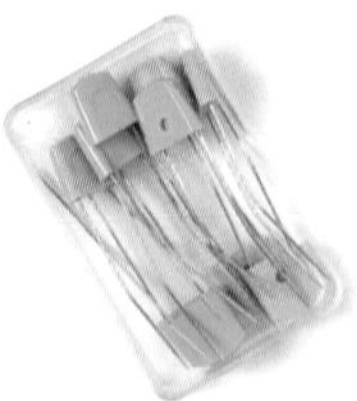

Forked blocking pins

Japanese pins with two shaped metal pins set in a plastic handle are good for blocking lace and pieces of lightweight crochet. Insert the pins so the plastic handle lies flat.

Knitting clips

Specially shaped plastic clips, originally designed as a knitting aid, are useful for holding pieces of crochet firmly together for seaming. Space several clips at regular intervals along a seam, removing them as you sew.

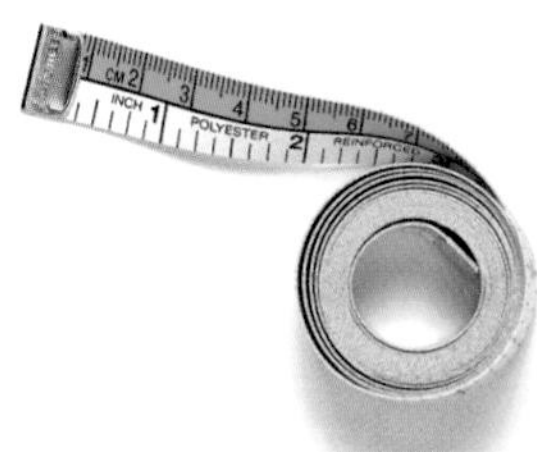

Tape measure

Choose a measure that shows both centimetres and inches on the same side so you can work from both European and American patterns. Replace the tape if it becomes worn or frayed as it will probably have stretched and become inaccurate.

Sharp scissors

Choose a small, pointed pair of scissors to cut yarn and trim off yarn ends. A folding pair of scissors is useful to carry when you are travelling. Alternatively, use a leather sheath to protect the points on an everyday pair.

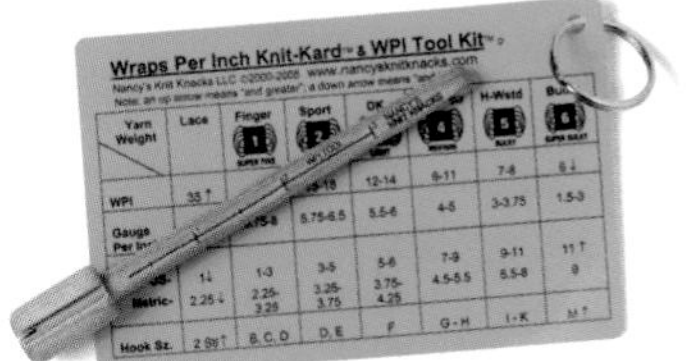

Wraps per inch tool

Originally used to determine the thickness of handspun yarn, this simple wooden tool is useful when comparing and substituting different yarns. Wind each yarn around the tool then count the number of wraps made over one inch. Compare the results to find matching yarn weights. The accompanying chart lists wraps per inch (WPI) for standard yarn weights.

Metal ruler

A short metal ruler is useful for measuring blocks and small items accurately. You will also need a metal yardstick to help you block large pieces of crochet such as shawls and wraps.

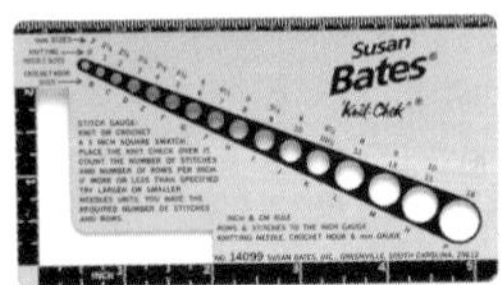

Size gauge

Use a size gauge to check the size of your hooks by slotting your hook though the different holes until you get a snug fit. It also includes a cm and inch rule, and a cut-out section for measuring stitch and row gauge.

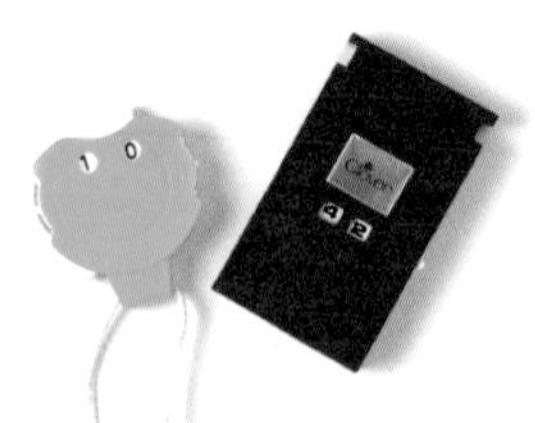

Row counter

Row counters keep track of how many rows you have worked. Simply click on the counter to record each row as it is completed. Use either a freestanding counter or one that hangs on a cord around your neck.

Stitch markers

Useful when counting stitches and rows, slide a split-ring marker directly onto a crochet stitch to mark your place. Locking stitch markers are similar to split-ring markers, but can be locked after placing on a stitch.

TRY IT

14 Making your own decorative markers

These are easy to make using beads and jewellery-making components. You will need headpins, seed beads, lightweight decorative beads and a lobster claw clasp.

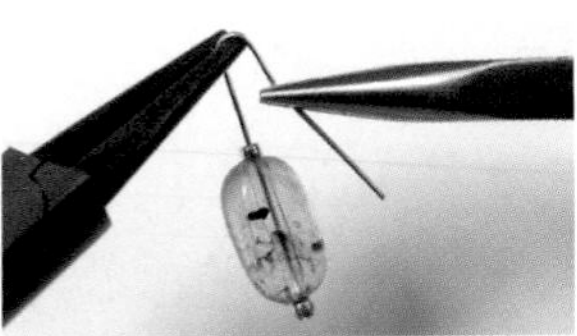

1 | Thread a seed bead, one large decorative bead and a final seed bead onto a headpin. Using round-nose pliers, hold the headpin a short distance above the beads and use the needle-nose pliers to bend the headpin to make a nice curve.

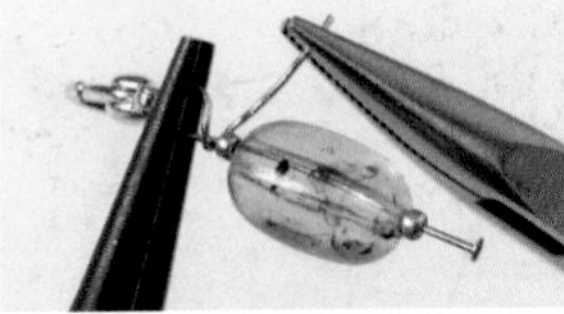

2 | Thread the clasp onto the headpin. Grip the headpin just below the clasp, and use the needle-nose pliers to wrap the end around the headpin to secure. Push beads down headpin, wrap once more.

3 | Use the side cutters to trim the surplus headpin. With the needle-nose pliers, squeeze the cut end of the headpin flat above the last seed bead to avoid snagging.

Looking after hooks

Store your hooks in a clean container such as a plastic or wooden box, or a zipped cosmetic bag. It is a good idea to store metal, wood and plastic hooks in separate compartments or bags to prevent metal hooks scuffing softer plastic or wooden hooks. If you look after your hooks, they will give you many years of crocheting.

15

Making a roll-up hook case

Make a colourful roll-up fabric case to house your hooks in style. Cotton dress-weight fabrics work best so you can be as bold as you like with pattern and colour. This case fits the shorter Japanese hooks. Make the case deeper to fit longer hooks.

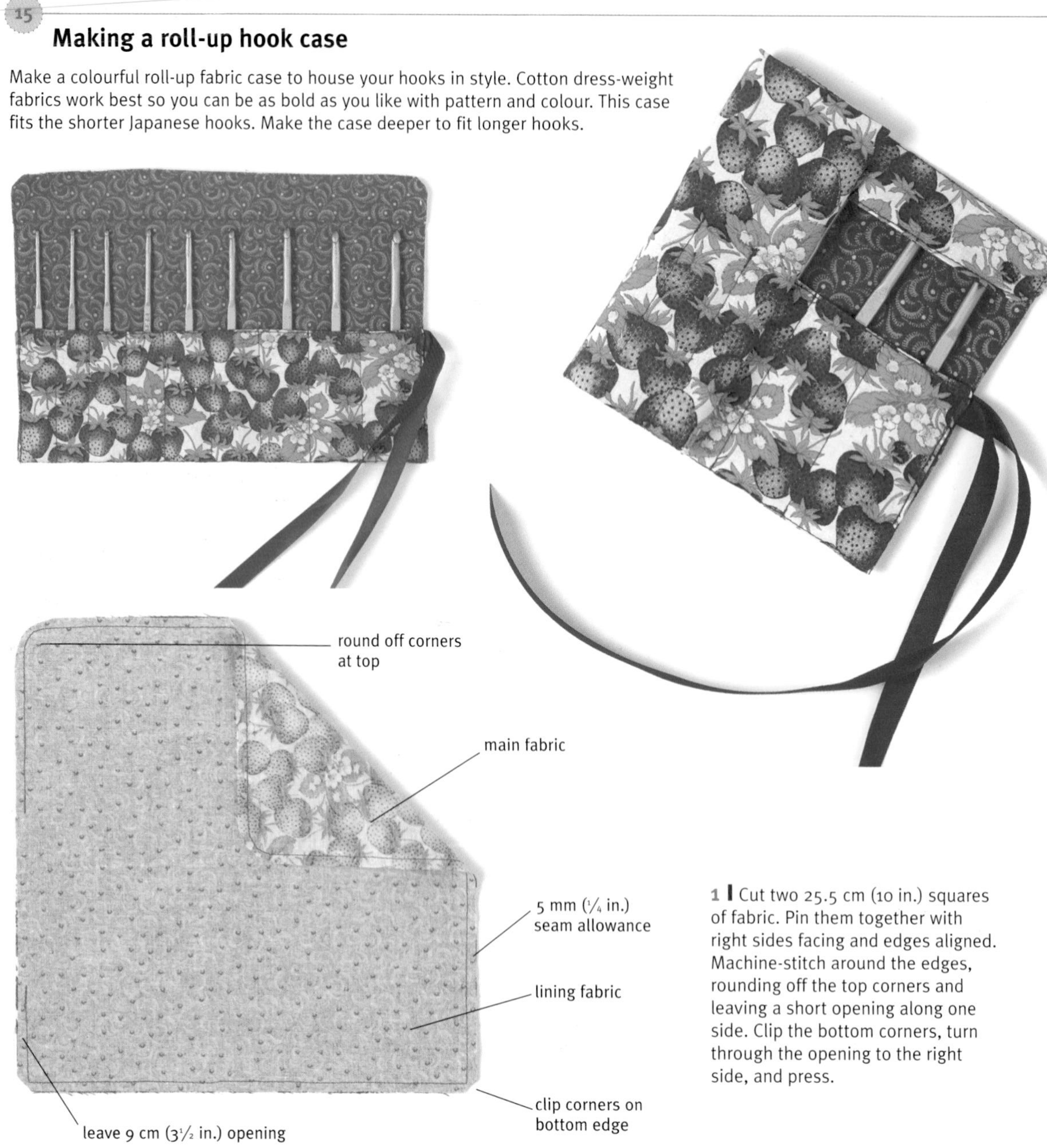

1 Cut two 25.5 cm (10 in.) squares of fabric. Pin them together with right sides facing and edges aligned. Machine-stitch around the edges, rounding off the top corners and leaving a short opening along one side. Clip the bottom corners, turn through the opening to the right side, and press.

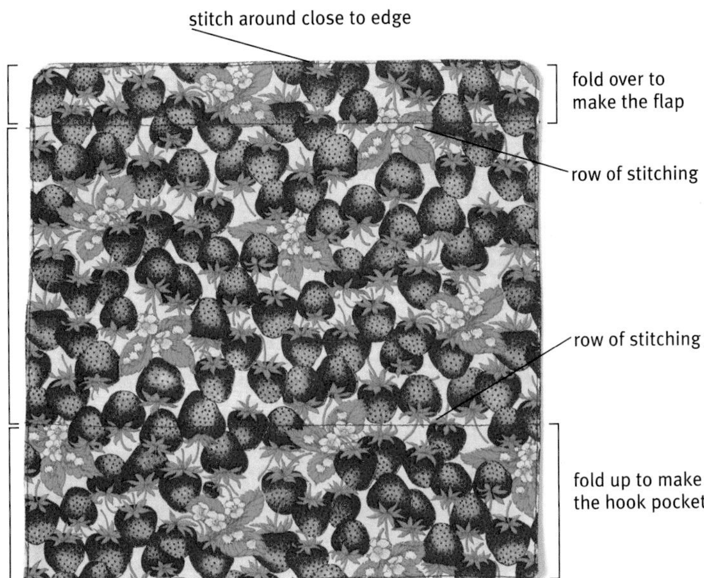

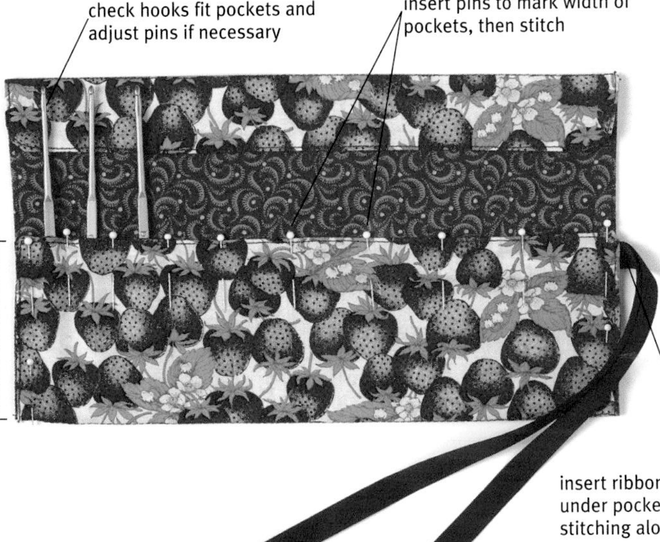

2 | Machine-stitch around the case close to the edge. Work two horizontal rows of stitching across the top and bottom of the case as indicated. Fold the top and bottom along these stitched lines to make flaps. Press the folds.

3 | Position crochet hooks under the larger bottom flap as desired. Insert a dressmaker's pin between each hook. Check each hook fits easily into its pocket, then remove the hooks. At the right-hand edge of the bottom flap, insert the folded ribbon between the layers and pin in place as indicated. Stitch the vertical lines marked by the pins to make the hook pockets. Finally, stitch down the side edges of the bottom flap, securing the ribbon ties on the right-hand edge. Insert a hook into each pocket, fold down the top flap, and roll up the case from left to right. Wrap the ties around the case and tie in a bow to secure.

FIX IT

16 *Metal or plastic hook starting to feel greasy or sticky?*

Wash in warm water with a little detergent, rinse with clean water, and dry thoroughly with a soft cloth.

17 *Yarn catching on a plastic hook?*

Remove snags and rough patches by rubbing gently with fine sandpaper or a jeweller's file.

18 *Wooden hook losing its lustre?*

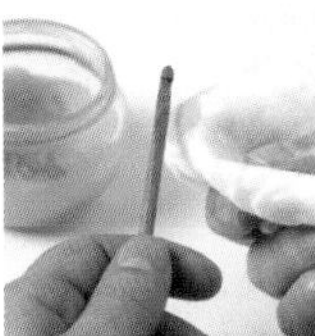

Clean using a cloth moistened with white spirit, allow to dry, then polish with a tiny amount of colourless beeswax furniture polish. Buff up to a nice sheen by rubbing the hook with a soft cloth.

Which yarn?

There is a huge range of yarns you can use for crochet, from very fine cotton to thick, chunky wool. Yarns can be made from one fibre or combine a mixture of two or three in varying proportions. As a general rule, the easiest yarns to use for crochet, especially for a beginner, have a smooth surface and a medium or tight twist to prevent splitting.

TRY IT

19 Using fun materials

Do not restrict yourself to crocheting only with yarn. There are many other fun materials to experiment with that can make fabulous bags and accessories. Try soft jeweller's wire, ribbon, string, strips of plastic bags or fabric, and marvel at the effects you can achieve.

Wire crochet

28-gauge jewellery wire worked with a 4.5 mm (size G) hook. Wire crochet looks best worked in narrow strips to make bracelets and necklaces – you can leave it plain or embellish it by adding some beads (page 134).

Plastic bags

1 cm (3/8 in.) strips of plastic bag cut in a spiral shape to make a continuous length and worked with a 6 mm (size K) hook.

Raffia

Artificial raffia worked with a 4.5 mm (size G) hook.

Twine

Polyester package twine worked with a 5 mm (size H) hook.

Ribbon

Narrow metallic ribbon worked with a 6 mm (size K) hook.

Yarn types

Woollen yarns and blended yarns with a high proportion of wool feel good to crochet with as they have a certain amount of stretch, making it easy to push the point of the hook into each stitch. Silk yarn has a delightful lustre, although it has less resilience than either wool or cotton and is much more expensive. Yarns made from cotton and linen are durable and cool to wear, but may be blended with other fibres to add softness. Yarns made of synthetic fibres, such as acrylic or nylon, are usually less expensive to buy than those made from natural fibres, but can pill more easily and lose their shape. A good solution is to choose a yarn combining a small proportion of synthetic fibres and a natural fibre like wool or cotton.

Yarn is sold by weight rather than by length, although the packaging of many yarns now includes the length of the ball (yardage) as well as other information. Yarn is usually sold in balls, although some yarns may still come in the form of hanks or skeins, which need to be wound by hand into balls before you begin to crochet.

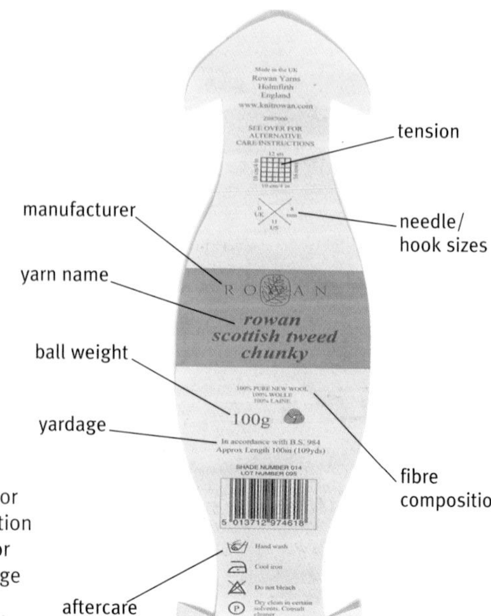

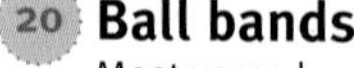

20 Ball bands

Most yarns have a paper band or tag attached with vital information such as the weight of the ball or skein, fibre composition, yardage and how to look after your finished item. The band may also recommend hook and needle sizes and give tension details.

Classic yarn

Classic yarns include wool, silk, cotton and some synthetic fibres. They usually have a smooth, even surface. Mohair yarn, although fluffy in texture, is generally categorized as a classic yarn.

Pure wool and cotton

Classic pure wool or cotton yarns are made from several strands plied together. They come in all thicknesses from lace weight right up to thick chunky and bulky weights. This swatch is worked in double knitting (DK) pure Merino wool using a 4 mm (size F) hook.

Lopi yarn

Lopi yarns are generally used for outer garments such as coats, jackets and heavy sweaters. Lopi is a strong, hardwearing woollen yarn originating in Iceland. It comes in two weights and feels less soft to the touch than classic wool. This swatch is worked in the lighter weight, Lite-Lopi (Létt-Lopi), using a 5 mm (size H) hook.

Mohair blended yarn

A garment made from a classic mohair yarn is light to wear yet very warm. Work with a fairly large hook to make sure the fabric is soft and has good drape. The swatch is worked in an Aran (worsted weight) yarn made from 82% mohair and 9% wool, with a 9% nylon core for strength, using a 6 mm (size K) hook.

Novelty yarn

Textured and ribbon yarns, yarn incorporating slubs, bobbles, flags, or tufts, and yarns made from different threads plied together are known as novelty yarns. Although slightly more difficult to use than the smoother classic yarns, they make interesting and unusual crochet fabrics.

Textured yarn

Textured yarns can be made from pure wool or from wool or cotton mixed with synthetic fibres. They come in a wide range of weights and textures, including loops, bobbles and slubs, and may vary from thick to thin at intervals along the length. The swatch is worked in a heavily textured blend of cotton and synthetic fibres using a 6 mm (size K) hook.

Eyelash yarn

Eyelash yarn comes in many varieties and is usually made from synthetic fibres. The lashes radiate from a central core and may be short – like velvet – or longer to give a shaggy effect when worked. The swatch is worked in a 100% nylon eyelash yarn using a 4.5 mm (size G) hook.

Effects yarn

Effects yarns are designed to be used with a classic yarn to add texture or sparkle. Many effects yarns are fine and will combine with a smooth yarn without adding extra weight. Others are thicker and you will have to adjust your hook size accordingly. This swatch is worked in a fine 100% nylon textured effects yarn and a pure wool double knitting (DK) yarn, using a 4 mm (size F) hook.

Changing yarn

There will be times when you love the shape and style of a garment on a pattern but do not like (or cannot buy) the original yarn. It is easy to substitute another yarn, preferably one of similar weight and yardage, but keep the following guidelines in mind.

Useful hook and yarn combinations

4-ply (Sportweight) 2 mm–3.5 mm (B–E)

DK (Double knitting) 3.5 mm–4.5 mm (E–G)

Aran (Worsted weight) 5 mm–6 mm (H–K)

Tips for substituting yarn

• When substituting yarn made from a different fibre, or mix of fibres, check the yardage carefully as you may need to buy more or less yarn than the quantity quoted in the pattern.

• Cotton yarn generally gives less yardage than a pure wool yarn, unless it is blended with lightweight fibres such as acrylic or microfibre.

• The way a yarn is constructed can also make a difference to the amount of yarn in a ball or skein. A dense, heavily twisted yarn generally has less yardage than a light, fluffy yarn.

• After you have done your calculations, it is a good idea to add an extra ball or two to the amount you buy, just to make sure that you do not run out.

• If the pattern yarn has been discontinued, or is unfamiliar to you, find out about its characteristics by consulting one of the online knitting yarn directories such as Yarndex (www.yarndexforyarn.com). Choose a yarn with similar weight and characteristics to the one quoted in the pattern.

• Measure the tension of your swatch carefully and compare it with the original. A difference of one or two stitches or rows may dramatically alter garment sizing.

• Swatch, swatch and swatch again until you are happy with the resulting fabric. If necessary, make several swatches with different brands and sizes of hook to get the drape and feel of fabric that you want.

• When your chosen yarn is thinner than the suggested one, consider adding a novelty yarn or an extra strand of finer yarn to bulk it up.

• A colourful, handpainted yarn will affect the look of a stitch pattern and may overpower a complex stitch visually.

• If your chosen yarn is bulkier than the original, try working the swatch with a smaller hook.

Comparing yarns

Here three yarns of similar weight have been worked in the same stitch patterns using a 4 mm (size F) hook. The stitch pattern shows up beautifully worked in a classic pure wool yarn (bottom). Worked in a synthetic suede-finish ribbon yarn, the stitch pattern holds its own visually against the changing colours (middle) but, worked in a heavily textured yarn, the stitch pattern almost disappears (top).

24

Making up yarn weights

If you cannot find the weight of yarn that you need, try combining two or more strands of finer yarns, holding them together as you crochet. This is not an exact science and you will need to experiment and make a number of swatches to get the correct gauge. Many yarns labelled at a particular weight can vary dramatically in actual thickness from brand to brand. Another problem is the variable tension of individual crocheters. For example, one stitcher could use three strands of 4-ply (light sportweight) yarn, two strands of DK (double knitting) yarn, or one strand each of Aran (worsted weight) yarn and light sportweight (4-ply) yarn, to make up a chunky thickness. Another crocheter working with exactly the same yarns and hook size may get a very different result, depending on how tightly or loosely the stitches were worked.

Recycling garments

Charity shop garments can be unravelled for a good source of inexpensive yarn. Pure wool garments are excellent finds, but do not ignore quality garments made from synthetics. If you do not like the original colour, remember that many yarns can be successfully dyed at home, depending on their fibre composition. Turn to page 136 to see how the yarn being unravelled in the photograph looks after dyeing.

Check garments carefully before buying them in charity shops. You are looking for either handknits or commercially made clothes that have proper stitched seams inside. Avoid garments made from sections cut out of larger pieces of knitting that have been overlocked (serged) together. Unravelling these garments will yield hundreds of short lengths of yarn, not the continuous lengths you need.

Begin by unpicking as many seams as you can, cutting away collars and neckbands if necessary, until the pieces are separated. Starting at the top of each piece, unravel the rows, winding the yarn into a ball as you go. When you are finished, wind the yarn into skeins (page 137) and wash or steam them to get rid of the crinkles. When dry, rewind the yarn into balls ready for use.

TRY IT

Estimating quantities

There is really no magic formula to work out how much yarn you will need to make a garment, but there are a few useful things you can try. Buy a ball of your chosen yarn and work a fairly large swatch at least 15 cm (6 in.) square – or larger – using the pattern stitch and suggested hook size. Weigh the swatch. Compare the number of stitches and rows worked in the swatch with those in the instructions for the back of the garment. This will help you guesstimate how many multiples of the swatch you would need to make the back of the garment. Multiply this number by the weight of yarn in the swatch, and then divide by the weight of yarn in each ball. Once you have worked out how many balls you need for the back, repeat with the front and the sleeves, adding extra for bands, collars and other trimmings. Finally add them together.

Buying extra yarn

It is always a good idea to buy one or two extra balls of yarn for a project. Many yarn shops will take back unused yarn and give you a refund, providing the yarn is in good condition and you return it within a specified time limit.

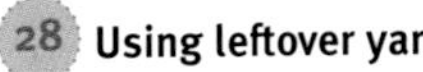

28 Using leftover yarn

If you cannot return unused yarn, consider making it into a small accessory such as a scarf, hat or pair of mittens. Small amounts of leftover yarn can be saved and combined at a later date in a multicoloured afghan or throw.

PATTERNS AND CHARTS

Working methods for crochet patterns are given as written instructions or shown in visual form as symbol charts. Filet crochet and colourwork designs are usually shown as charts accompanied by short instructions.

Understanding crochet patterns

When following a pattern, remember to make sure that you start with the correct number of stitches, then work through the instructions from the beginning exactly as stated.

Written pattern

As well as a complete set of instructions for crocheting a given garment, a written pattern supplies you with other details, including size, yarn and tension information.

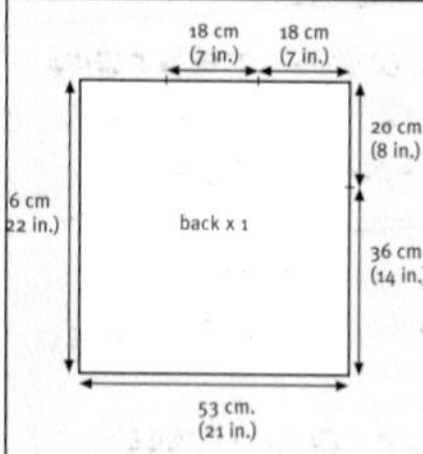

Schematic

A schematic is a diagram showing the shape of each piece of crochet used to make the garment in the pattern. Measurements of the finished pieces are shown on the diagram and these can be used in addition to the 'to fit' information to help you work out which size you should choose.

SIZES
One size to fit bust/chest 91–97 cm (36–
ACTUAL MEASUREMENT 107 cm (42 in.)
SIDE LENGTH 36 cm (14 in.) including ed
SLEEVE LENGTH (measured straight from
cuff edge) 46 cm (18 in.)

Sizing

Garment sizes may be quoted as 'to fit small, medium, or large', or to fit a specific bust or hip size, allowing for a certain amount of garment ease.

MATERIALS
QUANTITY 6 x 50 g balls of A, 3 x balls o
C, 3 x balls of D, 2 x balls of E, 3 x balls
of G
YARN "Extra Fine Merino" Double Knitt
pure wool DK yarn with 125 m / 137 yd

Yarn information

Yarn requirements for a garment may be quoted in different ways. The pattern may tell you how many balls of a specific yarn you will need to buy or it may give you a suggested yardage for a generic yarn.

CHECK YOUR TENSION
Make a foundation chain of 37 ch and
(6 in.) in pattern. Block the sample, allo
measure the tension. The recommende
stitches and 10 rows to 10 cm (4 in.).
If you have more stitches and rows, yo

Tension

A pattern will include a recommended tension for the yarn that has been used; match this tension exactly so your garment comes out the right size.

WINTER JACKET

Worked in a range of colours using yarn made from the finest merino wool, this loose-fi boxy jacket has an interlocking striped pattern consisting of two stitches of different he

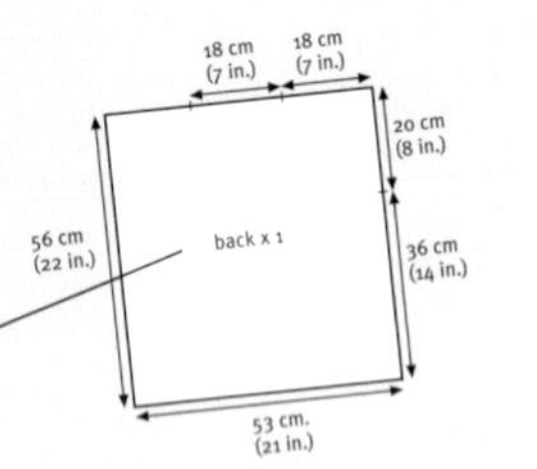

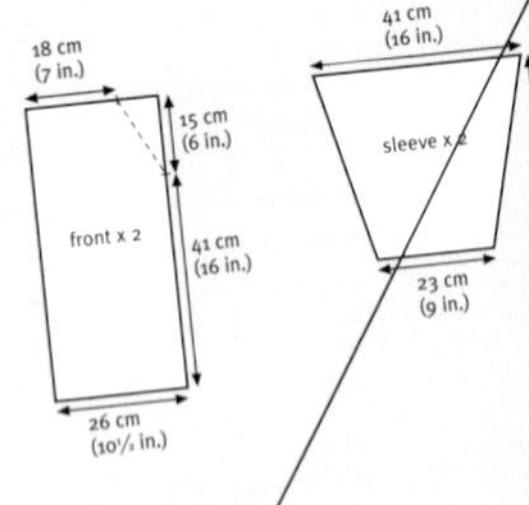

SIZES
One size to fit bust/chest 91–97 cm (36–38 in.)
ACTUAL MEASUREMENT 107 cm (42 in.)
SIDE LENGTH 36 cm (14 in.) including edging
SLEEVE LENGTH (measured straight from top of sleeve to cuff edge) 46 cm (18 in.)

MATERIALS
QUANTITY 6 x 50 g balls of A, 3 x balls of B, 2 x balls of C, 3 x balls of D, 2 x balls of E, 3 x balls of F, 2 x balls of G
YARN "Extra Fine Merino" Double Knitting by Jaeger (or pure wool DK yarn with 125 m / 137 yd per 50 g ball)
COLOUR 943 Raspberry (A) 944 Elderberry (B), 979 Tango (C), 984 Violet (D), 971 Loden (E), 920 Wineberry (F), 923 Satinwood (G)
HOOK SIZE 3.5 mm, 4 mm, 4.5 mm (E, F, G)
NEEDLE Large tapestry needle
7 beads to make buttons

CHECK YOUR TENSION
Make a foundation chain of 37 ch and work 15 cm (6 in.) in pattern. Block the sample, allow to dry and measure the tension. The recommended tension is 20 stitches and 10 rows to 10 cm (4 in.).
If you have more stitches and rows, your tension is too tight and you should make another sample using a larger hook.If you have less stitches and rows, your tension is too loose.

ABBREVIATIONS
ch—chain; dc—double crochet; tr—treb
inc—increase; st(s) —stitch(es)

BACK
Using yarn A and the 4.5 mm (G) hook, to the 4 mm (F) hook.
Row 1 (right side) Insert hook into 3r (counts as 1 dc), 1 dc into each of next each of next 4 ch, 1 dc into each of ne * to end, turn.
Row 2 1 ch, 1 dc into each of next 4 into each of next 4 sts, 1 dc into each 4 sts; rep from * to end, turn. Break
Row 3 Join in yarn B, 3 ch (counts a st, 1 tr into each of next 3 sts, * 1 dc 4 sts, 1 dc into each of next 4 sts, re working last tr into top of turning
Row 4 Rep row 3. Break off yarn B

HOOK SIZE 3.5 mm, 4 mm, 4.5 mm (E, F, G)
NEEDLE Large tapestry needle

Hook sizes

The pattern will tell you which size hooks were used to make the garment shown, as well as any other equipment required. Depending on how loosely or tightly you crochet, you may need to use smaller or larger hooks than those given if you are to achieve the correct tension.

ABBREVIATIONS
ch—chain; **dc**—double crochet; **tr**—treble crochet;
inc—increase; **st(s)** —stitch(es)

Abbreviations and techniques

Information about any unusual abbreviations used in the pattern are generally given at the beginning of the instructions.

Rows 5 & 6 Join in yarn A, rep row 2. Work straight in pattern, repeating rows 3, 4, 5, and 6 and changing the yarn colour after every two rows as previously given in the colour sequence, ending by working one extra row in yarn A.
Fasten off yarn.

FRONT (MAKE 2)
Using yarn A and the 4.5 mm (G) hook, 53 ch. Change to the 4 mm (F) hook.
Work in pattern exactly as for the back, changing the yarn colour every two rows as given in the colour sequence, ending by working one extra row in yarn A.

COLOUR SEQUENCE FOR SLEEVES
Work two-row stripes of pattern in the same colour sequence as the back and fronts, omitting stripes 1–5 and beginning with stripe 6, in yarn A.

SLEEVES (MAKE 2)
Using yarn A and the 4.5 mm (G) hook, 45 ch. Change to the 4 mm (F) hook.
Work in pattern exactly as for the back, changing the yarn colour after every two rows as given in the colour sequence, ending by working one extra row in yarn A.
Increase 1 st at each end of every 3rd row until there are 76 sts.
Work in pattern until the colour sequence is complete, then work one extra row in yarn A.
Fasten off yarn.

FINISHING
Weave in the short yarn ends, block each piece and allow to dry completely.
When dealing with the ends on the right front, weave them in on the right side for the top 19 cm (7½ in.) as the top of the right front will be turned back to form the collar, leaving the wrong side of the work visible. Weave in the ends as usual on the wrong side as here the joins occur on the armhole edge, not on the front edge.
With right sides together, join the fronts and back together at the shoulders, leaving the centre 18 cm (7in.) open.
Measure the top of the sleeves and mark the centre point with a pin. With right sides facing, join the sleeves to the fronts and back aligning the centre points with the shoulder seams.

With right sides together, join the sleeve and side seams.

WORKING THE EDGING
Row 1 With right side facing, join yarn A to the lower edge of the jacket. Using the 3.5 mm (E) hook, work one row of evenly spaced double crochet edging along the lower edge, front edges and neck, working 1 ch at corners, 2 dc into sts at either side of shoulder seams. Along front edges of left and right fronts, space stitches evenly by working 2 dc into each tr row end, 1 dc into each dc row end. Join with sl st into first dc.
Row 2 1 ch, work 1 dc into each dc in previous row, working 3 dc into ch sp at each corner and making 7 button loops along the right front as follows: 3 dc into 1 ch sp at bottom corner of right front, 1 dc into next dc, * miss 2 dc, 4 ch, 1 dc into each of next 10 dc; rep from * 6 times, continue as established in dc. Join with sl st into first dc.
Row 3 1 ch, work 1 dc into each dc in previous row, working 3 dc into 2nd stitch of 3 dc group at each corner and [3 dc, 3 ch, 3 dc] into each 4 ch button loop along right front. Join with sl st into first dc.
Fasten off yarn.

BACK
Using yarn A and the 4.5 mm (G) hook
to the 4 mm (F) hook.
Row 1 (right side) Insert hook into 3r
(counts as 1 dc), 1 dc into each of next
each of next 4 ch, 1 dc into each of ne
* to end, turn.
Row 2 1 ch, 1 dc into each of next 4 s
into each of next 4 sts, 1 dc into each
4 sts; rep from * to end, turn. Break o
Row 3 Join in yarn B, 3 ch (counts as

Round brackets and asterisks

Round brackets usually contain extra information, not instructions that have to be worked. Asterisks indicate that you must repeat the sequence of stitches (or the set of instructions) that follow the symbol.

rk 1 dc into each dc in previous row,
working 3 dc into 2nd stit
of 3 dc group at each
corner and [3 dc, 3 ch,
3 dc] into each 4 ch
button loop along
right front. Join wi

Square brackets

The sequence of stitches enclosed inside the square brackets must be worked as instructed and repeated for the number of times stated after the second bracket. Square brackets are sometimes used instead of asterisks.

FIX IT

30 *Confused by a pattern?*

Start at the beginning and work through the pattern and each instruction exactly as stated. When instructions are written in a small print size, it helps to have the pattern photocopied and enlarged so the words are easier to read.

31 *Having trouble following the right size?*

Mark all the directions for your size using a highlighter pen or use a coloured pen. Circle the correct number of stitches and rows throughout the pattern.

32 *Keep losing your place in the pattern?*

Buy a cross-stitcher's metal board with a movable magnetic strip. Place the board behind your pattern and move the strip down row by row so it tells you exactly where you are in the instructions.

33 *How many rows worked?*

Attach markers in the crochet fabric every few rows to help with counting. Buy special split-ring markers (or improvise with safety pins, hairgrips or short lengths of contrasting yarn) and thread them through the crochet at regular intervals, say every 10 rows, to make counting easier. Also use markers to keep track of increase and decrease rows.

Reading symbol charts

Some crochet patterns use symbol charts to show the working method in visual form. Indicating where and how different stitches should be placed in relation to one another, these symbols have now been standardized around the world. Although a crochet pattern with a symbol chart will still contain some written instructions, the stitch patterns are shown diagrammatically and not written out line by line.

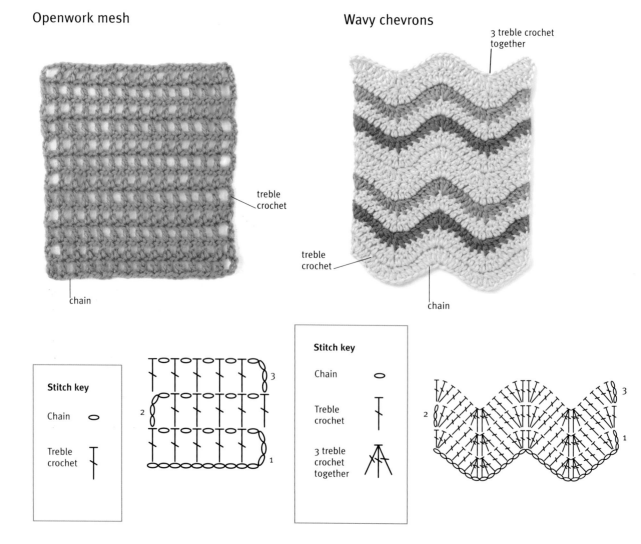

The meaning of symbols

To use a pattern with a symbol chart, first familiarize yourself with the different symbols and their meanings (pages 155–6). All of the symbols used in the swatches shown here appear in a key at the side of the chart. Each one represents a double stitch or instruction (such as chain or double crochet) and indicates exactly where to work it. Follow the number sequence on the chart regardless of whether you are working in rows or rounds. In the same way as using a written pattern, keep a note of which row or round you are working to avoid confusion.

Openwork mesh

treble crochet

chain

Stitch key

Chain

Treble crochet

3
2
1

Wavy chevrons

3 treble crochet together

treble crochet

chain

Stitch key

Chain

Treble crochet

3 treble crochet together

3
2
1

Cluster circle

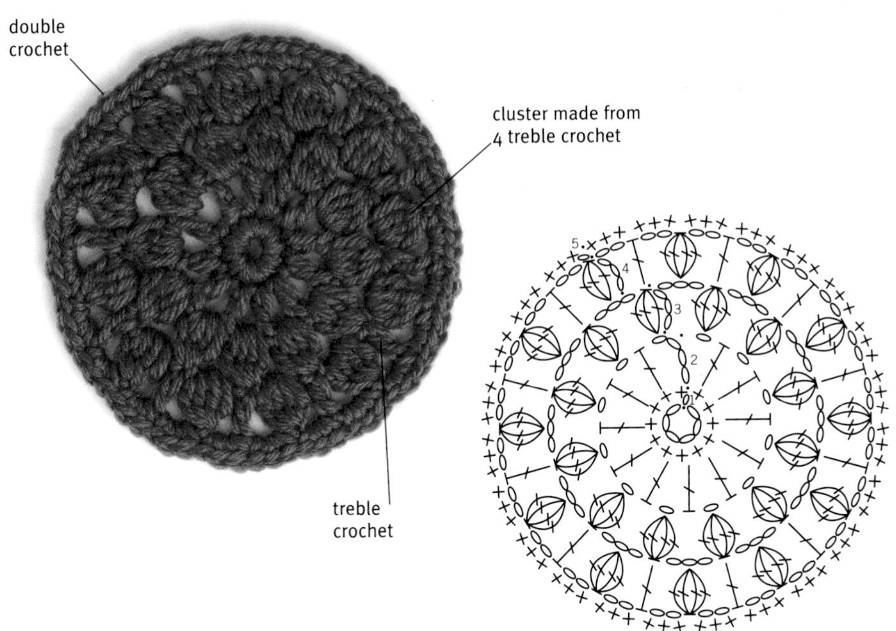
double crochet
cluster made from 4 treble crochet
treble crochet
5
4
3
2
1

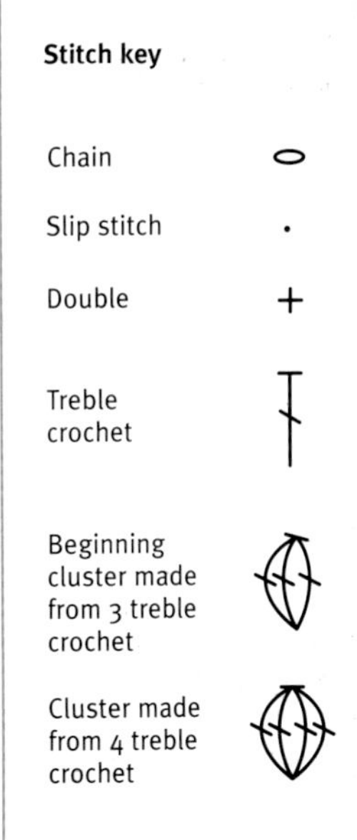
Stitch key
Chain
Slip stitch
Double
Treble crochet
Beginning cluster made from 3 treble crochet
Cluster made from 4 treble crochet

Croydon square

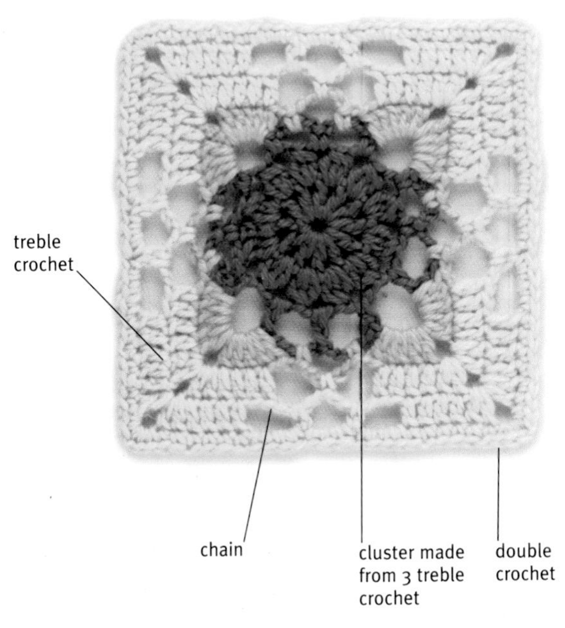
treble crochet
chain
cluster made from 3 treble crochet
double crochet

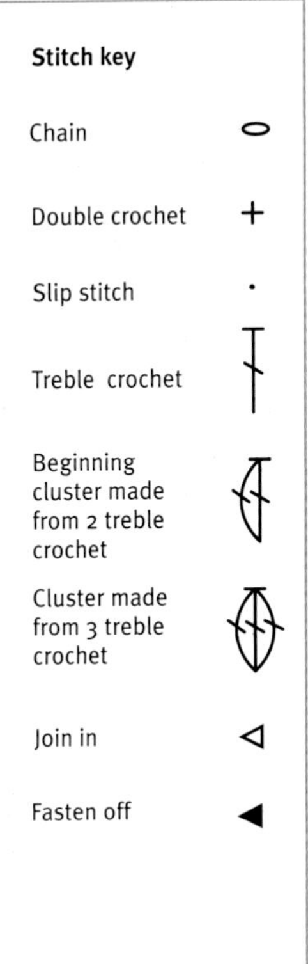
Stitch key
Chain
Double crochet
Slip stitch
Treble crochet
Beginning cluster made from 2 treble crochet
Cluster made from 3 treble crochet
Join in
Fasten off

Mixing and matching stitch patterns

There is a bewildering array of crochet stitch patterns to choose between at the start of a project. Looking at the type of fabrics created by different stitch patterns can help to narrow down your choice. Some stitch patterns create chunky textured fabrics decorated with bobbles, popcorns and other three-dimensional elements, while others may produce soft, light and lacy fabrics with a good drape. A smooth double crochet fabric may look rather dull and boring, but when colour is added in the form of cheerful stripes or an intarsia block, the surface comes to life.

The swatches shown below and opposite are all worked in the same type of yarn, a woollen DK (double knitting) yarn, and use a colour palette restricted to mauve, lavender, purple and lilac enlivened by a little green. Each swatch is attractive in its own right, but arranged together they begin to show some of the possibilities gained by working with different stitch patterns. From the smooth double crochet brought to life by bold areas of colour to the heavily ribbed chevron pattern, each stitch pattern has something different to offer the crocheter. Some stitches, particularly the lace patterns, are best used alone while others would combine happily in the same piece; horizontal stripes, bobbles and embroidered stripes could be used together as they are all based on double crochet. There is no substitute for sitting down with several balls of yarn and trying out the stitch patterns that most appeal to you. This will demonstrate how various stitch patterns are constructed, how easy or challenging they are to work, and how the fabric feels and drapes in your hand.

35 Chevrons

Based on treble crochet stitches, this pattern is made by increasing and decreasing at regular intervals along the rows. Chevrons are perfect for making scarves, wraps and afghans. Be as bold with colour choice as you like.

37 Textured chevrons

This heavily ribbed textured chevron pattern is easy to work in rows of double crochet. The ribs are made by working into the back loops only of the stitches on the previous row, rather than working through both loops in the usual way.

36 Filet pattern

Filet crochet patterns are easy to work, and make a light lace fabric with a combination of solid blocks and spaces on a mesh background. As these designs are charted, you can easily mix several border or block designs in the same piece, or create your own patterns on graph paper.

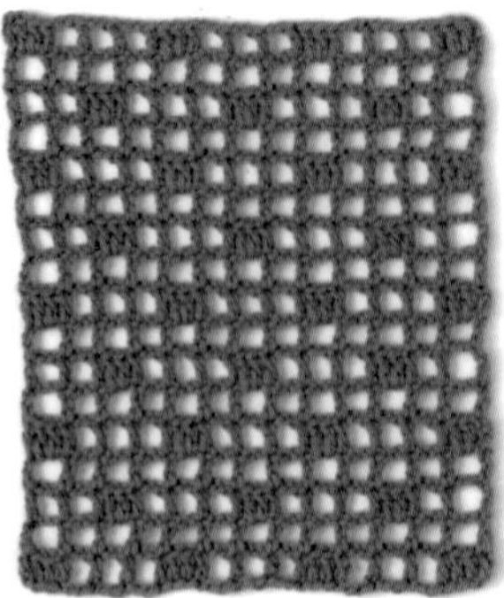

38 Criss-cross lace

This stitch pattern combines double crochet stitches and chains to make a delightfully lacy fabric. Lacy crochet combines well with plainer stitch patterns. For example, lace sleeves add lightness and a focal point to a solidly worked cotton top.

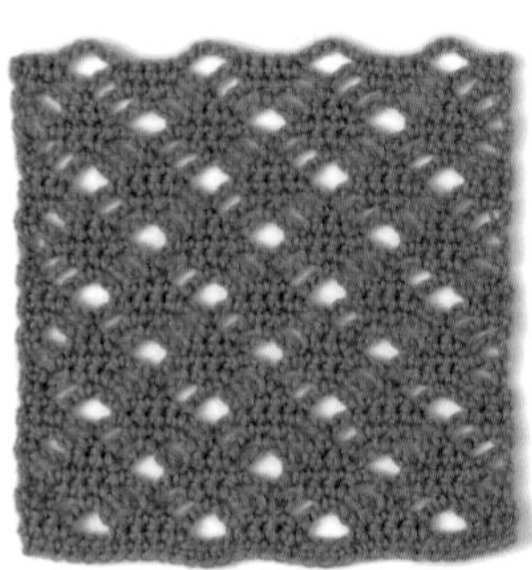

39 Lacy fans

Bands of treble crochet alternate with bands of lacy fans to make an attractive fabric. This type of lace would combine well with other treble crochet-based stitch patterns to make pretty, feminine garments.

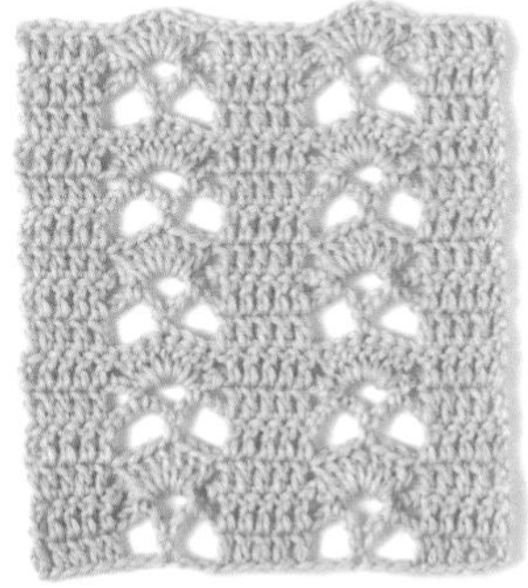

40 Stripes

Narrow stripes add interest to plain double crochet fabric. To avoid having lots of yarn ends to darn in at the end, work each one-row stripe in three different colours. Do not break off the yarn at the colour changes but carry the colours not in use up the side ready to work the next stripe.

41 Checkerboard

Blocks of colour make a bold statement on this swatch. Double crochet makes an attractive fabric that is a perfect background for Jacquard and intarsia colourwork designs.

42 Small-scale patterns

Many small-scale stitch patterns are unjustly overlooked in garment design. While not as showy as some of the more complicated patterns, they make neat, slightly textured fabrics that are perfect for classic, tailored styles.

43 Running stitches

Plain double crochet makes the perfect background for an allover pattern of regularly spaced running stitches. Make running stitches in a contrasting colour to the main yarn, or choose a shiny or matte embroidery thread.

44 Clustered lace

Clusters of treble crochet can be combined with chains to make a wide variety of lace stitches perfect for garments, light throws or baby shawls, depending on the weight of yarn used.

45 Textures

Highly textured stitch patterns look good worked in smooth yarns that show off the attractive stitch construction. Great for simple coats and jackets, you can combine textured crochet fabrics with areas of smoother, small-scale pattern on the collar, cuffs and bands.

46 Bobbles

Bobbles are great fun to work, and make an interesting fabric. Bobbles can be arranged in regular rows as shown, or worked in small groups to create simple blocks such as a heart, triangle or diamond.

Working from a colour block chart

Jacquard and intarsia patterns as usually worked from a chart rather than from rows of written instructions. The design is shown as a grid chart with each colour represented by a coloured square or a symbol. A chart may occasionally have coloured squares with a black symbol inside each square to help with recognizing yarns that are similar in colour. A key will accompany the chart to indicate which yarn is represented by which chart colour or symbol.

How does it work?

Each coloured square or symbol on the chart represents one stitch and you should always work upward from the bottom, reading odd-numbered rows (right-side rows) from right to left, and even-numbered rows (wrong-side rows) from left to right. Any repeating sections on Jacquard charts are indicated by large brackets or the repeat will be boxed in.

47

Getting started

Begin by working the foundation chain in the first colour. Starting at the bottom right-hand corner of the chart, work the pattern from the chart, joining in any new colours as they occur in the design. On the first row, work the first stitch into the second chain from the hook, then the rest of the row in double crochet. For more information about working Jacquard and intarsia designs, turn to pages 130–31.

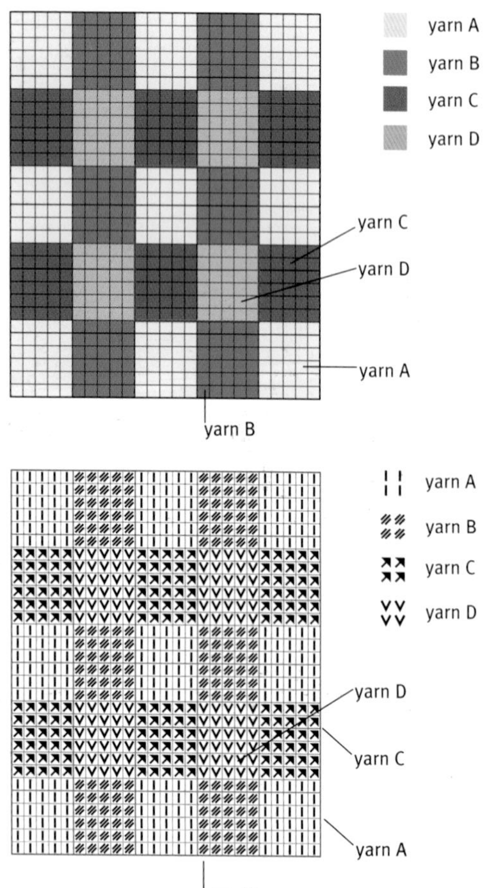

Jacquard swatch

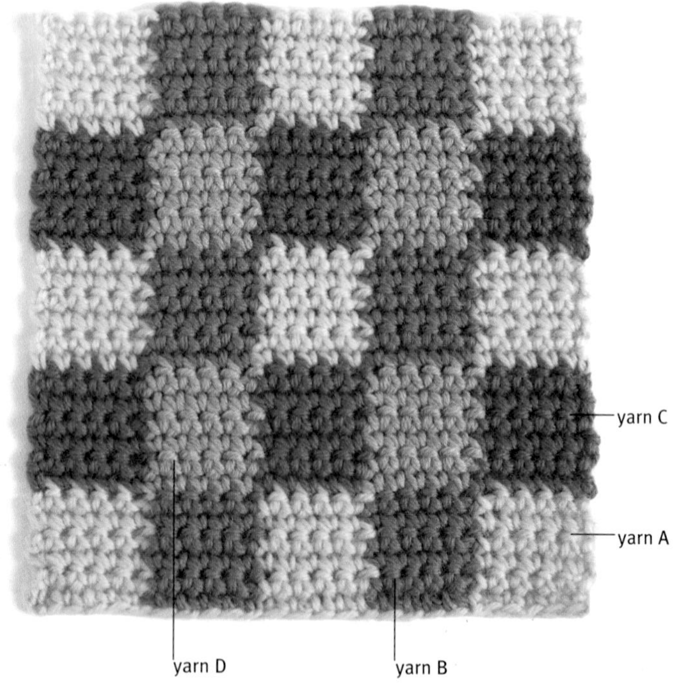

Intarsia swatch

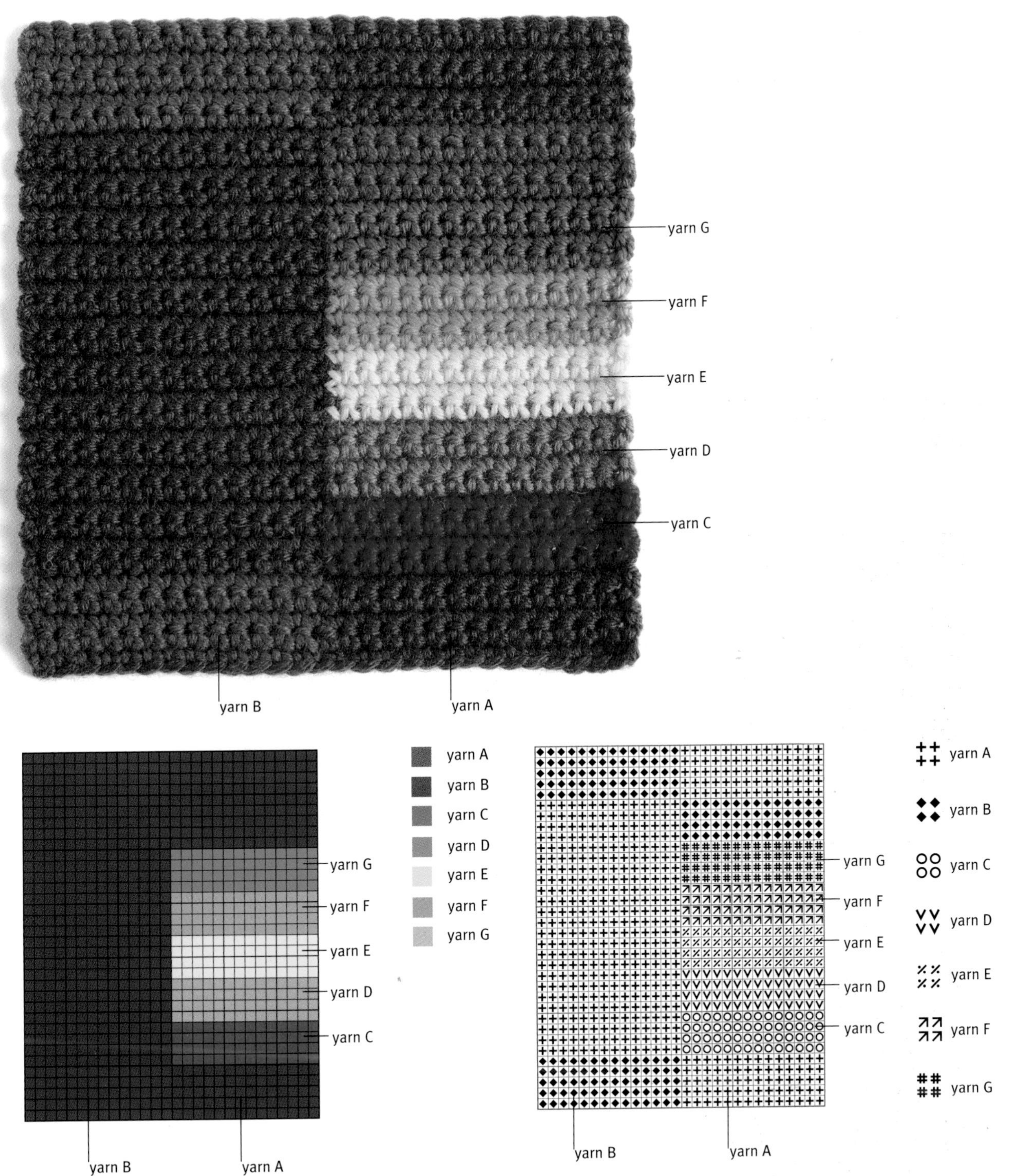

Working from a filet crochet chart

Like Jacquard and intarsia patterns, filet crochet is usually worked from a chart on a grid rather than from rows of written instructions. A symbol key accompanies the chart, giving details of how different elements are represented. Usually in black and white, the charts show the design as it will look from the right side of the fabric.

Reading filet crochet charts

Numbered down the sides, filet crochet charts show the pattern sequence from the right side of the work. Work up from the bottom and from one side to the other. Read the odd-numbered (right-side) rows from right to left and the even-numbered (wrong-side) rows from left to right.

Each open square equals one space made of two treble crochet stitches separated by two chains. When a square is filled in or has a dot or cross at the centre, chains are replaced by two treble crochet stitches to form a solid block of four stitches.

As filet crochet charts begin with the first row, the foundation chain is never shown. To calculate the number of stitches you will need to make, first multiply the number of squares across the chart by three and then add one. For a chart which is 20 squares across, for example, make a foundation chain 61 chains long (20 x 3 + 1). You also need to add the correct number of turning chains, depending on whether the first chart row begins with a space or a block. Two blocks together on the chart are filled by seven treble crochet stitches, three blocks by 10 stitches, and so on.

Swatch worked in blocks and spaces

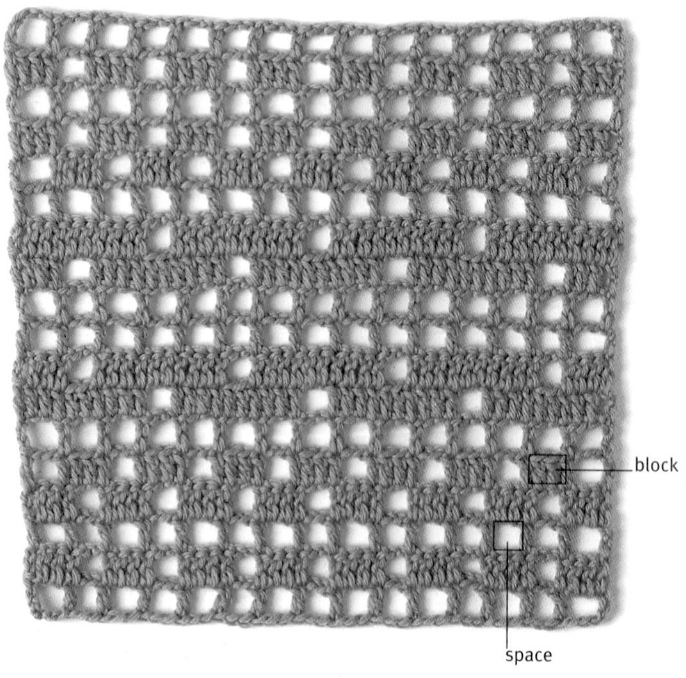

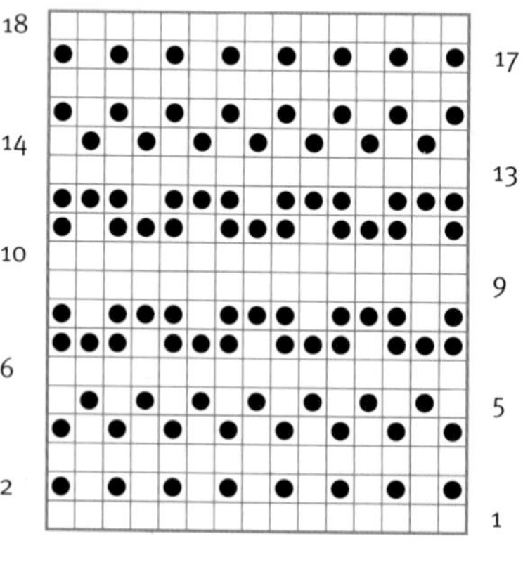

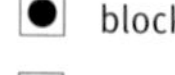

block

space

49

Reading a filet crochet chart with bars and lacets

In addition to the blocks and spaces used in ordinary filet crochet, there are also bars and lacets. Always combined with blocks and spaces, bars and lacets make larger holes in the crochet fabric (as shown below). A bar makes a double-sized space twice as wide as an ordinary space, takes up two horizontal squares in the chart, and acts as the base for a pair of blocks worked over seven stitches. A lacet creates a pretty 'V'-shaped stitch that adds a decorative touch to your work. Like a bar, a lacet takes up two horizontal squares on the chart.

Swatch worked in blocks, spaces, bars and lacets

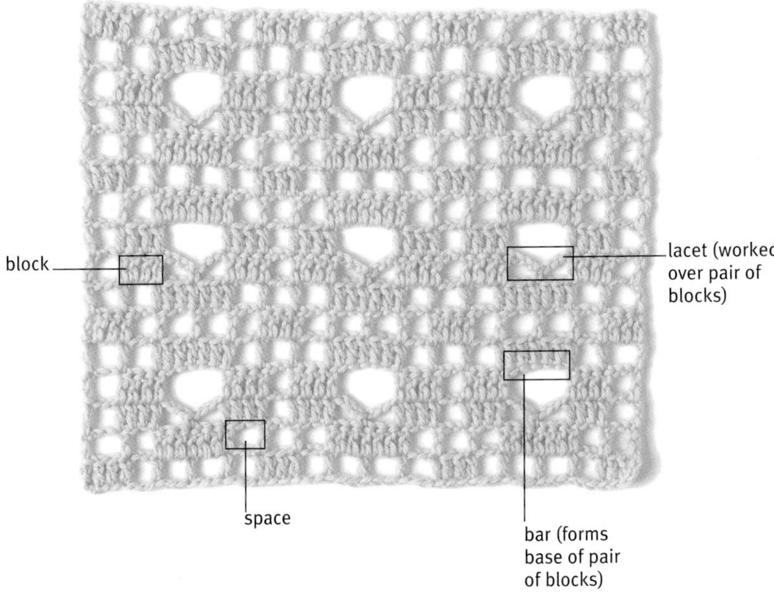

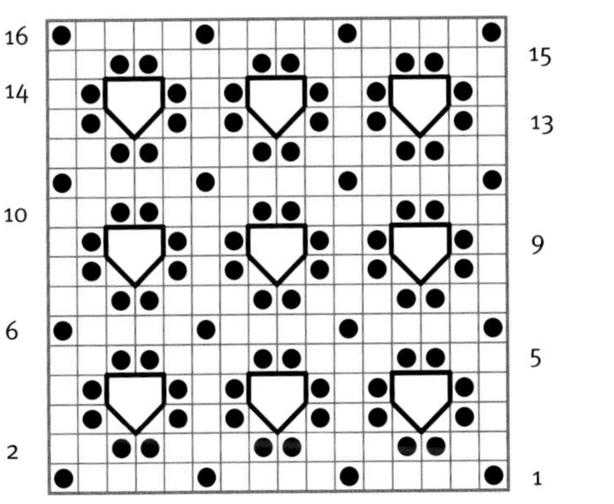

 block

space

bar/double space

lacet

TRY IT

Working with stitches of different heights

As well as working filet crochet charts conventionally as treble crochet and chains (page 30), try the same chart with stitches of different heights to change the proportions of the mesh and give a totally different fabric. Use taller stitches and try working more or fewer chains between the blocks.

Double treble variation

Using the basic chart shown left, work 4 dtr for each block and [1 dtr, 2 ch, 1 dtr] for each space. The resulting fabric is taller in proportion and much more lacy.

Single chain variation

Using the basic chart shown left, work 3 tr for each block and [1 tr, 1 ch, 1 tr] for each space. The resulting fabric is more solid, and less lacy.

DESIGN

Key elements such as tension and drape will dictate how well a garment fits and how good it feels to wear. Once you have added these considerations to the creation of your garment, simply draw a schematic and you are ready to begin designing.

All about tension

The term 'tension' refers to the number of stitches and rows contained in a given width and length of crochet fabric. Crochet patterns include a recommended tension for the yarn which has been used to make the item shown and it is important that you match this tension exactly so your work comes out the right size.

51

Choosing the correct tension

Tension measurements are usually quoted as x stitches and y rows to 10 cm (4 in.) measured over a certain stitch pattern using a certain size of hook. The information may also include a measurement taken across one or more pattern repeats. Working to the suggested tension will also make sure that the crochet fabric is neither too heavy and stiff, nor too loose and floppy when in use. Yarn ball bands or tags may also quote a recommended tension as well as giving information about fibre composition, yardage and aftercare. If you are not planning to use the exact yarn quoted in the pattern instructions, remember that even yarns of the same weight and fibre content made by different manufacturers will probably vary slightly in thickness.

52

Determining tension

Tension can be affected by the type of yarn used, the size and brand of the crochet hook, the type of stitch pattern and the tension of an individual crocheter. No two people will crochet to exactly the same tension, even when working with an identical hook and yarn. How you hold the hook and the rate at which the yarn flows through your fingers will affect the tension you produce. Crochet fabric has less 'give' and elasticity than a comparable knitted fabric so it is crucial to make and measure a tension swatch before you begin making anything. Accessories such as bags, socks, mittens and hats plus items such as cushion covers and lace edgings are often worked to a tighter tension than scarves, shawls, garments and afghans which require a softer type of fabric with better drape. For more information on evaluating drape, turn to page 34.

53

Making and measuring a tension swatch

Read the pattern instructions to identify the recommended tension. Working in the exact yarn you will use for the item, make a generously sized swatch 15–20 cm (6–8 in.) wide. If you are working a stitch pattern, choose a number of foundation chains to suit the stitch repeat. Work in the required pattern until the piece is 15-20 cm (6–8 in.) long. Fasten off the yarn. Block the swatch using the method suited to the yarn composition (pages 144–47). Allow to dry.

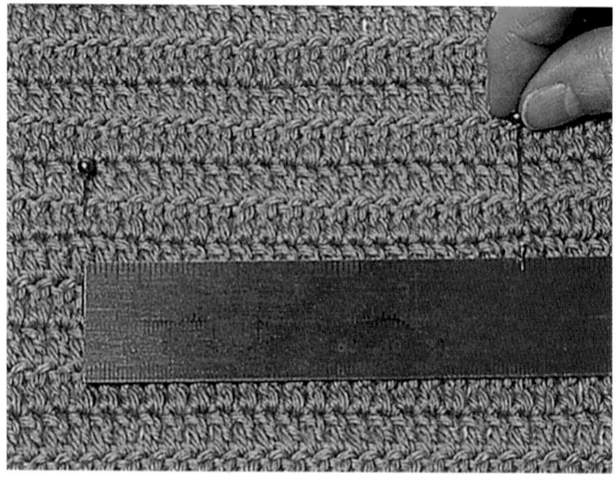

1 | Lay the swatch right side up on a flat surface and use a ruler or tape measure to measure 10 cm (4 in.) horizontally across a row of stitches. Mark this measurement by inserting two pins exactly 10 cm (4 in.) apart. Note down the number of stitches (including partial stitches) between the pins.

2 | Turn the swatch on its side. Working in the same way as step 1, measure 10 cm (4 in.) across the rows, once again inserting two pins exactly 10 cm (4 in.) apart. Make a note of the number of rows (including partial rows) between the pins.

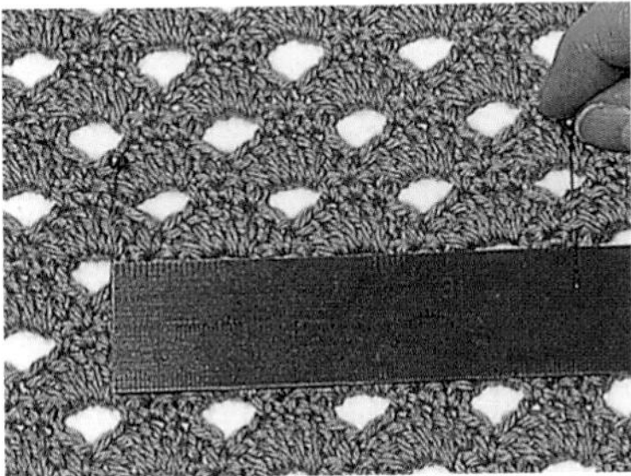

3 | When working a particular stitch pattern, tension information may be quoted as a multiple of the pattern repeat rather than as a set number of rows and stitches. Work your swatch in pattern but count repeats instead of rows and stitches between the pins.

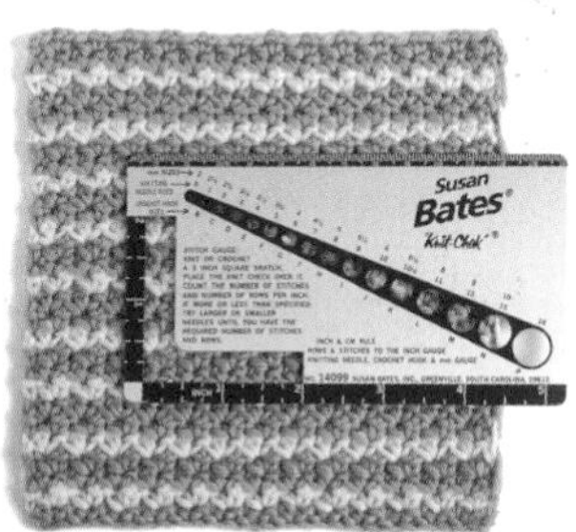

4 | Use a size gauge instead of a ruler to measure patterns with a small repeat but remember that the cut-out window usually measures 5 cm (2 in.) not 10 cm (4 in.). Work your swatch in pattern and count the number of stitches and rows showing in the gauge window. Multiply these numbers by 2.

54 Adjusting tension

If you have more stitches or a smaller pattern repeat between the pins inserted in your swatch (or your block is too small), your tension is probably too tight. Make another swatch using a hook one size larger. If you have less stitches and a larger pattern repeat between the pins inserted in your tension swatch (or your block is too large), your tension is probably too loose. Make another swatch using a hook one size smaller. Block the new swatch as before and measure the tension. Repeat this process until your tension matches that indicated in the pattern and you are happy with the feel of the fabric.

55 Measuring a block

Block tension is usually taken as a finished measurement after blocking. Blocks themselves are measured in different ways, depending on their shape.

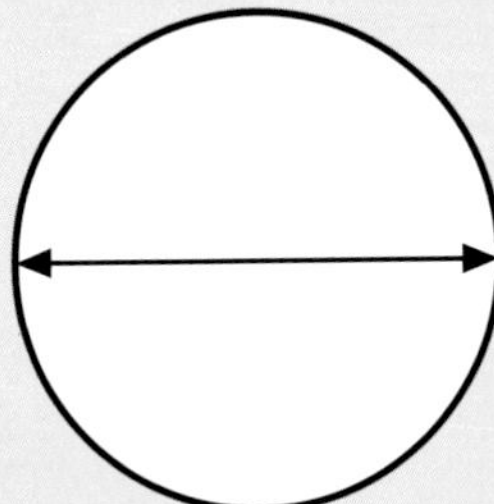

Round block
Measure across the diameter.

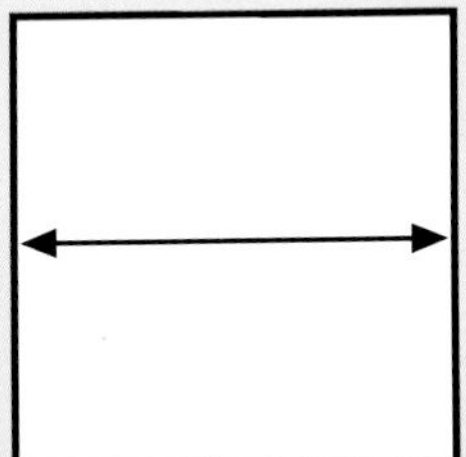

Square block
Measure across the centre.

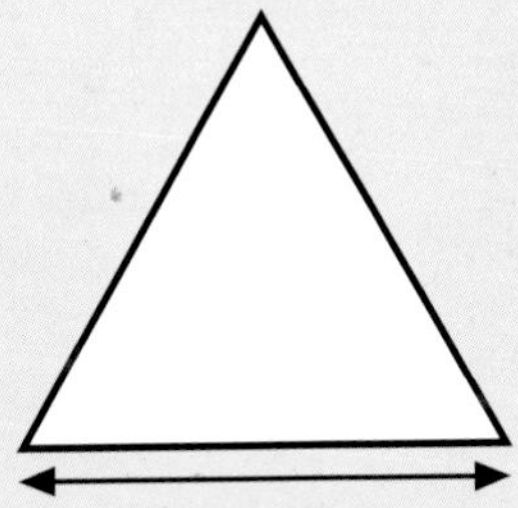

Triangular block
Measure across the base.

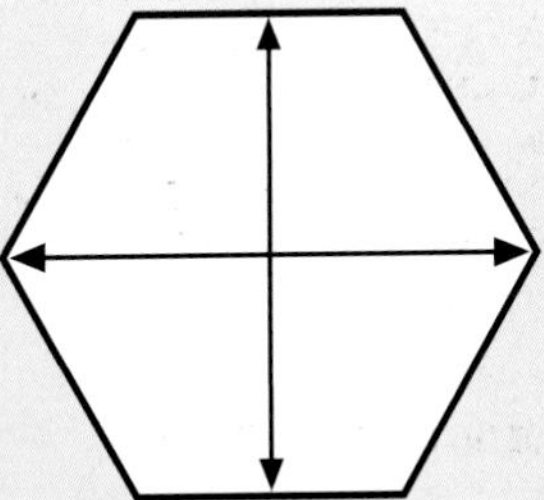

Hexagonal block
Measure from side to side or from point to point, depending on your pattern instructions.

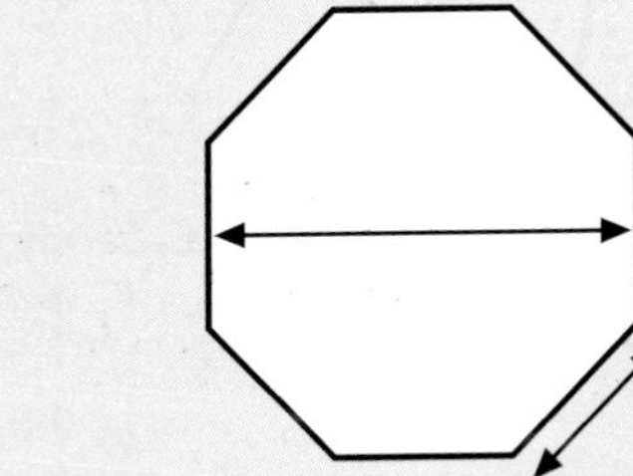

Octagonal block
Measure from side to side or along one edge, depending on your pattern instructions.

Evaluating drape

When making swatches, you need to consider the feel and drape of the crochet fabric as well as the tension. Crochet tends to produce a thicker, less stretchy fabric than knitting and this should be taken into consideration when choosing both your yarn and stitch pattern. A solid, unyielding fabric with little drape makes a great handbag but a stiff, uncomfortable garment. A loose fabric is suitable for a floaty shawl but will stretch out of shape if used for a jacket or coat.

56 Adjusting drape

If you have chosen a particular stitch but the swatches are coming out stiff, try a larger hook size or different yarn. When the fabric is loose, use a smaller hook size or different yarn. You may need to amend the pattern instructions to reflect the new tension or work a smaller or larger garment size to compensate for the changes. As well as changing hook size and yarn to alter the feel and drape of your swatch (page 71), you can substitute lighter or heavier stitch patterns to get the exact drape of fabric you require.

Cool cotton yarn and a mesh stitch pattern combine to make this summer tunic with trimmed beaded neckline. It is perfect for the beach or worn over cut-off jeans.

57 Lightweight crochet fabrics

Soft, light crochet fabrics with plenty of holes, such as mesh, openwork, filet crochet and many lace stitches, have excellent drape. Worked in finer yarn weights, they are suitable for lightweight summer garments, scarves, shawls, wraps, light afghans and blankets. This type of fabric weight can also be used for babywear and shawls but avoid those with large holes as they may trap tiny fingers. Suggested yarn weights are Super Fine and Fine from the chart on page 157.

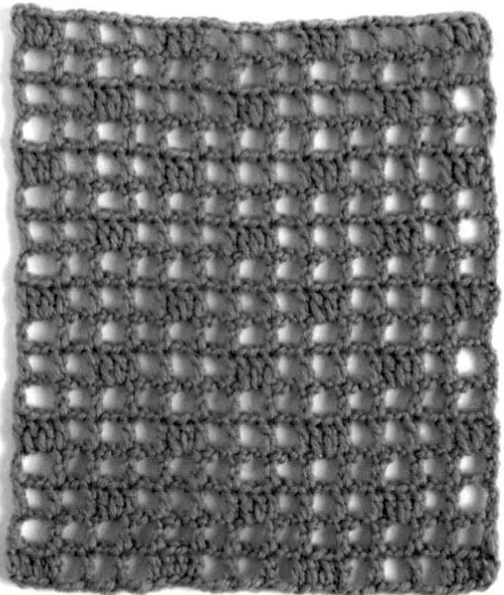

58 Lightweight to medium-weight crochet fabrics

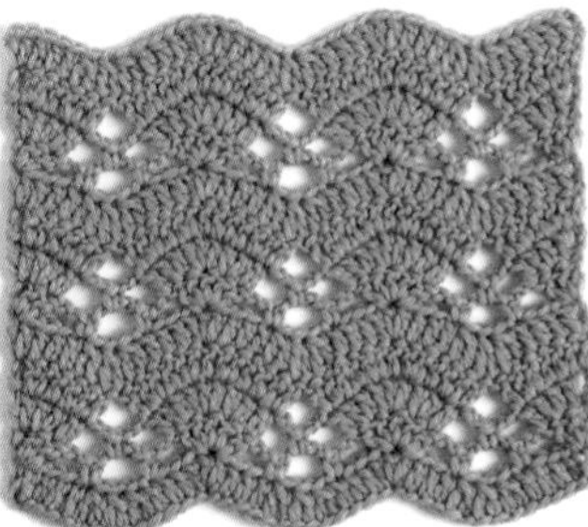

These lace stitch patterns are more solidly worked than lightweight crochet fabrics and incorporate areas of lace mixed with solid areas of stitching. This type of fabric weight is good for sweaters, cardigans, light jackets and skirts, babywear, plus wraps, shawls and scarves that are slightly heavier and warmer to wear than those in the previous category. Suggested yarn weights are Fine and Light from the chart on page 157.

59 Medium-weight crochet fabrics

These solidly worked stitch patterns are worked in suitable yarns to produce pliable crochet fabrics. Good for making light, warm garments and outerwear, including jackets, ponchos and coats, plus accessories like scarves, hats and mittens. Medium-weight fabrics also work well when making throws, afghans and blankets. Suggested yarn weights are Light and Medium from the chart on page 157.

60 Heavy crochet fabrics

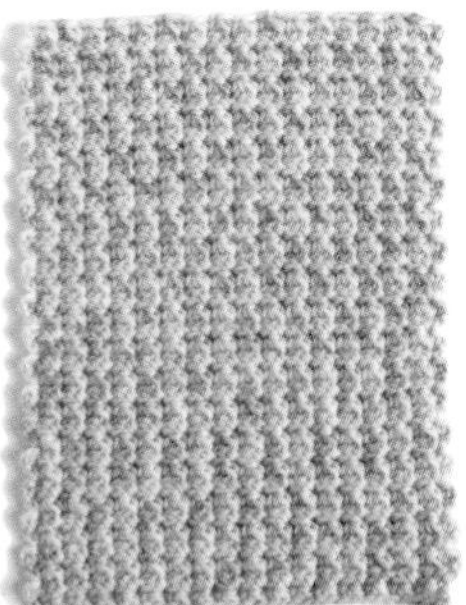

Heavy stitch patterns and textured crochet fabrics have less drape than any of the previous categories. Solidly worked stitch patterns with a small amount of texture are good for semi-tailored garments such as boxy jackets. Heavily textured patterns (bobbles, post stitches) are best used for simply shaped garments or accessories.

TRY IT

61 Making a pot holder

Do not waste your swatches! A swatch worked in a thick, durable stitch makes a good pot holder if you add a hanging loop to one corner. With a little extra work, you can make an even better one from two swatches of similar size. Avoid using swatches worked in synthetic yarns as the yarn may melt.

1 | Place the swatches together with the wrong sides facing and work a round of double crochet edging through both to join them together and make a chain loop at one corner. Work another round of double crochet and several stitches into the chain loop to make a sturdy hanger.

2 | If you do not have two swatches of a similar size, crochet a plain piece of double crochet fabric for the back then proceed as above.

Garment shapes

Very few people will be the same body shape as the model on a printed crochet pattern and sometimes it is difficult to know whether a particular style of garment will suit you, particularly if you are tall, petite or take a plus size. Try sketching a croquis of your shape on paper, then experiment with different styles and shapes to see which ones work best.

62 Preparing a croquis

Once you have settled on a design, ensure that the instructions are written in your size and that measurements are accurate. Check the pattern to see whether the garment is a standard fit, tight, loose or oversized. Different fittings can make a noticeable difference to the size of a finished piece. Review all the information available before deciding which size fits you best.

Start by making a sketch called a croquis – a simple line drawing of your body shape – and use it as a tool to test different styles, garment shapes and colour combinations. Ask a friend to take digital photographs of you in your underwear or wearing a body leotard. You will need full-body shots taken from the front, back and sides.

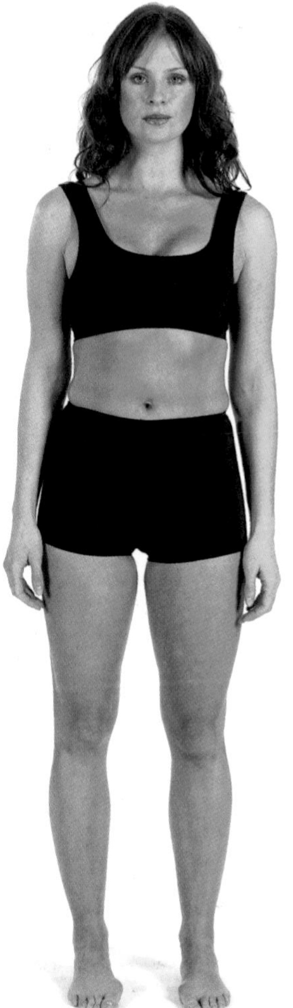

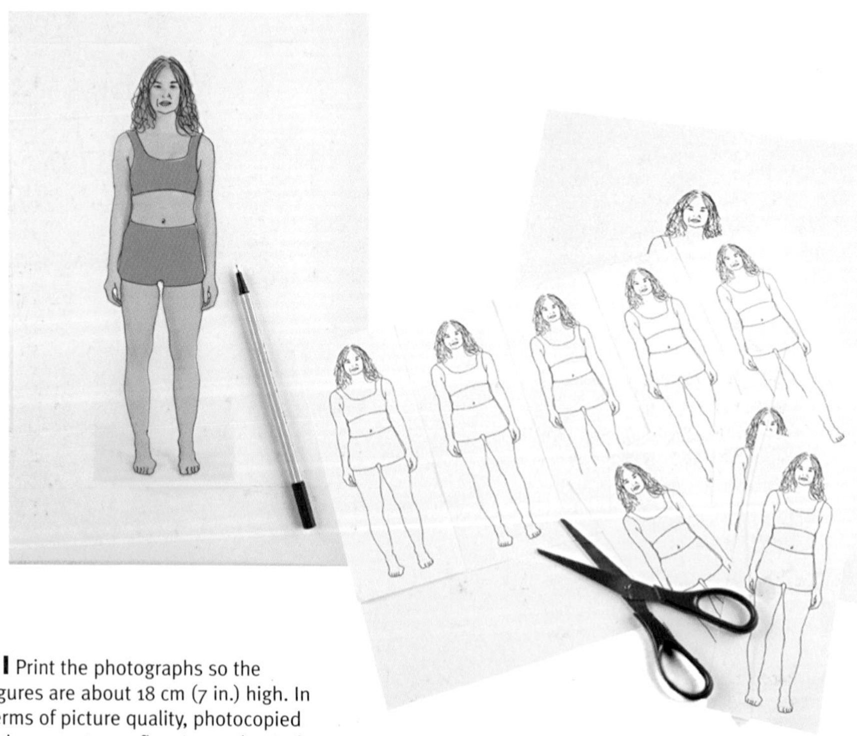

1 | Print the photographs so the figures are about 18 cm (7 in.) high. In terms of picture quality, photocopied enlargements are fine. Lay a sheet of tracing paper over each figure and trace its outline, adding details such as the waistline, neckline and bust points. These tracings constitute your croquis.

2 | Reduce the front-view figures so they are about 8 cm (3 in.) high. Make six to eight same-size copies. Cut out and stick the copies onto a larger piece of paper to make your croquis sheet.

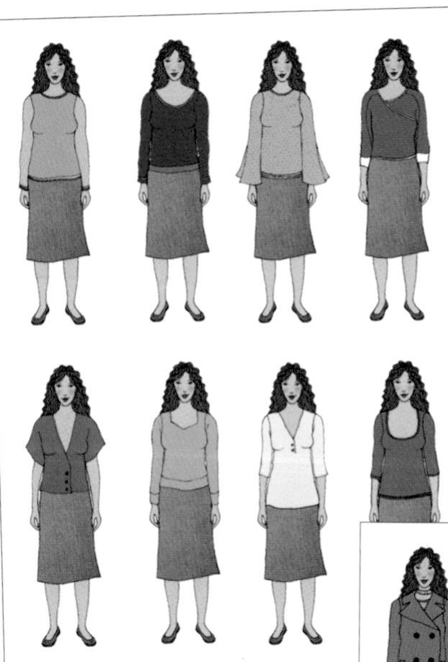

3 | Block in different garment shapes using the marker pens. Start with a roundneck sweater, for instance, and see whether it suits your body shape. Experiment using different necklines, make the sweater shorter, longer or simply add different sleeves.

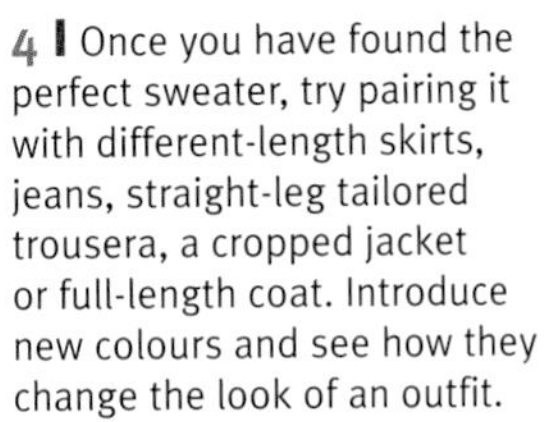

4 | Once you have found the perfect sweater, try pairing it with different-length skirts, jeans, straight-leg tailored trousera, a cropped jacket or full-length coat. Introduce new colours and see how they change the look of an outfit.

63 A good fit

Accurate body measurements are vital but the fit of a finished item can vary from the actual body measurements by an extra 15 cm (6 in.) or more. This difference is known as ease. Although the pattern might describe a garment as fitting a particular bust size, a close-fitting sweater, for example, will differ from one designed to fit loosely.

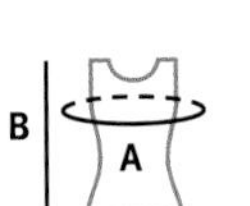

very close fit
actual bust/chest size

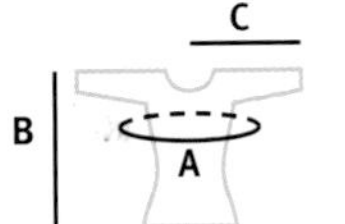

close fit
actual bust/chest size plus 2.5–5 cm (1–2 in.)

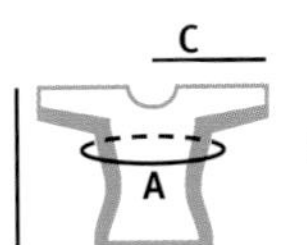

standard fit
bust/chest plus 5–10 cm (2–4 in.)

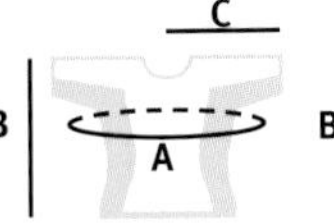

loose fit
bust/chest plus 10–15 cm (4–6 in.)

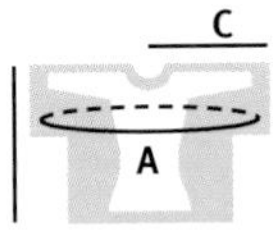

oversized fit
bust/chest plus 15 cm (6 in.) or more

A bust/chest

B garment length from back neck

C centre back neck to cuff with arm slightly bent

TRY IT

64 Body measurements

Once you have measured yourself, keep a record of when these measurements were taken.

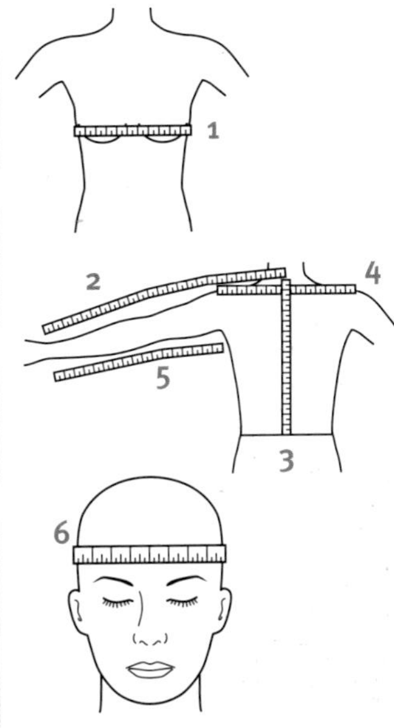

1 | Bust: without pulling the tape measure too tightly, measure around the fullest part of your chest.

2 | Centre back from the neck to the cuff: with one elbow slightly bent, measure from the back of the neck, across the shoulder and elbow to the wrist.

3 | Back waist length: measure from the base of the neck to the waistline.

4 | Cross back: measure from shoulder to shoulder.

5 | Sleeve length: measure from the armpit to the wrist.

6 | Head: measure across the forehead and around the circumference of the skull.

Getting a good fit from a readymade pattern

It pays to choose your pattern with care so it suits your height, weight and body shape (page 36). You may love the look of a photographed garment but it may not be flattering on you.

65 Check the schematic

Compare the measurements given on a schematic against those of an existing garment that fits you well. Make any necessary adjustments to the pattern at this stage.

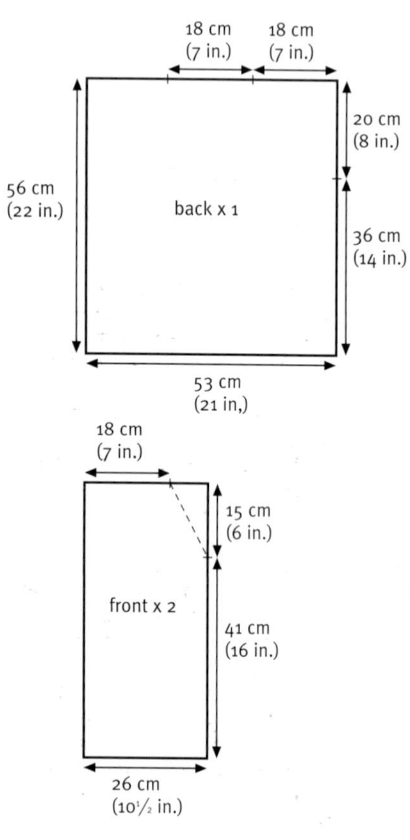

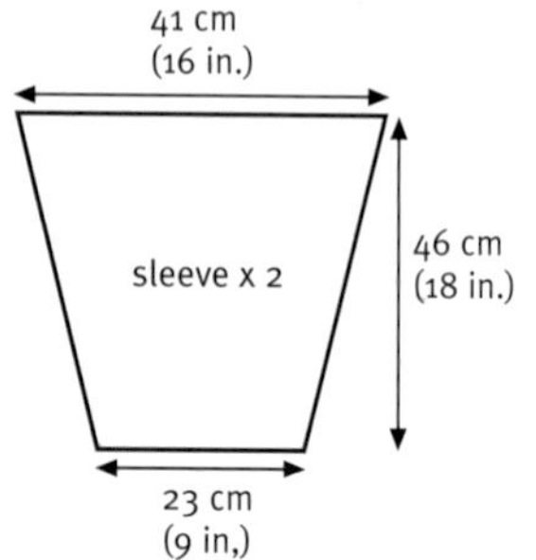

It is easy to lengthen a sleeve by working a deeper edging around the cuff.

Make a more generous collar by altering the position of the buttons and loops or try eliminating the top button and loop.

To widen the neckline, make slightly shorter shoulder seams.

Shorten the sleeves by working less rows between the increases. Make sure that you spread the increases evenly along the sleeve length.

If you need to make a garment wider or narrower, remember that you will have to add or subtract a complete pattern repeat.

66

Checklist for a well-fitting garment

Now that you have chosen your pattern and yarn, consider the ways in which a readymade pattern can be altered.

- Take your body measurements correctly (page 37).
- Decide whether you want your garment to be loose or tight fitting and how much ease you require (page 37).
- Check your requirements against the fit of the garment pattern before deciding on the size.
- If substituting yarn, choose one of a similar weight and composition to the pattern yarn.
- Swatch and re-swatch as necessary until you like the feel of the fabric (page 34) and get tension (page 32).
- Always block your swatches before measuring to ensure the tension measurements are accurate.
- When lengthening or shortening sleeves, change where the increases or decreases fall, moving them closer together for a shorter sleeve or wider apart for a longer sleeve.
- Alter the length of the shaped front and back pieces. For straight styles, simply work either more or less rows.
- On a set-in sleeve, leave the armhole shaping as written (even if this means working a smaller or larger size on the pattern and adjusting other measurements to compensate).
- Pin or tack the garment pieces together then try them on before blocking and seaming. If you need to make drastic alterations, it is less damaging to the yarn to undo the garment pieces at this stage than after they are blocked.
- Block the garment pieces before seaming to ensure even seams and a good finish.

Design basics

The first step toward designing your own garment is working out what you want it to look like. Will it be a tank, vest, sweater, cardigan or jacket? Do you want it to be long, cropped, loose or fitted? With short sleeves or long sleeves? Before starting to swatch, select your type of yarn, the stitch pattern and make sure you draw a schematic, an accurate outline of the garment pieces and their measurements.

67

Making a schematic

Use a pencil to rough out your schematic on squared paper. Once you are happy with the shapes you have drawn, block them in with ink and erase any pencil marks to tidy up your sketch.

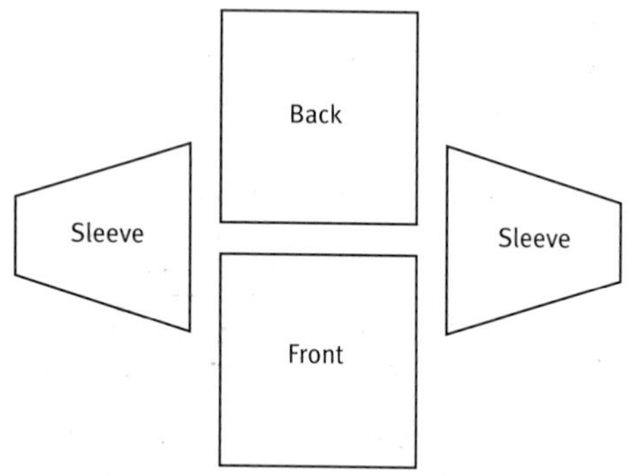

1 | Sketch a rough outline without any shaping or details of the front, back and sleeves on your garment.

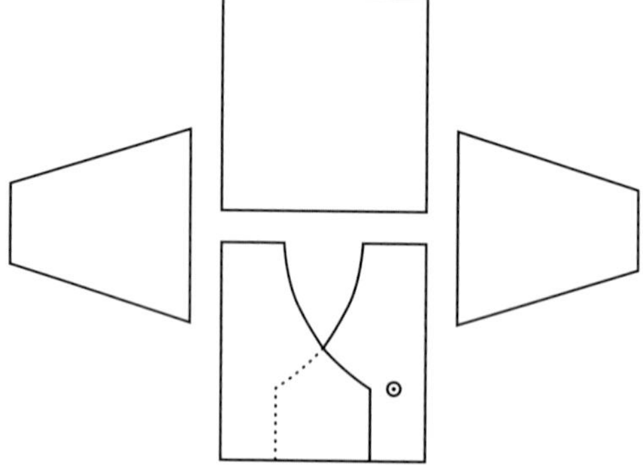

2 | Draw in the details of the front piece. Notice how it has been divided into two to make a crossover top with a button fastening and a 'V'-shaped neckline. The back piece remains unchanged.

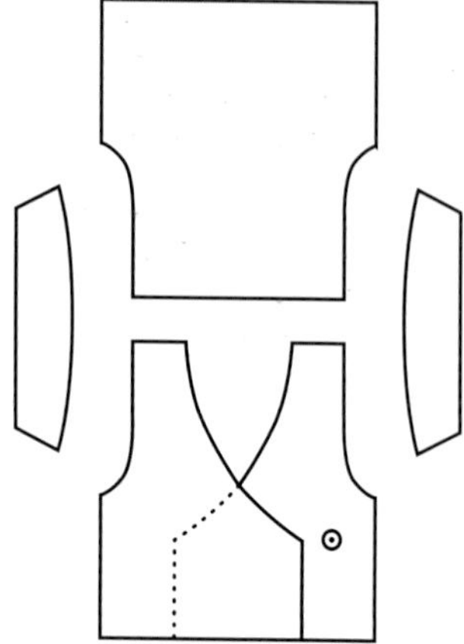

3 | Decide on the sleeves for your garment and alter your template accordingly. Add armhole shaping to the front and back to suit the shape of the chosen sleeves.

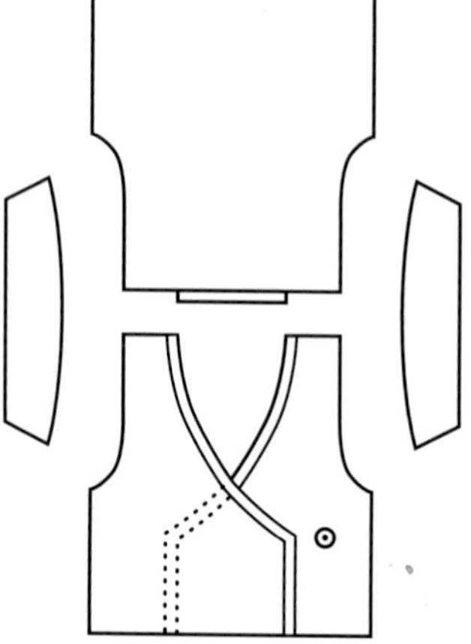

4 | Add more detail to your schematic such as edgings. Give accurate measurements for each piece, taken either from a well-tailored garment or from the charts on pages 152–4. Design features add style and individuality to even the simplest item.

Two kinds of coloured beads (page 134) trim the edging and the cross-over shape is enhanced by the stylish single-button fastening.

This light and dainty summer top with cap sleeves and a cross-over front can be worn on its own or slipped over a long-sleeved cotton top or a T-shirt.

68

Guidelines for using your swatch and schematic

- Measure the tension of your swatch (page 32) to determine how many rows and stitches you need to work to make 10 cm (4 in.) of crochet fabric. Include any partial stitches and rows if these occur.
- Divide each of these numbers by four to give the average number of stitches and rows to 2.5 cm (1 in.) of fabric. Include any partial stitches and rows if these occur.
- Divide the desired width of the garment by the stitch tension. The resulting number will tell you how many stitches you need to work the correct width.
- Divide the desired length of the garment by the row tension. The resulting number will tell you how many rows you need to work the correct length.
- Use these numbers to help you calculate how many stitches you need to increase or decrease when shaping, and how many rows you need to work between increases or decreases.
- When making the foundation chain, add the number of turning chains (page 54) for the stitch that you intend to use.
- Make a note of your calculations on the schematic and work the garment pieces from that information. You may prefer to write down the instructions as a conventional pattern instead.

Designing scarves

As long strips of fabric that do not require any shaping, scarves are the perfect accessory and quick to make from expensive or luxury yarn as they use up relatively little material. Crocheting a scarf is also a good way of using up the odd lengths of yarn in your stash that you cannot bear to throw away.

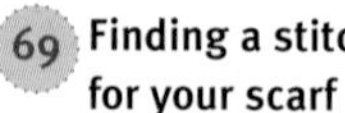

TRY IT

69 Finding a stitch pattern for your scarf

From plain mesh to more elaborate patterns, lace crochet stitches make great scarves, are fairly quick to work using medium-weight yarn, and drape beautifully around the neck.

mesh

trellis

trellis and shells

fans and shells

large lace pattern

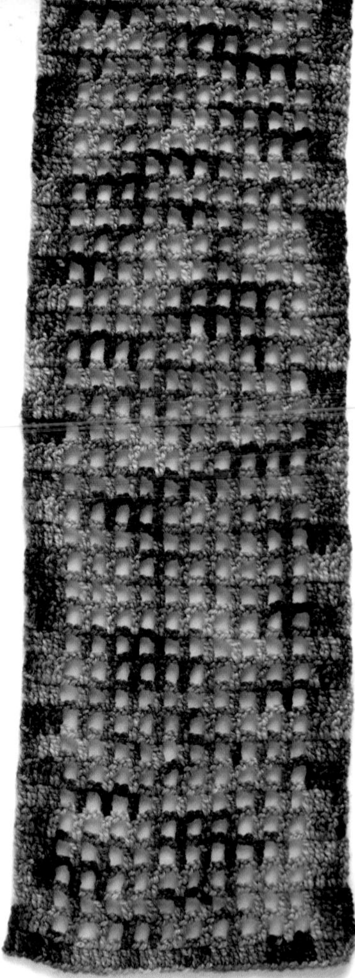

Narrow filet crochet mesh

Random stripes using yarn leftovers

70

Narrow filet crochet mesh

Worked in handpainted merino wool using a 3 mm (size D) hook, the pattern is a simple 1 tr, 2 ch mesh edged with 4 tr on the long edges and one row of dc on the short edge. The mesh pattern breaks up the yarn colours well and helps to avoid areas of pooling colour.

71

Random stripes using yarn leftovers

This stripy scarf in a slightly textured variation of double crochet makes a soft yet sturdy fabric. Worked using small amounts of leftover DK yarn, each end is finished off with a fringe in a different colour of yarn.

Lengthwise stripes with self fringe

Solid colour with double crochet edging

72 Lengthwise stripes with self fringe

Make a long foundation chain and work your scarf along the length instead of from side to side. Use a different yarn for each row, mixing textures and leaving long yarn ends as you change colour. Do not darn in the yarn ends. When the crochet is finished, neatly knot and trim the ends to make a fringe.

73 Solid colour with double crochet edging

This lovely plain scarf featuring a ripple stitch pattern is made from merino wool. This type of wool wears well and is warm, soft and gentle against the skin. The edges are finished with a single row of double crochet edging (page 100).

FIX IT

74 *Scarf ends that do not match up when working a ripple stitch pattern?*

Begin your scarf at the centre and work outwards from each side of the foundation chain. This technique works well for most stitches that make a shaped edge but is unsuitable for heavily zigzagged or wavy ripple stitches.

1 | Make the desired length of foundation chain as stated in the pattern. Work the first pattern row as directed.

2 | Work the first half of the scarf in the usual way, finishing at the end of a pattern repeat. Fasten off the yarn and darn in the end.

3 | Return to the start of the scarf, join the yarn and work the first pattern row into the other side of the foundation chain. If the first row is an RS row, make sure the RS of the work is facing you.

4 | Work the second half of the scarf to match the first, making sure that you finish both halves on the same pattern row.

Designing shawls and wraps

Popular both as a fashion accessory and practical way of keeping the chills at bay, shawls and wraps are enjoyable pieces to crochet. Usually triangular, square or round, they can be made up from one piece of crochet fabric or from blocks joined together. Wraps and stoles are long rectangles with either plain ends or fringed trims. When wearing them, fold a round shawl in half to make a half-moon shape that is double the thickness, fold a square across the width to make a shallow rectangle, or from point to point to make a triangle.

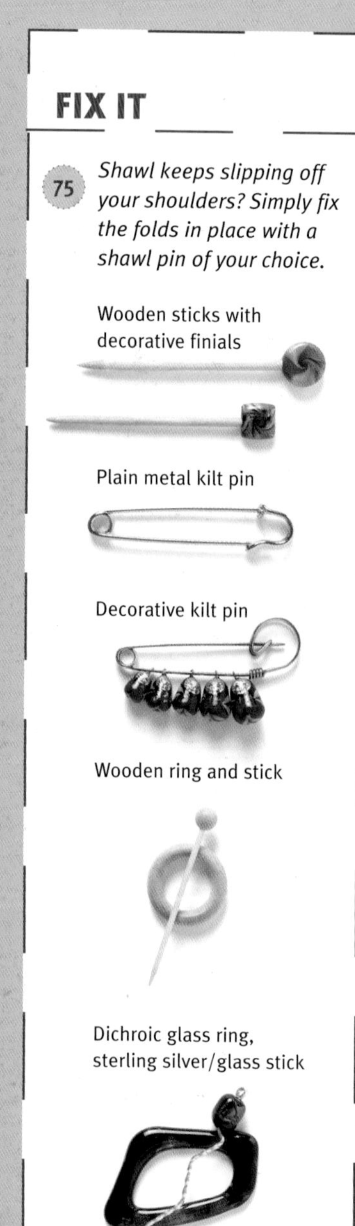

FIX IT

75 *Shawl keeps slipping off your shoulders? Simply fix the folds in place with a shawl pin of your choice.*

Wooden sticks with decorative finials

Plain metal kilt pin

Decorative kilt pin

Wooden ring and stick

Dichroic glass ring, sterling silver/glass stick

Shawl and wrap shapes

Shawls and wraps can be made in many different sizes and shapes, from a tiny decorative shoulder shawl to a warm, enveloping wrap. The sizes given below are only suggestions so feel free to experiment.

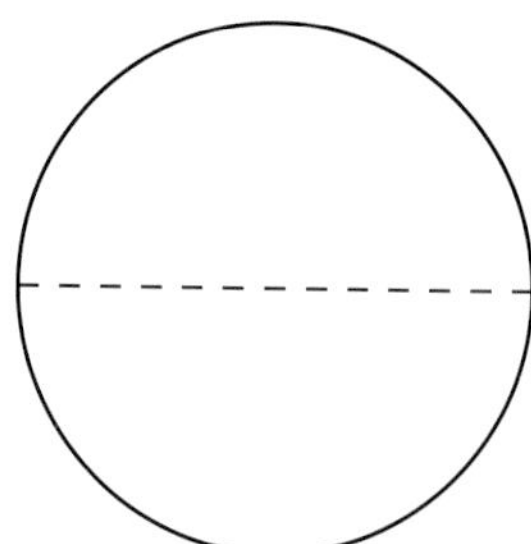

Round shawl

This shawl is normally worn folded in half. A good, all-purpose size is around 102 cm (40 in.) in diameter.

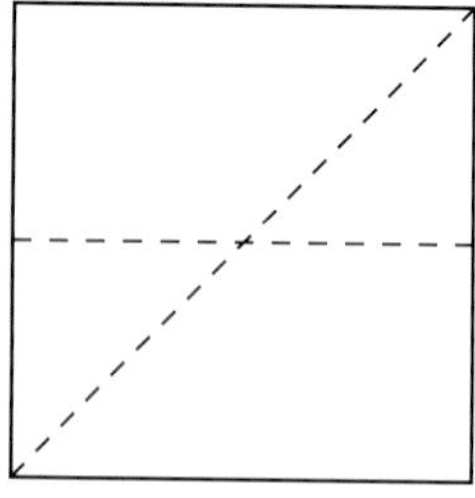

Square shawl

A square shawl can be folded to make a triangle or rectangle which are usually larger than a round shawl at 122–152 cm (48–60 in.) square.

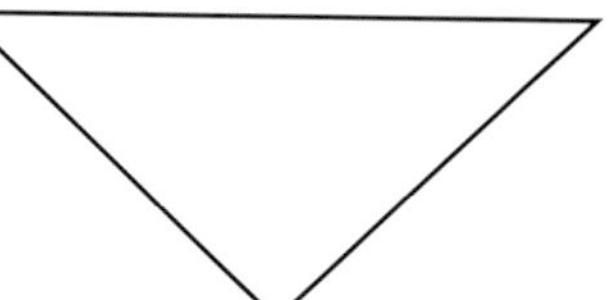

Triangular shawl

A triangular shawl needs to be wide enough to sit easily across the shoulders. Make sure it is 122–183 cm (48–72 in.) across the wingspan, depending on the effect you require, and about 32–40 in. (81–102 cm) deep.

Rectangular stole

A stole is normally 46–51 cm (18–20 in.) wide and 183–203 cm (72–80 in.) long.

Rectangular wrap

Wider and shorter than a stole, a wrap can measure 61–76 cm (24–30 in.) wide and 168–183 cm (66–72 in.) long.

77 Triangular shawl in wool

This large shawl was worked outwards from the centre of the neck edge in a shell pattern and finished with three rows of double crochet edging. Yarn: DK-weight yarn leftovers in blue, mauve, purple, jade green and grey worked with a 4 mm (size F) hook.

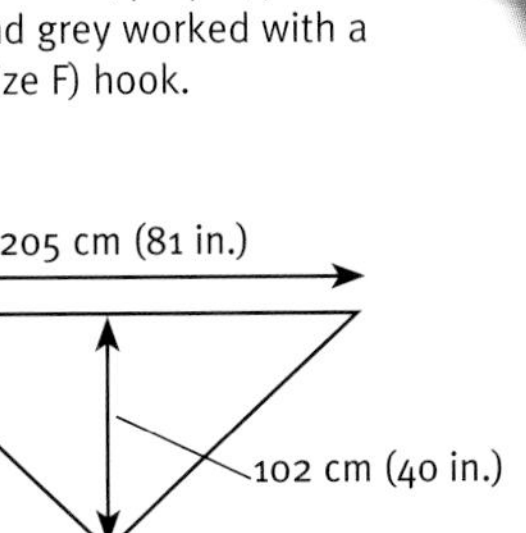

78 Evening wrap in a luxury yarn

Worked in lacy blocks crocheted together and finished with a delicate looped edging, this wrap is perfect for special occasions. Yarn: pure silk 4-ply (sportweight) worked with a 2.5 mm (size C) hook.

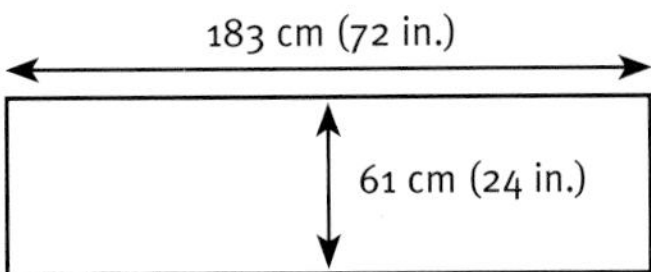

79 Filet crochet wrap in wool

Filet crochet makes lovely wraps and shawls. Although this wrap looks delicate and lacy, it is warm and cosy when worked in woollen yarn. Worked in plain mesh, it is dotted with tiny motifs and each end is decorated with a border. Yarn: superwash pure wool DK worked with a 4 mm (size F) hook.

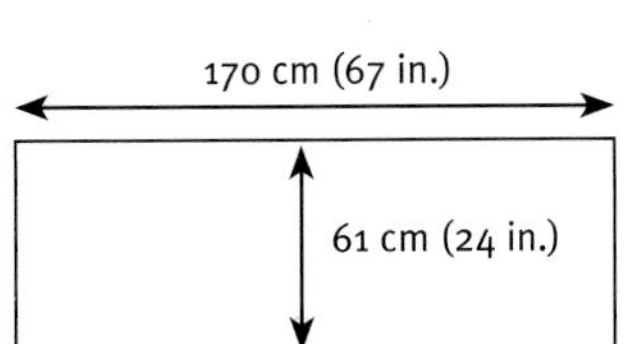

TRY IT

80 Working out a shawl shape

Experiment with different small-scale shapes using yarn leftovers. Label each swatch and give the construction details. Finally, make a proper swatch using the project yarn and hook. The four shapes below were worked in sock yarn using a small hook.

Start with a 6 ch ring to form the centre point of the neck edge. The inner blocks of stitches are made from 3 tr with 1 ch separating the blocks. Each edge block has four stitches and the centre line of increases is made by working [3 tr, 2 ch, 3 tr] into the same space.

Work two lines of increases instead of one and three stitches into every edge block. A shawl worked in this shape sits nicely on the shoulders because of the curved neck edge.

Start this triangle at the point with 4 ch, 2 tr into the fourth ch from the hook, turn. 3 ch (counts as 1 tr), 2 tr into first st, 1 ch, 3 tr into the third of 3 ch, turn.

Worked similarly to the third shape but with an extra stitch added to every side group. To stop the edges from pulling, try turning with 4 ch instead of 3 ch, making the last st of every row a dtr instead of a tr.

CROCHET TECHNIQUES

Crochet fabric is made from a combination of chains and basic stitches. To begin practising the basics, choose a smooth woollen yarn and suitable hook. Woollen yarn is very easy to work with and the smooth surface lets you see the stitches clearly as they are formed. You can find more information on hooks and yarns on pages 10–21.

Working a foundation chain

The foundation chain is the crochet equivalent of casting on in knitting and it is important to make sure that you have made the required number of chains for the pattern you are going to work. Chains (ch) are also used to bring the hook up to the correct level when turning at the end of a row (page 54), and as a component of lace and other fancy stitches (pages 62–9). The foundation chain is started with a slipknot, which anchors the yarn on the hook.

TRY IT

81 Using markers to help count long chains

When counting a long foundation chain, it is a good idea to slip a stitch marker or piece of spare yarn into the chain to mark every 10 or so stitches. This will make counting the foundation chain quicker, and it will be easier to check that you have worked the correct number of chains.

82 Making a slipknot

1 | With a 15 cm (6 in.) tail of yarn on the left, loop the ball end of the yarn around your right index finger. Carefully slip the loop off your finger. Holding the loop in your right hand, push a loop of the tail end through the first loop.

2 | Insert the hook into the second loop. Gently pull the tail end of the yarn to tighten the loop around the hook and complete the slipknot.

83 Holding the yarn

To control the supply of yarn from the ball, loop the tail end of the yarn over your left index finger, and take the yarn coming from the ball loosely around the ring finger on the same hand to tension it. Use your thumb and middle finger to help hold the work as you crochet. If it feels more comfortable, control the yarn by taking it around your little finger instead.

84 Working the foundation chain

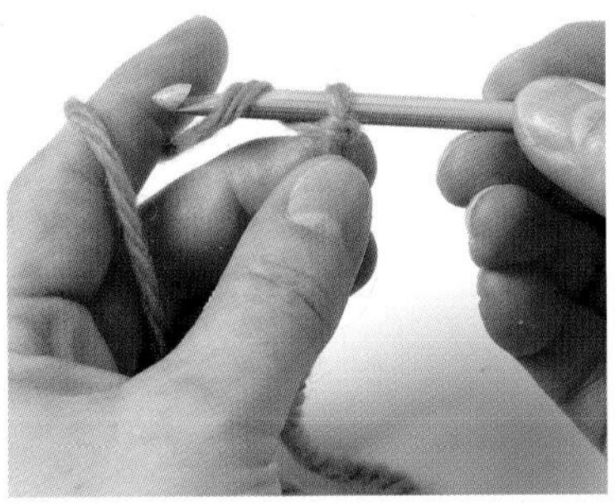

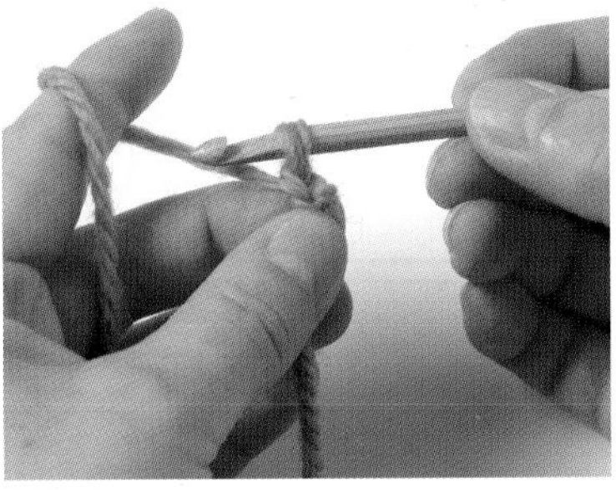

1 | Holding the hook with the slipknot in your right hand, and the yarn in your left, wrap the yarn over the hook. This is known as *yarn over* (yo) or *yarn over hook* (yoh). You should always wrap the yarn over the hook in the same way: around the back of the hook first (as shown).

2 | Draw the yarn-over loop through the slipknot, leaving a new loop on the hook to complete the first stitch of the chain.

3 | Repeat this process, drawing a new yarn-over loop through the stitch on the hook until the chain is the required length. Move your thumb and middle finger along the chain every few stitches to keep even tension on the yarn.

85 Counting chains

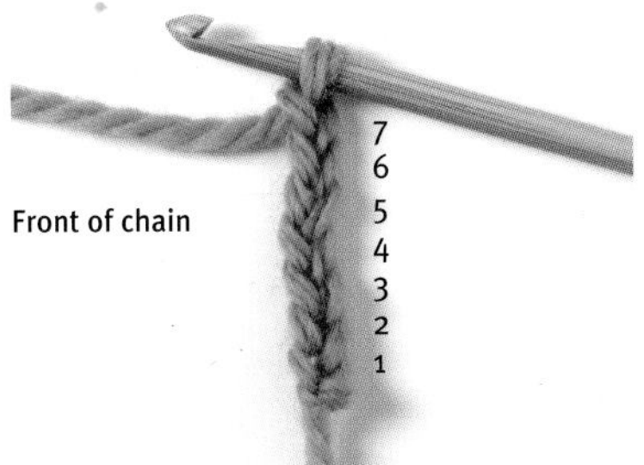

Front of chain

Back of chain

The front of the chain looks like a series of 'V' shapes or little hearts, while the back of the chain forms a distinctive 'bump' of yarn behind each 'V'. Working up the chain from the slipknot, count each 'V'-shaped loop on the front of the chain as one chain stitch. The loop on the hook is never counted. You may find it easier to turn the chain over and count the bumps on the back of the chain instead.

86 Working into the foundation chain

1 | You are now ready to work the first row of stitches into the chain. There are different ways of inserting the hook into the chain, but this is the easiest way for the beginner—although it makes a rather loose edge. Holding the chain with the front (the 'V' shapes) facing you, insert the hook into the top loop of the chain closest to the hook, and work the first stitch as required by the pattern.

2 | To make a stronger, neater edge that does not require an edge treatment, turn the chain so the back of it (the bumps) is facing you. Work the first row of stitches as instructed in the pattern, inserting the hook into the bump on the back of each chain stitch.

87 Making an approximate foundation chain

To eliminate counting errors when making a large piece of crochet, such as an afghan or shawl, work your foundation chain a few inches longer than you need. Work the first few rows of stitches following your pattern, then unravel any extra chains at the beginning by cutting off the slipknot and carefully pulling out the unwanted chains.

Working basic stitches

The basis of crochet fabric is a small number of basic stitches of differing heights. The shortest stitch is double crochet (dc); half treble crochet (htr), treble crochet (tr) and double treble crochet (dtr) are progressively taller. Basic stitches can be worked in rows to make solid fabric, while grouped or combined stitches create lacy or textured fabrics.

88 Working a slip stitch

Slip stitches (sl st) are rarely used to create a crochet fabric. Instead the stitch is used to join rounds of crochet or to move the hook and yarn across a group of existing stitches to a new position. To work a slip stitch into the foundation chain, insert the hook from front to back under the top loop of the second chain from the hook. Wrap the yarn over the hook and draw it through both the chain and the loop on the hook. One loop remains on the hook and one slip stitch has been made.

89 Double crochet

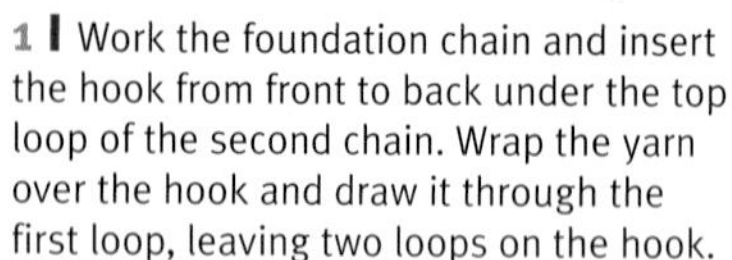

1 I Work the foundation chain and insert the hook from front to back under the top loop of the second chain. Wrap the yarn over the hook and draw it through the first loop, leaving two loops on the hook.

2 I To complete the stitch, wrap the yarn over the hook and draw it through both loops on the hook. Continue in this way along the row, working one double crochet stitch into each chain.

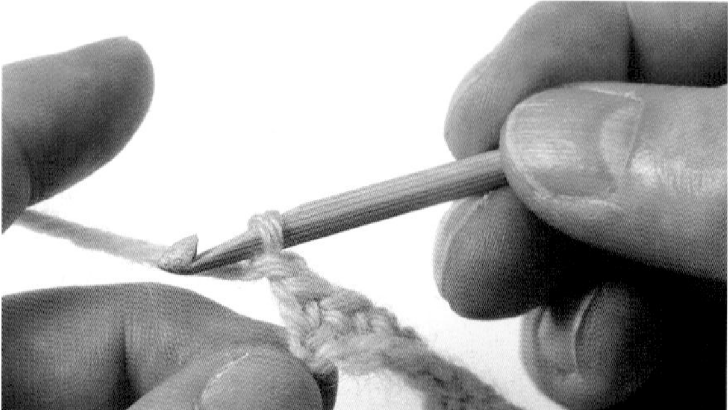

3 I At the end of the row, make one chain for the turning chain (this chain does not count as a stitch on the next row). Turn the work over, ready to begin the next row.

4 I Insert the hook from front to back under both loops of the first double crochet at the beginning of the row. Work a double crochet stitch into each stitch of the previous row, being careful to work the final double crochet stitch into the last stitch of the row below, but not into the turning chain.

90 Half treble crochet

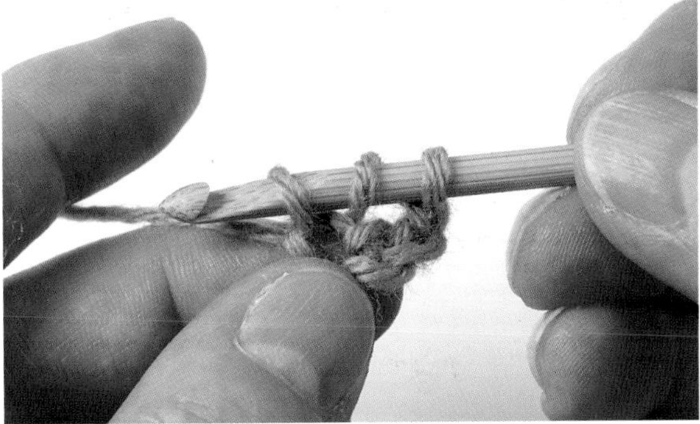

1 I Wrap the yarn over the hook and insert the hook from front to back into the work. If you are at the start of the first row, insert the hook under the top loop of the third chain from the hook. Draw the yarn through the chain, leaving three loops on the hook.

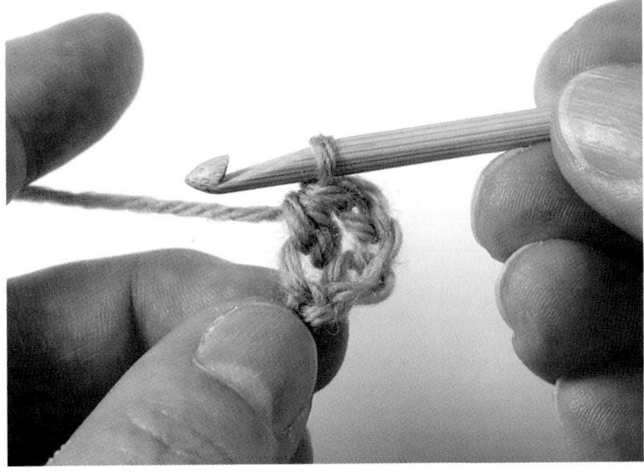

2 I Wrap the yarn over the hook and draw through all three loops on the hook. One loop remains on the hook, and one half treble crochet stitch has been made.

3 I Continue along the row, working one half treble crochet into each chain. At the end of the row, work two chains for the turning chain before turning the work.

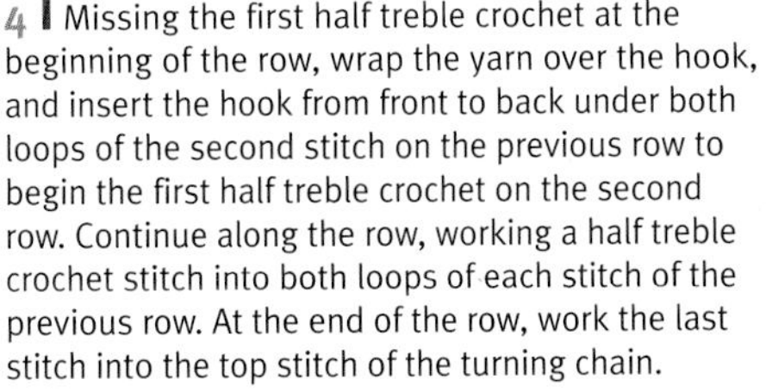

4 I Missing the first half treble crochet at the beginning of the row, wrap the yarn over the hook, and insert the hook from front to back under both loops of the second stitch on the previous row to begin the first half treble crochet on the second row. Continue along the row, working a half treble crochet stitch into both loops of each stitch of the previous row. At the end of the row, work the last stitch into the top stitch of the turning chain.

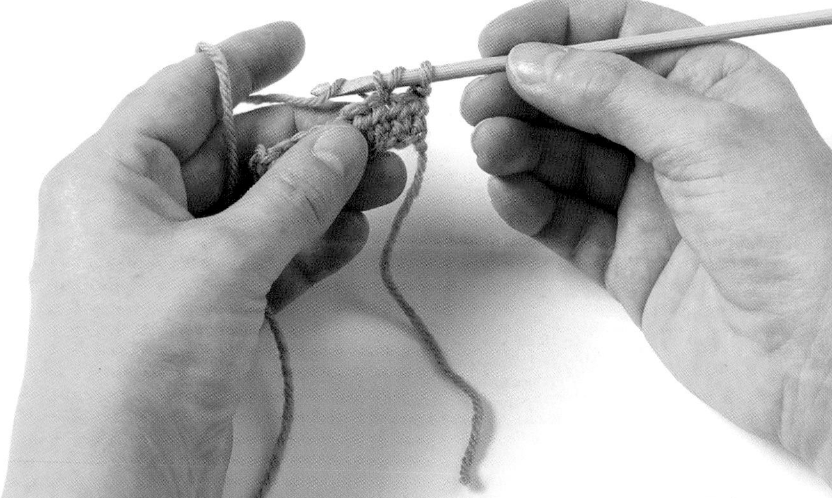

91

Treble crochet

1 | Wrap the yarn over the hook and insert the hook from front to back into the work. If you are at the beginning of the first row, insert the hook under the top loop of the fourth chain from the hook. Draw the yarn through the chain, leaving three loops on the hook.

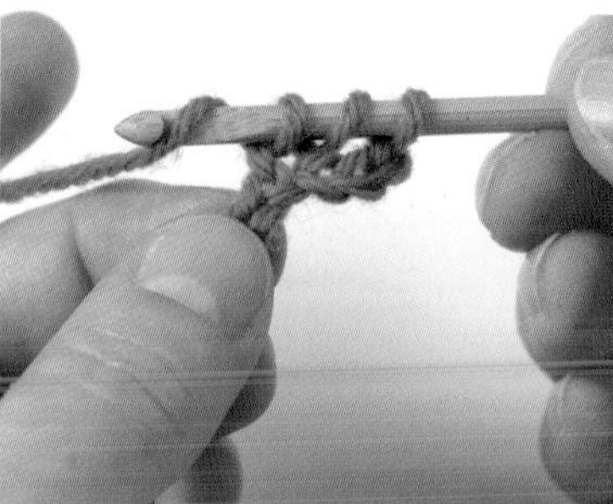

2 | Wrap the yarn over the hook and draw it through the first two loops on the hook. Two loops remain on the hook.

3 | Wrap the yarn over the hook. Draw the yarn through the two loops on the hook. One loop remains on the hook and one treble crochet stitch has been worked.

4 | Continue along the row, working one treble crochet into each stitch on the previous row. At the end of the row, work three chains for the turning chain and turn the work over.

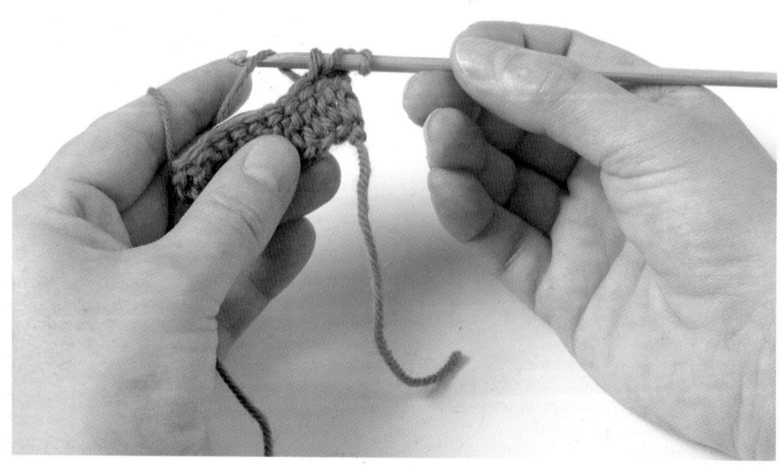

5 | Missing the first treble crochet at the start of the previous row, wrap the yarn over the hook and insert the hook from front to back under both loops of the second stitch on the previous row to make the first treble crochet stitch. Continue along the row, working a treble crochet into each stitch of the previous row. At the end of the row, work the last stitch into the top stitch of the turning chain.

92

Double treble crochet

1 | Wrap the yarn over the hook twice. Insert the hook from front to back into the work. If you are at the beginning of the row, insert the hook under the top loop of the fifth chain from the hook. Wrap the yarn over the hook and draw through, leaving four loops on the hook. Wrap the yarn over the hook again.

2 | Working in a similar way to treble crochet, draw the yarn through two loops leaving three loops on the hook. Wrap the yarn over the hook again and draw through two loops, leaving two loops on the hook.

3 | To complete the stitch, wrap the yarn over the hook again and draw through the remaining two loops on the hook. Repeat along the row.

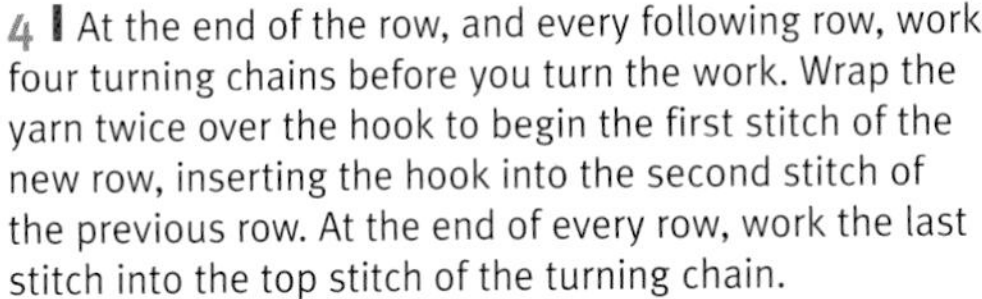

4 | At the end of the row, and every following row, work four turning chains before you turn the work. Wrap the yarn twice over the hook to begin the first stitch of the new row, inserting the hook into the second stitch of the previous row. At the end of every row, work the last stitch into the top stitch of the turning chain.

Extended stitches

Extended stitches (also called Elmore stitches) are variations of four basic stitches: double, half treble, treble and double treble crochet stitches. Each variation makes a slightly taller stitch than the corresponding basic stitch. They are useful ways of adding shaping when a gradual height increase is needed. Each stitch can also be used to form an attractive fabric in its own right.

93

Extended double crochet

Work the first stage of an ordinary double crochet (insert hook into work, yarn over and draw through) so you have two loops on the hook. Wrap the yarn over the hook and draw it through the first loop on the hook, leaving two loops on the hook. To complete the stitch, wrap the yarn over the hook and draw it through both loops on the hook.

94

Extended half treble crochet

Work the first stage of a half treble crochet (yarn over hook, insert hook into work, yarn over, draw hook back through work) so you have three loops on the hook. Wrap the yarn over the hook. Draw it through the first loop, leaving three loops on the hook. To complete the stitch, wrap the yarn over the hook and draw it through the three loops on the hook.

95

Extended treble crochet

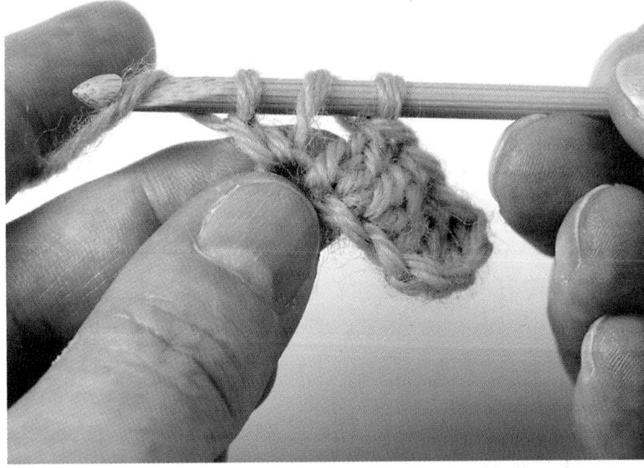

Work the first stage of an ordinary treble crochet (yarn over, insert hook into work, yarn over and draw back through the work) so you have three loops on the hook. Wrap the yarn over the hook and draw it through the first loop on the hook, leaving three loops on the hook. Wrap the yarn over the hook again, and draw it through the first two loops on the hook. To complete the stitch, wrap the yarn again and draw it through the two remaining loops on the hook.

96

Extended double treble crochet

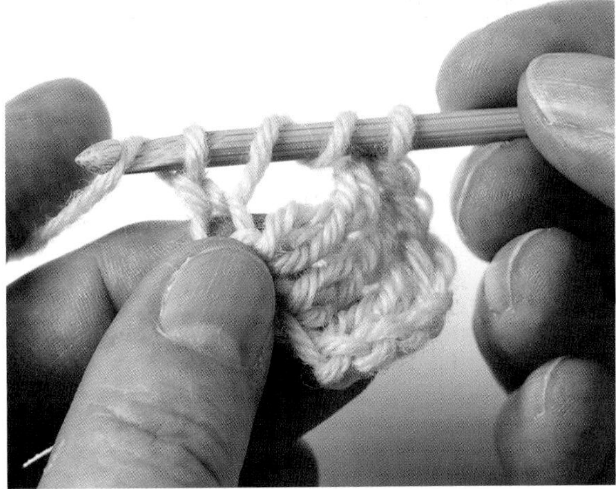

Work the first stage of an ordinary double treble crochet (yarn over twice, insert hook into work, yarn over and draw back through the work), so you have four loops on the hook. Wrap the yarn over the hook and draw it through the first loop on the hook, leaving four loops on the hook. Wrap the yarn over the hook again, and draw it through the first two loops, leaving three loops on the hook. Wrap the yarn over again, and draw it through the first two loops, leaving two loops on the hook. To complete the stitch, wrap the yarn over again and draw it through the remaining two loops on the hook.

Turning and starting chains

When working crochet in rows or rounds, you will need to work out the number of extra chains at the start of each row or round required to bring the crochet hook up to the correct height for the subsequent stitch. Worked at the end of a straight row, these additional chains are called a turning chain. Worked at the start of a round, these extra chains are known as a starting chain.

97

Number of turning chains

The diagram on the right shows the number of chain stitches required to make a turn for each stitch. If you tend to work chain stitches tightly, you may need to keep the edges of your work loose by working an extra chain.

The turning or starting chain is counted as the first stitch of the row – except when working double crochet where the single turning chain is ignored. For example, 3 ch (counts as 1 tr) at the start of a row or round means the turning or starting chain contains three chain stitches (counted as the equivalent of one treble crochet stitch). When working a stitch pattern, a turning or starting chain may be longer than the number required for the stitch (counts as one stitch plus the number of chains). For example, 5 ch (counts as 1 tr, 2 ch) means that the turning or starting chain is equivalent to one treble crochet stitch plus two chain stitches.

At the end of the row or round, the final stitch is worked into the turning or starting chain worked on the previous row or round. The final stitch may be worked into the top chain of the turning or starting chain or into another specified stitch of the chain. For example, 1 tr into 3rd of 3 ch means that the final stitch is a treble crochet stitch worked into the third stitch of the turning or starting chain.

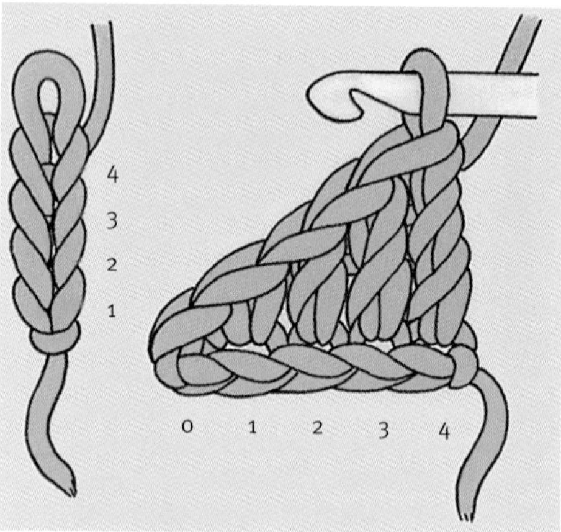

Double crochet stitch	1 turning chain
Half treble crochet stitch	2 turning chains
Treble crochet stitch	3 turning chains
Double treble crochet stitch	4 turning chains

98

Working into the front and back loops

Unless stitch pattern instructions tell you otherwise, most crochet stitches are worked by taking the hook under both loops of the stitches made on the previous row. By changing the way of working by inserting your hook under a single loop, either the back or the front loop of the stitch, you get a different effect. The unworked loop becomes a horizontal bar and the character and appearance of the fabric changes. Although treble crochet stitches are shown here, you can use this technique with any crochet stitch.

Working into the front loop

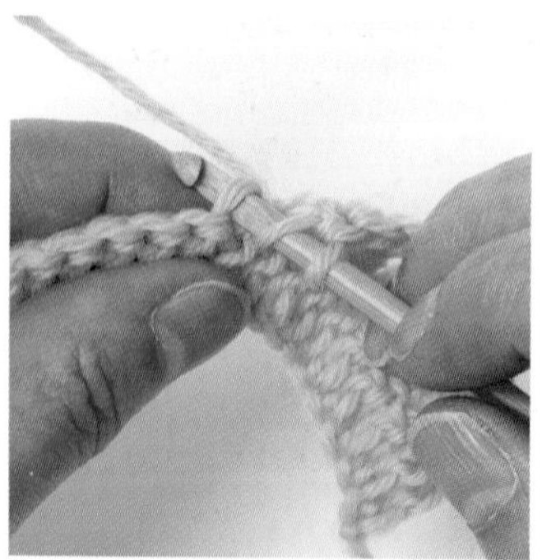

To work into the front of a row of stitches, insert the hook only under the front loops of the stitches made on the previous row.

Swatch worked into the front loops

Working only into the front loops produces a fabric with slight horizontal ridges.

Working into the back loop

To work into the back of a row of stitches, insert the hook only under the back loops of the stitches on the previous row.

Swatch worked into the back loops

The ridges are more defined than those produced by working into the front loops.

99

Counting rows

When counting rows of basic crochet fabric, remember that basic stitches have different heights, ranging from the shortest double crochet to the tallest treble crochet.

Double crochet

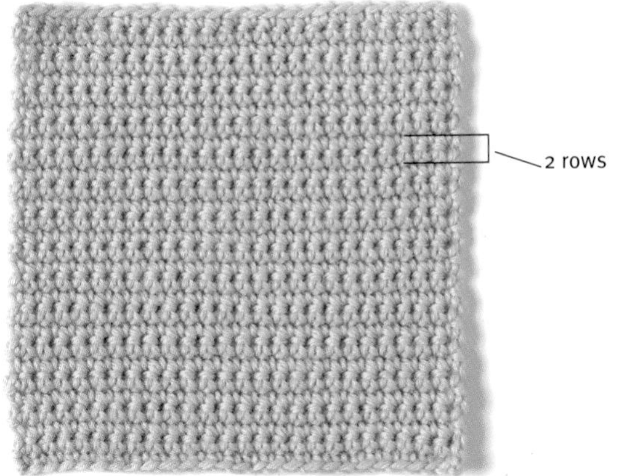

Treble crochet

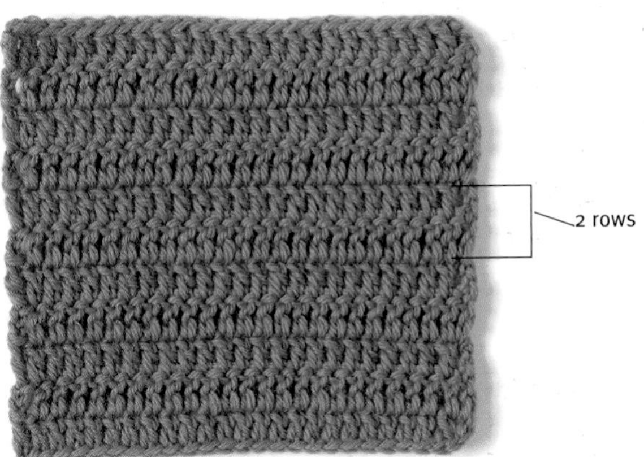

Half treble crochet

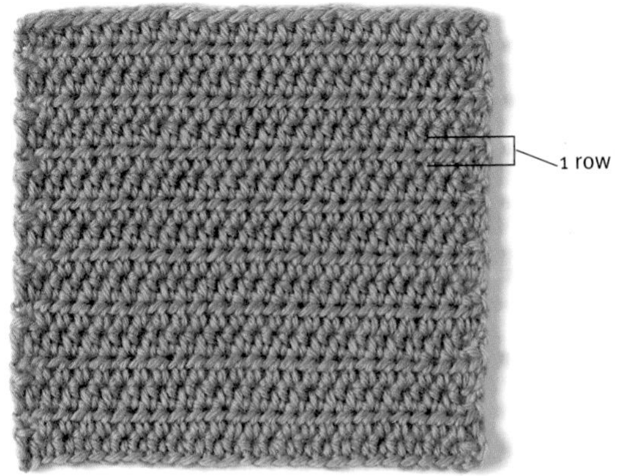

Double treble crochet

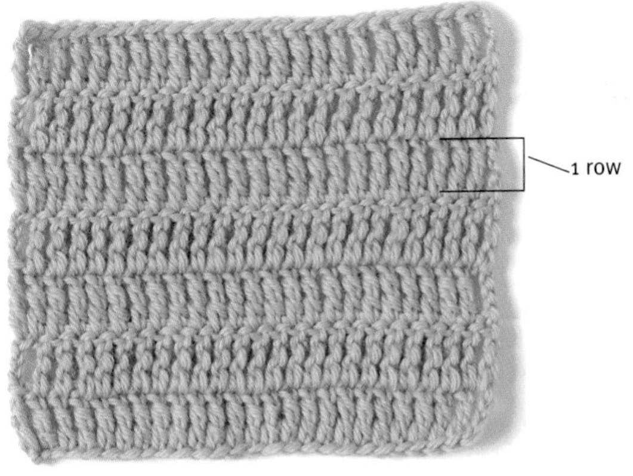

Understanding stitch patterns, multiples and repeats

Stitch patterns are worked over a set number of chains. It is vital that you work the correct number of foundation chains before the first pattern row. After you have worked the chain, follow the pattern row by row. Work any instructions inside the square brackets the number of times stated and repeat the sections between asterisks as directed. After working all the rows of instructions once, the pattern will tell you how to continue and which row or rows you should repeat. If you are working a striped pattern as shown, the instructions will tell you how many rows of each yarn colour you should work.

100 Working the soft wave stitch pattern

Working the foundation chain

The foundation chain for this stitch pattern is worked in multiples of 12 (12, 24, 36, 48), adding three chains to the total to ensure the pattern works correctly. To check that you work the correct number, insert a marker into every twelfth chain. Remember to add the extra three chains at the end.

Working row 1

1 | Begin by working a tr into the fourth chain from the hook to account for the three extra chains (the three missed chains count as the first stitch of the row). Work the series of instructions between * and repeat. This equals one complete repeat of the stitch pattern over 12 chains.

2 | Removing markers as you reach them, repeat this set of instructions along the row until you reach the last ch. Instead of working the usual [2 tr into next ch] twice, end the last repeat by working 2 tr into the last chain to make the end of the row match the beginning.

Working row 2

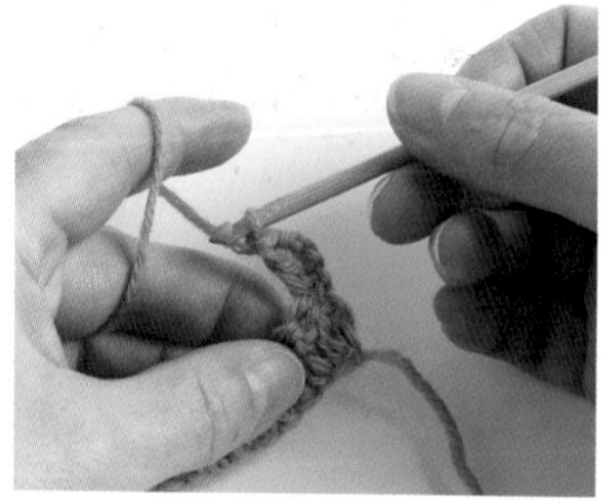

1 | First work 3 ch (the turning chain that counts as the first stitch of the row) then a tr into the same stitch shared as the base of 3 ch.

2 | Repeat the series of instructions from * to rep across the row until you reach the missed chains of the previous row. As before, the last repeat has a different ending so work 2 tr into the third of the missed chains.

Working row 3

1 | Begin with 3 ch (this counts as the first tr of the new row), then work a tr into the same stitch. Repeat the instructions from * to rep, stopping when you reach the turning chain of the previous row.

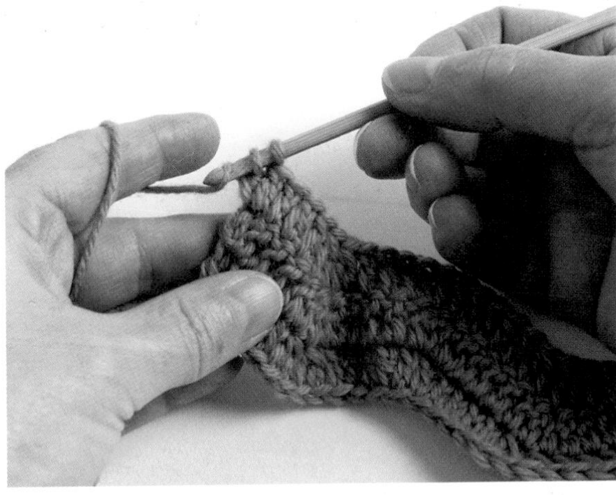

2 | Work the last 2 tr of the row into the third chain of the previous row's turning chain. The pattern's next and subsequent rows are made by repeating the instructions for row 3.

101

Working a repeating colour sequence

Yarn colours in a stitch pattern can be referenced in different ways. Each one may be represented by a letter (as shown here), a colour name (lavender, pearl, amethyst), or by one colour designated as the Main Colour (MC) with the remaining ones shown as Contrast Colour (CC) plus a number or letter.

Colours from left to right; yarn A, B, C, D, and E.

Soft wave stitch pattern

Foundation chain: multiple of 12 chains plus 3.
Using yarn A, make the required length of foundation chain.
Row 1: (RS) 1 tr into 4th ch from hook, *1 tr into each of next 3 chs, [tr2tog] twice, 1 tr into each of next 3 chs, [2 tr into next ch] twice; rep from * ending last rep with 2 tr into last ch, turn.
Row 2: 3 ch, 1 tr into same st, *1 tr into each of next 3 tr, [tro2tog] twice, 1 tr into each of next 3 tr, [2 tr into next tr] twice; rep from * ending last rep with 2 tr into 3rd of beg missed 3 ch, turn.
Row 3: 3 ch, 1 tr into same st, *1 tr into each of next 3 tr, [tr2tog] twice, 1 tr into each of next 3 tr, [2 tr into next tr] twice; rep from * ending last rep with 2 tr into 3rd of 3 ch, turn.
Repeat row 3, changing yarns in the following colour sequence: 4 rows in yarn A, 1 row in yarn B, 2 rows in yarn C, 3 rows in yarn D, 4 rows in yarn E.
Repeat for the length required. Fasten off yarn.

Joining in new yarns

When working all in one colour, try to join a new ball of yarn at the end of the row rather than in the middle to make the join less noticeable. You can do this at the end of the row you are working by making an incomplete stitch and using the new yarn to finish the stitch. Alternatively, join the new ball of yarn at the beginning of the row you are about to work by using the slip stitch method shown below. It is important to join a new colour of yarn neatly when working blocks. There are two ways to do this – both make neat joins and can be used when working any stitch. When working colour patterns in treble or double crochet, join the new colour of yarn into the last stitch worked in the old colour using the methods shown below.

102

Three methods for joining a new yarn in treble crochet

1 | Join the new colour on the last stitch of the final row worked in the previous colour. Leaving the last stage of the final stitch incomplete, loop the new yarn around the hook and pull it though the two loops on the hook to complete the stitch. Turn the work and continue working in the new yarn.

2 | When working colour patterns in treble crochet, join the new yarn colour where the pattern or chart indicates. Leave the last stitch worked in the previous colour incomplete and proceed as for step 1.

3 | When joining a new yarn, you may find it easier to knot the two loose ends together on the back of the work before you cut the yarn no longer in use, leaving a tail of about 10 cm (4 in.). Always undo the knot before darning in the yarn ends (page 142).

103

Two methods for joining a new yarn in double crochet

1 | Join a new colour on the last stitch of the final row worked in the previous colour. To work the last stitch, insert your hook into the work, wrap the first yarn around the hook, and draw through so there are two loops on the hook. Wrap the new yarn around the hook and pull through both stitches on the hook. Turn and work the next row with the new colour.

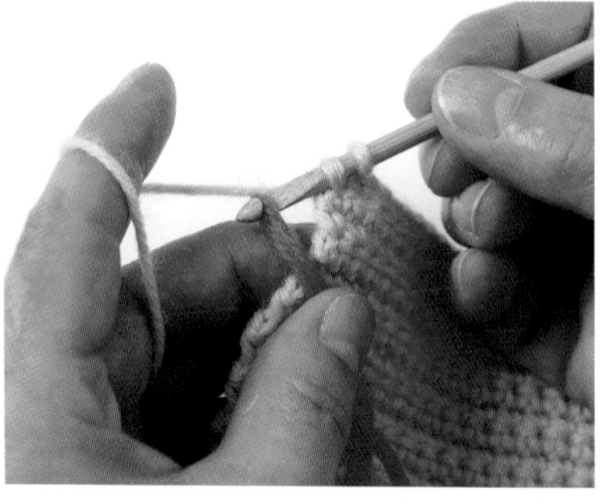

2 | When working colour patterns in double crochet, join the new yarn colour where the pattern or chart indicates. Leave the last stitch worked in the previous colour incomplete and proceed as for step 1.

104

Joining a new yarn using slip stitch

This method can be used when working any stitch. At the beginning of the row, make a slipknot in the new yarn and place it on the hook. Insert the hook into the first stitch of the row, wrap the new yarn around the hook and draw through both the stitch and the slipknot to make a slip stitch. Continue along the row using the new yarn.

105

Two methods for joining a new yarn in the round

1 | Work to the end of the round, leaving the last stitch incomplete. Use the new yarn to complete the stitch, and then join the round with a slip stitch worked in the new colour. Continue to work the next round in the new colour.

2 | For method two, complete the last stitch of the round using the old colour. Insert the hook ready to make the slip stitch that joins the round, wrap the new yarn over the hook and pull it through to complete the slip stitch.

3 | Work the turning chain in the new colour and continue the next round. When changing colours using this method, you may find it easier to knot the old and new yarn together on the wrong side before working the slip stitch. Always undo any knots before darning in the yarn ends.

Fastening off yarn

It is very easy to fasten off the yarn when you have finished a piece of crochet. Use the first method for wool, cotton and other yarns that do not slip, and the second method when working with silk, viscose and other slippery yarns. Remember not to cut the yarn too closely to the work, as you will need enough yarn to darn in the end neatly and securely.

106

Slippery yarns

When working with slippery yarn, finish the row and work one chain stitch to help lock the yarn in place. Cut the yarn and pull the loop with the hook until the cut end is free. Gently pull the yarn to tighten the chain.

107

Non-slippery yarns

Finish the last stitch and cut the yarn about 15 cm (6 in.) from the stitch. Pull the loop with the hook until the cut end is free. Pull the cut end gently to tighten the last stitch.

Joining lengths of yarn

Although it is always best to join new lengths of yarn at the edges of a piece of crochet (page 58), there are occasions when you will need to join a new yarn in the middle of a row. When a knot appears in the yarn as it unwinds from the ball and you have almost completed a row, a join is necessary – especially if you are using an expensive yarn and you want to waste as little as possible. It is also important to join a new ball during a row if you are worried that you might run out of yarn before the project is completed and every inch of yarn is precious.

Joining with a temporary knot

This method can be used to join lengths of almost any yarn in any stitch pattern. Leave yarn ends at least 10 cm (4 in.) long to make sure you have sufficient length to finish the ends securely. Always undo the knots before darning in the yarn ends.

1 | Stop crocheting when you are 10–15 cm (4–6 in.) away from the end of the old ball of yarn by working an incomplete stitch in the old yarn.

2 | Leaving the hook in position, knot the old and new yarns together on the wrong side. Tie the yarns together as close to the work as possible with a reef knot.

3 | If you were originally working a right-side row, keep the knot and yarn ends at the back of the work. Complete the stitch on the hook using the new yarn and continue along the row.

4 | If you were originally working a wrong-side row, bring the knot and the yarn ends to the front. Complete the stitch on the hook using the new yarn and continue along the row.

109

Joining with a looped splice

Use this joining method when working with a yarn that divides easily into two or four strands. For two-strand yarn, splice one strand from each yarn end as shown, or for four-strand yarn, work with two strands from each end.

1 | Stop crocheting when you are about 20 cm (8 in.) away from the end of the old ball of yarn, finishing with a complete stitch in the old yarn. Carefully divide the remaining yarn end into two strands by easing them apart with your fingers.

2 | On the new ball of yarn, divide the first 20 cm (8 in.) of yarn into two strands as before.

3 I Leaving the hook in position, fold one strand of the old yarn in half to make a loop. Leave the remaining strand loose at the back of the work.

4 I Thread one strand of the new yarn through the loop and fold it in half to make another loop that interlocks with the first one made from the original yarn. Let the remaining strand hang free.

5 I Carefully continue working the next few stitches with the looped yarn, and then continue along the row with the new yarn, leaving the two unused strands from both balls hanging. Darn in the two hanging strands on the wrong side.

110

Joining with a felted splice

Also known as a spit splice, this method of joining only works with woollen yarns than can be felted. It is not suitable for woollen yarns labelled 'superwash', 'machine washable' or for yarns made of cotton or any other type of natural or man-made fibre.

1 I Stop crocheting when you are about 30 cm (12 in.) away from the end of the old ball of yarn, finishing with a complete stitch in the old yarn. Carefully fray or tease out the last 10 cm (4 in.) of yarn by gently pulling it apart with your fingers until it is soft and fluffy.

2 I Repeat the fraying process on the first 10 cm (4 in.) of the new yarn. If you are working with a yarn that divides into strands, tease out each individual strand until it is fluffy.

3 I Using a sharp pair of scissors, carefully snip away some of the fluffy strands on both yarns. This will help to minimize bulk at the point where the yarns will be joined.

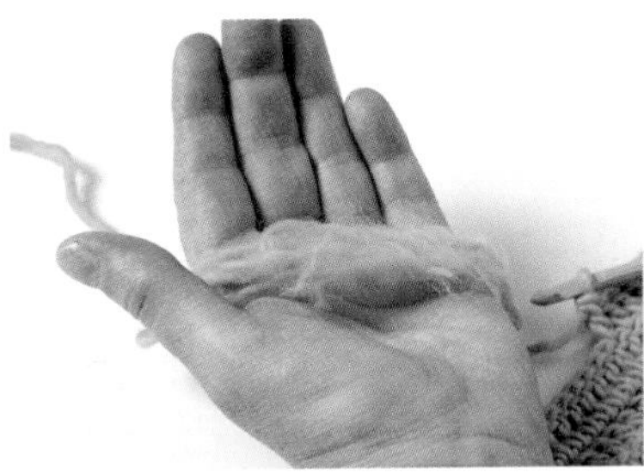

4 I Place the frayed end of the original yarn over your palm. Overlap with the end of the new yarn so the frayed part of both yarns lies across your palm.

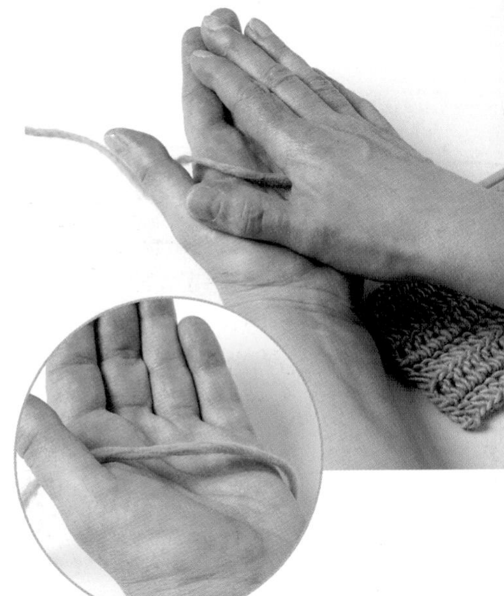

5 I Sprinkle the overlapping yarns with a little warm water and roll vigorously up and down between your palms for a few minutes. The moisture, warmth and friction of your hands will make the yarn ends felt securely together. Allow to dry, then continue working along the row.

Working filet crochet

This lacy type of crochet has a mesh background and a pattern picked out in solid blocks of stitches. Usually worked in fine cotton thread, it also looks effective in any smooth yarn.

111

Working the first row of a simple filet crochet design

Using the filet crochet chart on page 30, work rows of blocks and spaces to create this simple design. Also turn to this page for more information about how to follow and read filet crochet charts in general.

Starting the first row with a space

1 | Make the foundation chain. Follow the chart from the bottom right corner, along the row of squares marked. When the first square is a space, add four turning chains and work the first treble crochet stitch into the eighth chain from the hook.

2 | Continue working spaces and blocks along the row, reading the chart from right to left and working spaces and blocks as they occur.

Starting the first row with a block

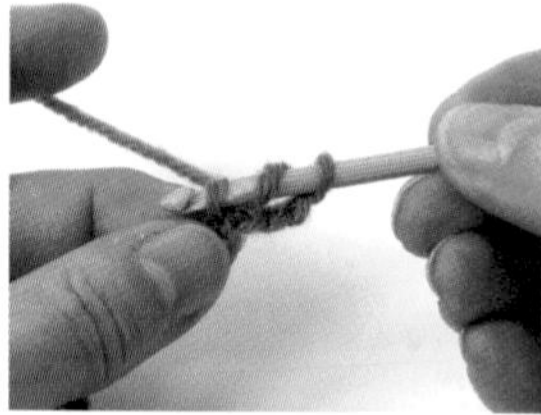

1 | When the first square on the chart is a block, add two turning chains and work the first treble crochet stitch into the fourth chain from the hook.

2 | Work one treble crochet stitch into each of the next two chains to complete the first block. Continue along the row, reading the chart from right to left and working spaces and blocks as they occur.

112

Working the rest of the chart rows

At the end of the first row, turn the work and follow the second row of the chart, reading from left to right. Work spaces and blocks at the start and end of the second and subsequent rows as follows.

Working a space over a space on the previous row

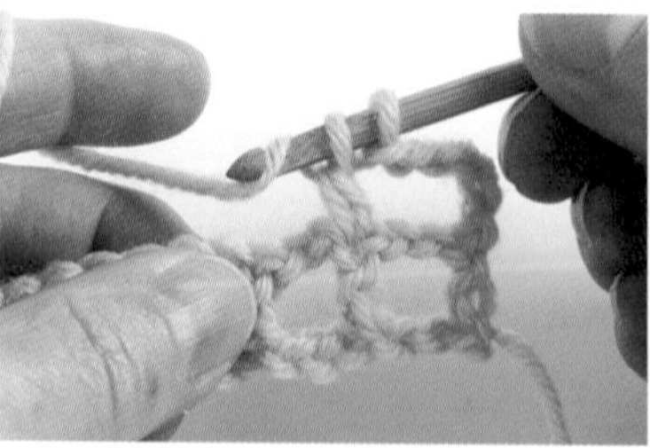

1 | At the start of a row, work five turning chains (counts as 1 tr, 2 ch), miss the first stitch and the next two chains, and work one treble crochet stitch into the next one. Continue working the spaces and blocks from the chart.

2 | At the end of a row, finish with one treble crochet stitch into the last treble crochet stitch, work two chains, miss two chains, work one treble crochet stitch into the third of five chains, turn.

Working a space over a block on the previous row

1 | At the start of the row, work five turning chains (counts as 1 tr, 2 ch), miss the first three stitches, and work a treble crochet stitch into the next one. Continue working spaces and blocks from the chart.

2 | At the end of a row, work to the last four stitches. Work one treble crochet stitch into the next stitch, work two chains, miss two stitches, work one treble crochet stitch into the top of three chains to complete the space, turn.

Working a block over a space on the previous row

1 | At the start of the row, work three turning chains (counts as 1 tr), miss one stitch, work one treble crochet stitch into each of the next two chains and one treble crochet stitch into the next stitch to complete the block. Continue across the row working spaces and blocks from the chart.

2 | At the end of a row, finish with one treble crochet stitch into the last treble crochet stitch, one treble crochet stitch into each of the next three chains of the turning chain and turn.

Working a block over a block on the previous row

1 | At the beginning of the row, work three turning chains (counts as one treble crochet stitch), miss one stitch, work one treble crochet stitch into each of the next three treble crochet stitches to complete the block. Continue across the row working spaces and blocks from the chart.

2 | At the end of a row, finish with one treble crochet stitch into each of the last three treble crochet stitches, one treble crochet stitch into the top of three chains, turn.

Simple filet design

Classic filet crochet designs rely on the interplay between solidly worked blocks and empty spaces to create a geometric pattern or pictorial design. Filet crochet looks good worked in almost any yarn or thread, providing it has a smooth surface. See pages 62–3 for the instructions and page 30 for the filet crochet chart.

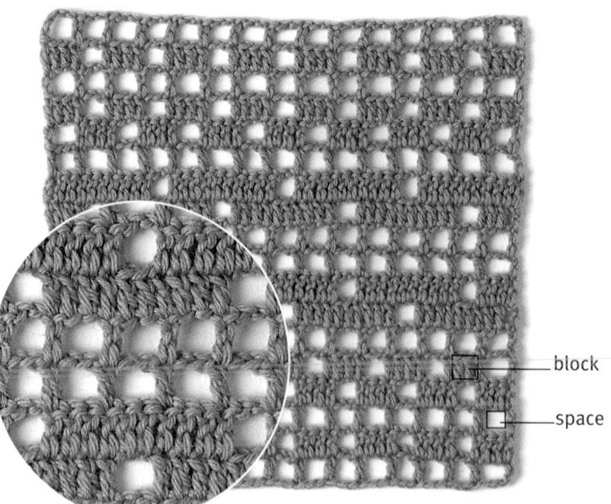

113

Working a more intricate design

This delicate filet crochet piece features bars and lacets as well as ordinary blocks and spaces. Find out more about bars and lacets and how they are shown on a chart by turning to page 31.

Working a bar over a pair of blocks

1 | Work to the position of the bar, then work one treble crochet into the first stitch of the pair of blocks. Work five chains to form the bar, then work a treble crochet into the last stitch of the blocks to complete the bar.

2 | To work a pair of blocks over the bar on the return row, work a treble crochet into the first stitch of the bar and one treble crochet into each of the five chains. Finish the block by working the last treble crochet into the next stitch.

Working a bar over a pair of spaces

1 | Work to the position of the bar, then work one treble crochet into the first stitch of the two spaces. Work five chains to form the bar, then work a treble crochet into the last stitch of the spaces to complete the bar.

2 | To return to the ordinary grid of spaces on the return row, work a space of two chains and a treble crochet, working the treble crochet into the third chain of the bar. Work two chains and a treble crochet into the next stitch to complete the grid.

Working a lacet over a pair of blocks

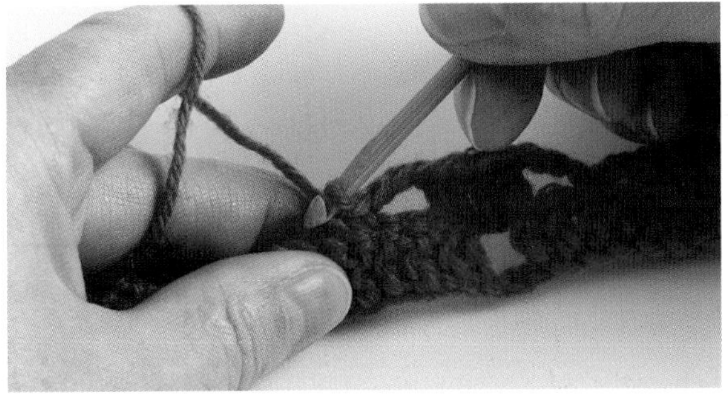

1 Work to the position of the lacet, then one treble crochet into the first stitch of the two blocks. Work three chains to form the right half of the lacet, a double crochet into the centre stitch, three chains and a treble crochet into the last stitch of the blocks to complete the lacet.

2 To work a bar over the lacet on the return row, work a treble crochet into the first stitch, then five chains to form the bar and a treble crochet into the last stitch to complete the bar.

Working a lacet over a pair of spaces

1 Work to the position of the lacet, then work one treble crochet into the first stitch of the two spaces. Work three chains to form the right half of the lacet, a double crochet into the centre stitch of the spaces and three chains to make the left half. Work one treble crochet into the last stitch of the spaces to complete.

2 To return to the ordinary grid of spaces, you must first work a bar over the lacet on the return row (see step 2, Working a lacet over a pair of blocks), then work two spaces into the bar on the next row (see step 2, Working a bar over a pair of spaces).

Intricate filet design

Adding bars and lacets to a filet crochet chart makes a much more intricate design than one produced by working only blocks and spaces. Bars and lacets take up two horizontal chart squares and they are usually surrounded by blocks and spaces.

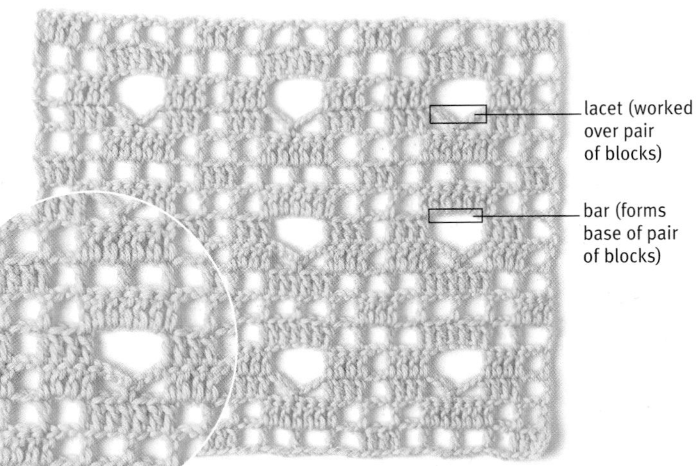

Working lace stitches

The simplest lace stitches are those that make a mesh or net of chains and stitches. They are straightforward and quick to work, but it is essential to work the correct number of foundation chains for the stitch you are using.

Trellis stitches create a fabric from short lengths of chains that are secured at intervals either by slip stitches or double crochet stitches. They are less easy to shape than mesh stitches but give a beautifully soft, lacy fabric. Both mesh and trellis stitches are often combined with many other stitches such as shell, fans, and clusters (pages 68–70).

Mesh patterns

Mesh stitches are versatile and can be used to make accessories, including shawls and wraps, as well as simple, lightweight summerwear garments.

1 | When working the first row of a mesh pattern directly into the foundation chain, make a neat edge by working each stitch into the back of the chain (page 47).

2 | Take care to insert the hook into the correct place stated in the pattern. In this stitch, the hook is inserted into the top of each stitch made on the previous row.

115

Offset mesh patterns

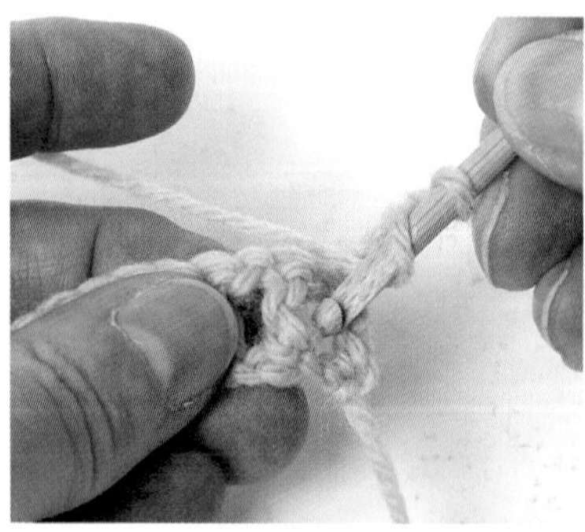

1 | When working the first stitch of the row, work the turning chain, then the first stitch into the first chain space.

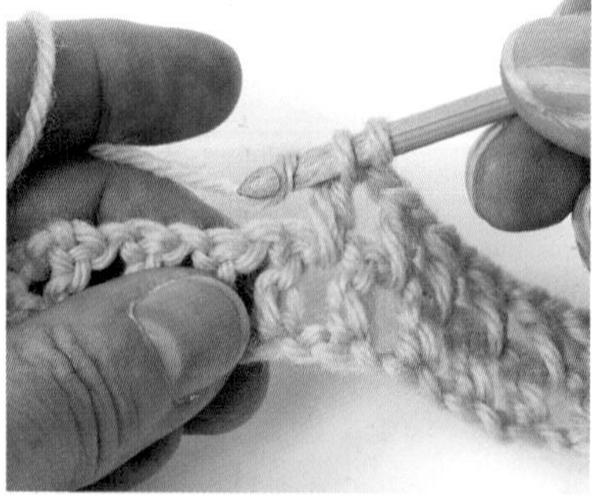

2 | Continue along the row, working each stitch into the chain spaces between the stitches worked on the previous row. Remember to insert your hook directly into the chain space not the chain.

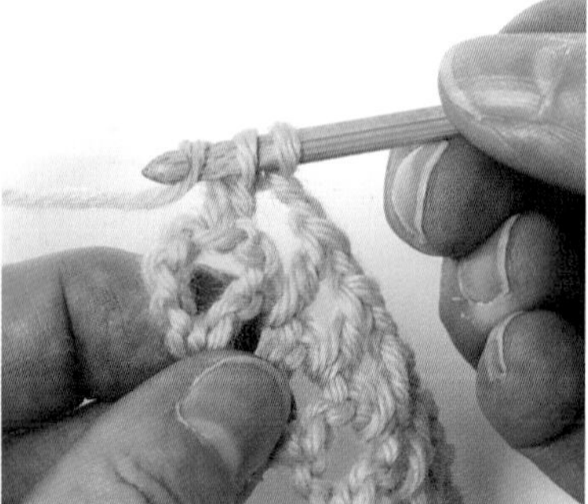

3 | When working the final stitch of the row, work it into the third stitch of the turning chain not the last chain space. This makes a neater, stronger edge.

116

Trellis pattern

1 | The chain spaces in trellis patterns are longer than those used in mesh patterns, allowing them to curve upward to create delicate arches.

2 | The chain spaces are usually anchored by slip stitches or, as shown, double crochet stitches worked into the space below each arch of chains.

Classic mesh

A classic mesh pattern made from treble crochet stitches and single chain spaces. This type of mesh is similar in construction to that produced by filet crochet (page 62).

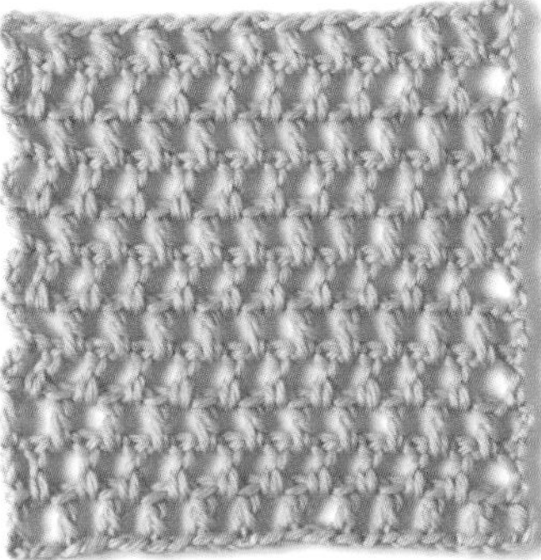

Classic offset mesh

Although the stitches and chain spaces are the same as for the classic mesh pattern, the construction changes to create a different style of mesh.

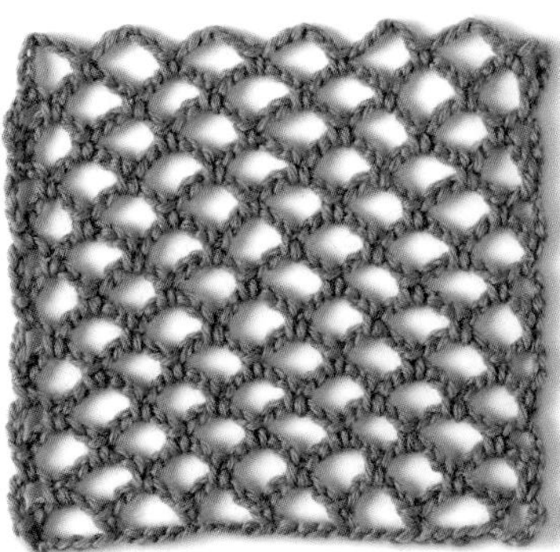

Classic trellis

Trellis patterns are quick and easy to work and make fabulous wraps and shawls. You can work them in a medium-weight wool, as shown here, or get a different effect by working in a fine thread with a small hook.

Combination stitches

Combining elements of mesh and trellis stitches, this stitch pattern creates a pretty fabric which, although straightforward to make, looks deceptively intricate.

Working shells and fans

Shell stitches are formed from three or more stitches which share the same chain, stitch or chain space and result in a triangular group of stitches that look a lot like tiny clam shells.

Usually chains or stitches at either side of a shell are missed to compensate for the space taken up by the shell and each stitch making up a shell is counted as one stitch. Large groups of treble crochet or double treble crochet stitches worked in the same way are often also known as fan stitches. Shell stitches often form the base for a larger fan-shaped stitch pattern that requires several rows to complete. You may also find shells and fan stitches mixed in the same pattern.

117 Basic three-stitch shell in treble crochet

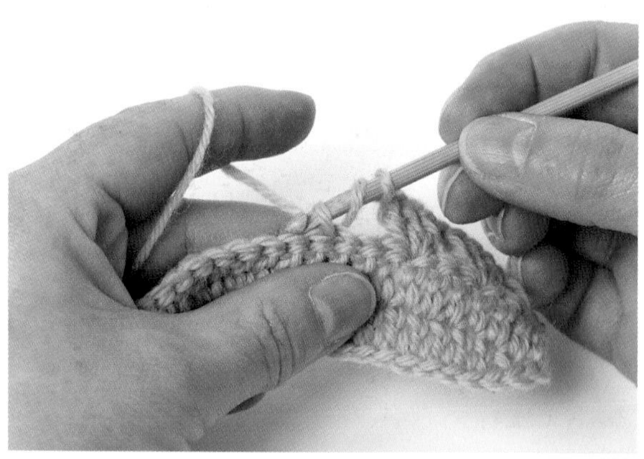

1 | Miss the stated number of chains or stitches and work the first treble crochet of the shell into the correct chain or stitch.

2 | Work the second treble crochet of the group into the same place as the previous stitch. In the three-stitch shell shown, this stitch forms the centre stitch of the shell.

3 | Work the remaining stitches into the same place as the previous stitches.

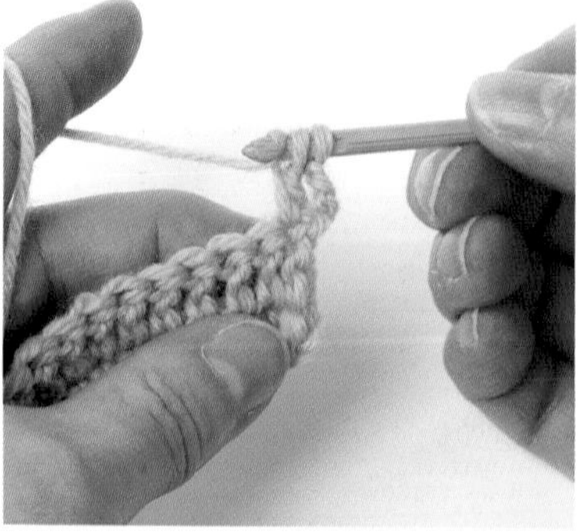

4 | At the start and end of the rows, you may have to work half shells to keep the continuity of the pattern. To start with a half shell, count the turning chain as the first stitch, then work a second treble crochet into the same place to complete the half shell.

5 | At the end of the row, make a half shell by working two treble crochet stitches into the turning chain of the previous row.

118

Working a fan stitch pattern over several rows

1 | The first pattern row may be worked into the foundation chain or into a solid row of stitches. Make sure that you work the correct number of stitches in each base shell (a five-stitch shell is shown).

2 | On the next row, increase as directed into the top of the stitches forming the shell. This makes a wider band of stitches which form the fan pattern's middle row.

3 | To complete each fan, work further increases as directed into the top of the group of stitches on the previous row. The finished fan shape has been worked over three rows.

119

Working a fan stitch into a chain space

1 | Many lacy stitch patterns combine shells, fans, and chain spaces. To work into a chain space, insert the hook through the space rather than into a stitch (a seven-stitch fan is shown).

2 | On the return row, the lacy section of the pattern is often formed by attaching short lengths of chains to the centre stitch of the shell or fan on the previous row.

Large fans

Large fans combine well with chain loops to make vertical bands of lace. The lace bands are separated by five-stitch columns of treble crochet which give the stitch pattern stability.

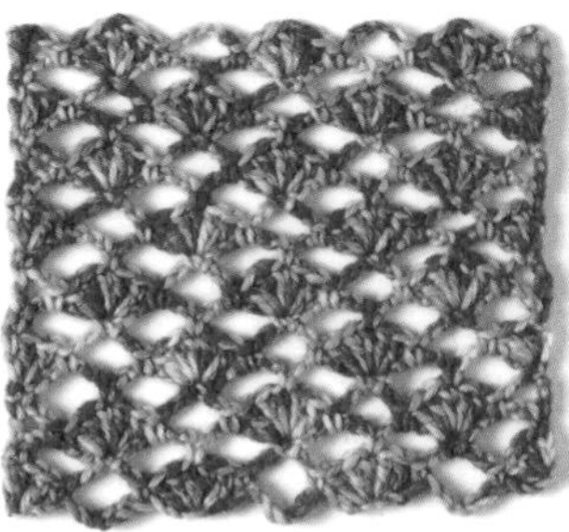

Combining stitches

This pattern combines five-stitch shells with a trellis arrangement of chain spaces (page 67) to make a stitch suitable for a lightweight shawl or wrap.

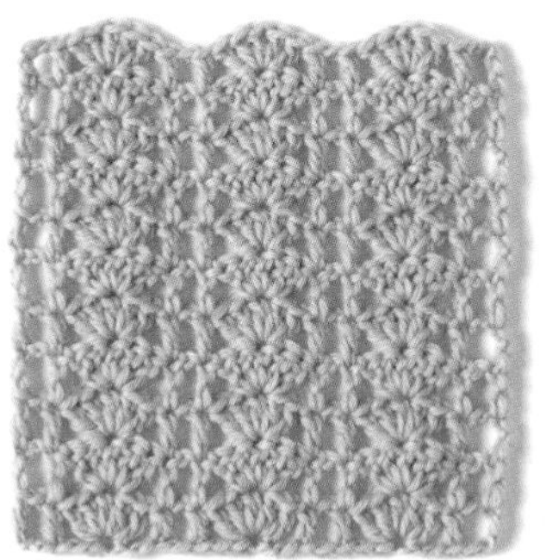

Shells and lace

This stitch pattern creates a compact piece of fabric. Shells are worked on top of one another to produce vertical bands divided up by lacy columns.

Large fan

The large fan-shaped pattern shown here is worked over four rows. The effect is light yet substantial, perfect for making a simply shaped garment or small afghan.

Working clusters

Clusters are groups of two, three or more stitches joined together at the top by leaving the last loop of each stitch on the hook, then drawing the yarn through all the loops to secure the stitch.

Clusters can be worked into two, three or more stitches made on the previous row or directly into a chain space. This technique is used as a way of decreasing one or more stitches (see Shaping, page 83) but double and treble crochet clusters are also used to make attractive stitch patterns in their own right.

120

Basic three-stitch cluster in treble crochet

1 | Wrap the yarn over the hook and work the first treble crochet stitch, leaving out the last stage so you end up with two loops on the hook. Work the second stitch in the same way so you now have three loops on the hook.

2 | Work the last stitch in the same way so you end up with four loops on the hook. Wrap the yarn over the hook.

3 | Draw the yarn through all four loops on the hook to complete the cluster and secure the loops. Repeat as required.

121

Working a cluster into a chain space

Work as above but each time insert the hook into the centre of a chain space rather than into the stitches themselves (a four-stitch cluster is shown being worked here).

Stitch cluster patterns

Clusters can be arranged in neat horizontal rows or to face in alternate directions for a lightly textured effect (as shown).

Changing scale

Many crochet stitch patterns, particularly delicate and lacy stitches, can look and feel completely different when worked in lighter or heavier yarn weights than those suggested in the pattern. The swatches on this page show how one lace pattern can change when worked in a different yarn using a suitable size of hook for the yarn weight. All the swatches were worked over the same number of stitches and rows.

Exploring scale

As well as appearance and drape, changing the yarn weight will also affect the tension and overall size of the piece you are making. Using a lighter yarn weight than the one recommended will make a smaller finished item, and using a heavier yarn will result in a larger item. (For more information on tension, see page 32. For hook sizes, see page 13.)

Lace-weight yarn

Swatch 1 is worked in Jamieson's Shetland lace-weight yarn with a 2 mm (size B) hook. It measures 7.5 cm (3 in.) by 8 cm ($3\frac{1}{4}$ in.) and the fabric feels soft with good drape.

4-ply merino

Swatch 2 is worked in Jaeger Matchmaker Merino 4-ply yarn with a 3 mm (size D) hook. It measures 9.5 cm ($3\frac{3}{4}$ in.) by 9 cm ($3\frac{1}{2}$ in.). The fabric is still soft with good drape but the holes in the pattern are now much larger.

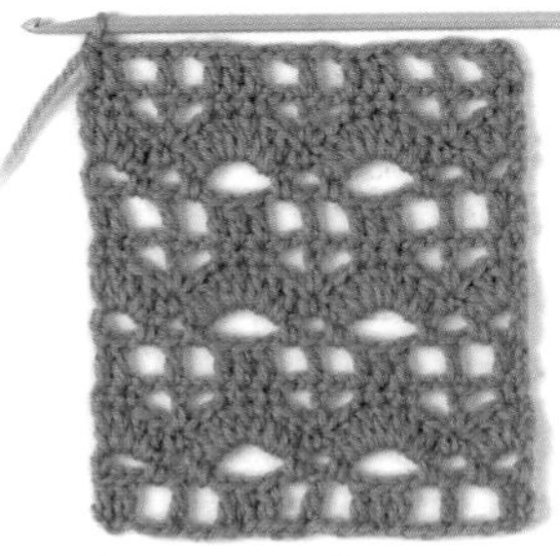

Double knitting merino

Swatch 3 is worked in Jaeger Matchmaker Merino DK with a 4 mm (size F) hook. It measures 11 cm ($4\frac{1}{4}$ in.) by 11.5 cm ($4\frac{1}{2}$ in.). The fabric still feels soft but does not drape as freely, and the stitch pattern is starting to look less delicate.

Cotton blend

Swatch 4 is worked in Rowan All Seasons Cotton with a 4.5 mm (size G) hook. It measures 12 cm ($4\frac{3}{4}$ in.) by 14 cm ($5\frac{1}{2}$ in.). The fabric no longer feels soft, while the stitch pattern looks heavy and coarse.

Worsted yarn

Swatch 5 is worked in Brown Sheep Lamb's Pride Worsted yarn, with a 5 mm (size H hook. It measures 14 cm ($5\frac{1}{2}$ in.) by 15 cm (6 in.). The fabric feels heavy and the stitch pattern no longer looks attractive.

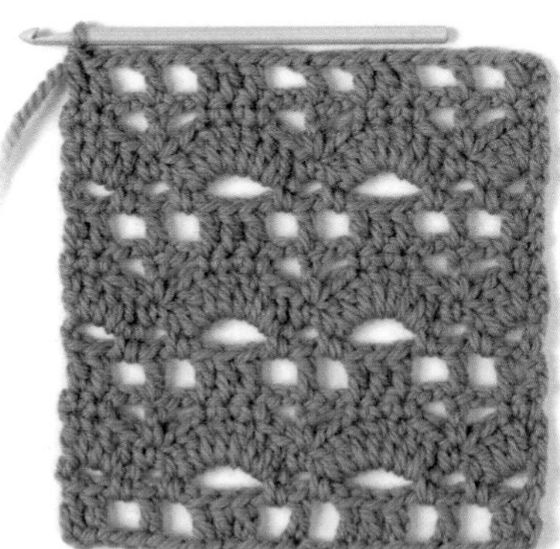

Chunky wool

Swatch 6 is worked in Texere Pure Wool Chunky with a 6 mm (size K) hook. It measures 16.5 cm ($6\frac{1}{2}$ in.) by 17 cm ($6\frac{3}{4}$ in.). The fabric feels stiff and looks unattractive.

Working chevron patterns

Worked in a similar way to plain horizontal stripes (page 128), in this type of stripe pattern extra stitches are added and subtracted at regular intervals along each row. This forms a pattern of regular peaks and troughs separated by blocks of stitches and creates attractive patterns known as ripple stitches. The peaks and troughs can either form sharp points or gentle waves, depending on how and where the increases and decreases are worked. The effect varies depending on the number of stitches in blocks between the peaks and troughs.

With basic chevron patterns, the pattern repeat is usually set on the first row after you have worked the foundation row of stitches into the foundation chain. This row is then repeated until the work is the required length. More complex chevron patterns combining smooth, textured and lace stitches are made up of peaks and troughs in a similar way but each pattern repeat may take several rows to complete. Always join new colours at the ends of the rows (page 58).

123

Chevron pattern in double crochet

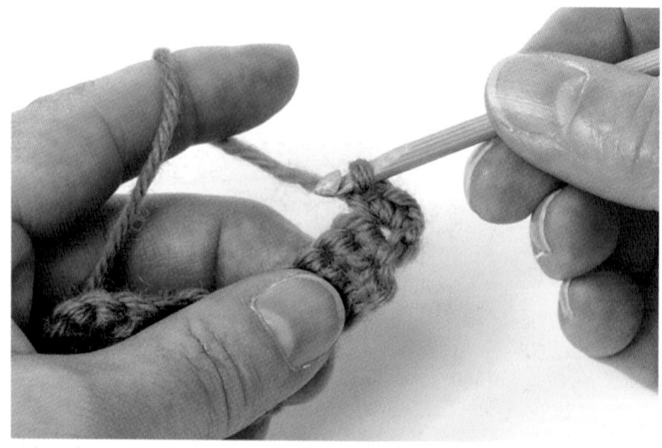

1 I To keep the peaks and troughs correctly spaced, you may need to work one or more extra stitches at the start of every row. In this pattern, two double crochet stitches are worked into the first stitch of every row.

2 I Balance the opposite end of the row by working two double crochet stitches into the last stitch of the row. This creates the correct number of stitches ready to work the next row.

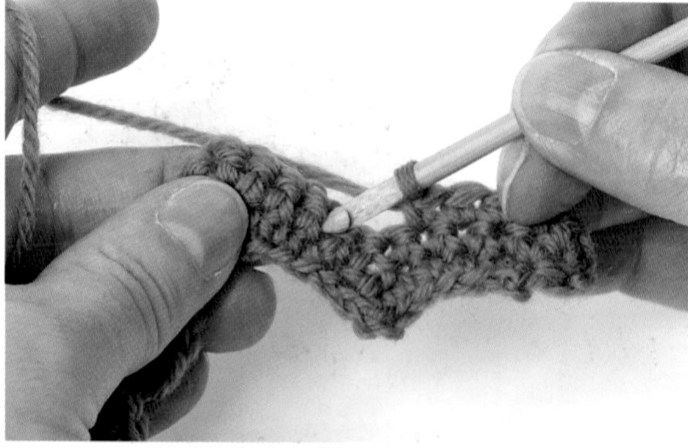

3 I To make the bottom 'V'-shapes of the chevron pattern (troughs), decrease two stitches by missing two double crochet stitches at the bottom of each trough, then continue working the next block of stitches.

4 I To make the top 'V'-shapes of the chevrons (peaks), increase two stitches by working three double crochet stitches into the same stitch at the top of each peak.

124

Chevron pattern in treble crochet

1 | At the start of the row, work one or more slip stitches to move the yarn and hook to the correct place for working the next row. Work a slip stitch into the second treble crochet of the row. Work the turning chain and continue.

2 | To form the peaks, work three stitches into the same stitch from the previous row. Work the block of stitches before the peak, then work three treble crochet stitches into the next stitch.

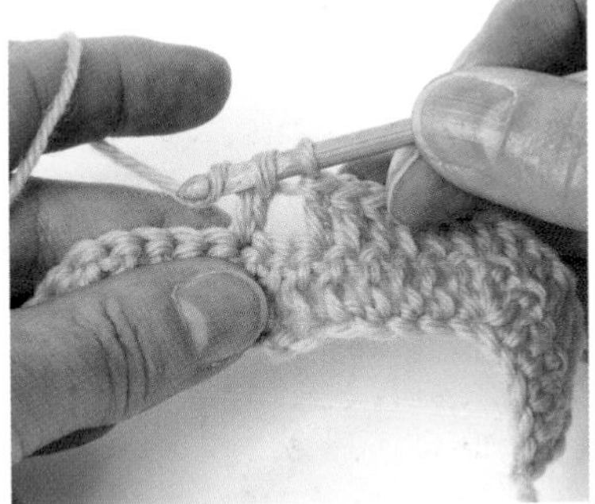

3 | To make the troughs, miss two stitches at the bottom of each trough in the same way as for the double crochet pattern on page 72. Extra stitches are not needed at the end of the row.

125

Wave pattern in treble crochet

1 | To make soft waves, work two sets of increases and decreases into the peaks and troughs instead of one set. To make the troughs, work three treble crochet stitches together (tr3tog) over the six stitches at the bottom of each trough.

2 | To make the peaks, work three treble crochet stitches into each of the central two stitches at the top of the peaks.

Wavy chevron

When pairs of increases and decreases are worked to form the peaks and troughs, a chevron pattern takes on a softly rounded wave formation.

Solid colour chevron

Although chevron patterns are usually worked in bands of colour to show off the stitch formation, they can be worked in a solid colour to make an attractive fabric.

Classic chevron pattern

This chevron stitch pattern is worked in double crochet. The crisp, pointed peaks and troughs of the pattern are accentuated by a careful use of colour.

Working puff stitches

These soft, puffy groups of stitches are less textured than either bobbles (pages 76–7) or popcorns (opposite). Each puff stitch is made from three or more half treble crochet stitches all worked into the same chain or stitch. They require a little practice as the half treble crochet stitches need to be worked loosely.

126

Basic puff stitch

1 | Wrap the yarn over the hook, insert the hook into the chain or stitch, wrap the yarn again and draw a loop through so there are three loops on the hook.

2 | Repeat this step twice more, each time inserting the hook into the same place, so there are seven loops on the hook. Wrap the yarn again and draw it through all the loops on the hook.

3 | Wrap the yarn and draw it through the loop on the hook to close the puff stitch and secure the loops. Repeat as required.

Puff stitch fabrics

Good for working baby blankets and afghans, puff stitches make a soft, slightly textured fabric. Depending on the stitch pattern used, puff stitch fabrics are often reversible.

Working popcorns

A popcorn stitch is a cluster of three, four, or five treble crochet stitches folded over and closed at the top with a chain. The popcorn gives a highly textured effect and looks like a tiny folded pocket that sticks out on the right side of the crochet fabric.

127

Basic five-stitch popcorn

1 | Work a group of five treble crochet stitches into the same chain or stitch. Elongate the working loop by pulling it gently with the hook.

2 | Remove the hook from the working loop and insert it under both loops of the group's first treble crochet stitch.

3 | To close the popcorn, pick up the working loop with the hook and draw it through so you fold the group of stitches. Close it at the top. Some stitch patterns may require you to secure the popcorn by wrapping the yarn over the hook and drawing it through the loop on the hook.

Popcorn combinations

When combined with other stitches, including lace, shells and fans, popcorns add texture to an otherwise flat surface. They look just as good worked on a small scale in fine yarn as they do worked in chunky yarn.

Working bobbles

A bobble is a group of stitches, usually treble crochet stitches, worked into the same stitch at the base and closed at the top. Made from three, four or five stitches, bobbles are usually worked on wrong-side rows and surrounded by flat, solidly worked stitches to throw them into high relief.

When calculating yarn requirements for a project, remember that bobbles use up more yarn than most other stitches. Multicoloured bobbles are a great way of using up short lengths of leftover yarn.

Basic five-stitch bobble

1 | On a wrong-side row, work to the position of the bobble. Wrap the yarn over the hook, work the first stitch, and skip the last stage to leave two loops on the hook.

2 | Work the second and third stitches in the same way. You now have four loops on the hook.

3 | Work the remaining two stitches of the bobble in the same way, so you end up with six loops on the hook.

4 | Wrap the yarn over the hook and draw it through all six loops to secure them and complete the bobble. You may find it helpful to gently poke the bobble through to the right side with the tip of one finger as you draw the securing loop through.

5 | Continue along the row, working bobbles as required. When working the following right-side row, take care to work one stitch into the securing stitch at the top of each bobble.

129

Multicoloured bobble

1 | Working in the main yarn, leave the last double crochet stitch incomplete with two loops on the hook. Use a separate length of contrast yarn to complete this stitch. Work a bobble as usual into the next stitch.

2 | Holding down both ends of the contrast yarn with your thumb, bring the main yarn across the bobble and work the securing stitch with this yarn. Continue working in the main yarn until you reach the position of the next bobble.

Grouped bobbles

Bobbles can be arranged in rows for all-over texture or grouped together to create a simple shape such as a diamond (shown here), triangle, square, heart or flower.

Individual bobbles

Individual bobbles can be used to work remnants of plain, textured, metallic or handpainted yarns with striking results.

Adding texture with post and spike stitches

Post stitches create a heavily textured surface made by wrapping the yarn as if you were going to work a treble crochet stitch, inserting the hook around the post (stem or body) of the stitches made on the previous row and then completing the stitch. Insert the hook from the front or back of the work to give a differently textured effect each way. Spike or dropped stitches are worked over the other stitches to add colour or texture to a piece of crochet.

130

Working a front post stitch

1 | Wrap the yarn once over the hook, insert the hook into the front of the fabric under the post and bring the point through at the front of the work.

2 | Wrap the yarn over the hook and draw a loop through on the front of the work. There are now three loops on the hook. Complete the treble crochet stitch in the usual way.

131

Working a back post stitch

1 | Wrap the yarn once over the hook, insert the hook into the back of the fabric under the post and bring the point through at the back of the work.

2 | Wrap the yarn over the hook and draw a loop through the back of the work so there are now three loops on the hook. Complete the treble crochet stitch in the usual way.

Chessboard pattern

Depending on the desired effect, these can be used separately or combined. This heavily textured stitch looks like a woven basket and is made by working blocks of front and back post stitches arranged in a chessboard pattern.

132

Working spike stitches

Spike or dropped stitches are worked individually over other stitches to give colour or texture to a piece of crochet. The stitches can also be worked in groups over one or more rows usually against a background of double crochet stitches. The stitch pattern you are following will tell you exactly where to insert the hook into the crochet fabric. As well as making interesting colour patterns when worked in two or more contrasting colours, spike stitches worked in a solid colour create a thick, densely worked fabric without much drape (ideal for adult outerwear and accessories such as hats, purses and bags).

Working a basic double crochet spike stitch

1 | Insert the hook as directed in the pattern instructions, taking the point right through the fabric to the wrong side.

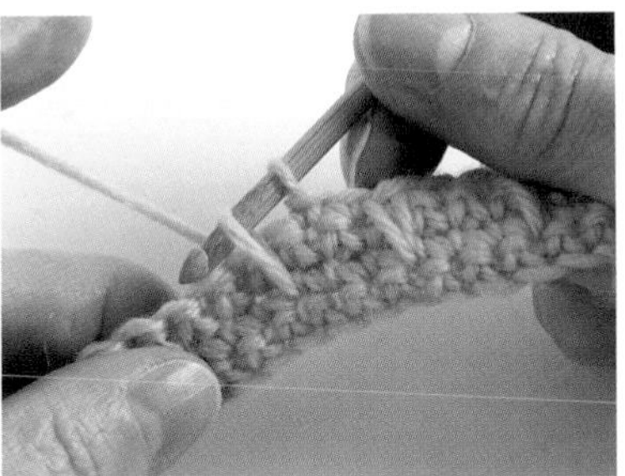

2 | Wrap the yarn over the hook and draw through to the front, lengthening the loop to the height of the working row.

3 | To finish the spike, complete the stitch in the usual way and continue along the row, following the pattern instructions. When working spike stitches, take care not to pull the loop too tightly as this will distort the fabric.

133

Stripe patterns

Contrasting colour stripes show off spike stitches to perfection; colour changes every two rows work well, too, with the yarn not used being loosely carried up the side to avoid having lots of yarn ends left over, or you can work repeating bands of stripes.

Contrasting stripes

Contrasting yarn colours highlight the stitch construction and make a busy and interesting surface pattern.

Subtle stripes

By changing the yarn colours to a pair with similar tonal values, the same stitch pattern looks less busy but still attractive.

Repeating stripes

Repeating bands of colour against a solid colour background gives a totally different effect. Turn to page 128 to find out more about stripe patterns.

Working crossed stitches

This type of stitch is worked in two distinct ways but each method requires two or more stitches to complete the crossing. In the first method, usually worked in treble crochet stitches, the second stitch both crosses and encloses the first stitch. In the second method, usually worked in double treble stitches, the second stitch crosses behind the first stitch but does not enclose it. Rows of crossed stitches worked by either method are usually separated by one or more plain rows of double crochet.

134

Working crossed treble crochet stitches

1 I Work to the position indicated on the pattern. *Miss one stitch and work a treble crochet into the next one.

2 I Wrap the yarn once over the hook. Insert the hook from front to back into the missed stitch.

3 I Wrap the yarn once over the hook and draw it through to the front, making three loops on the hook.

4 I Complete the treble crochet stitch in the usual way with this stitch crossing and enclosing the first stitch. Repeat from * as required.

Crossed treble crochet stitches

In this swatch, pairs of treble crochet stitches cross and the second stitch encloses the first. This type of crossed stitch is reversible: although the right and wrong sides look slightly different, either one can be used as the right side of a finished piece.

135

Working crossed double treble stitches

1 I Work to the position indicated on the pattern. *Miss one stitch and work a double treble stitch into the next one.

2 I Wrap the yarn twice over the hook. Take the hook behind the first stitch and insert it from front to back into the missed stitch.

3 I Wrap the yarn once over the hook and draw it through to the front, making four loops on the hook.

4 I Complete the double treble stitch so that it crosses behind the first stitch. If you find this manoeuvre tricky, try tilting your work slightly forwards. Repeat from * as required.

Crossed double treble stitches

Pairs of double treble stitches cross so that the second stitch is worked behind the first stitch. This creates a more textured fabric than working crossed treble crochet stitches. Like the crossed treble crochet stitches, either side can be used as the right side of a finished piece.

Shaping

There are several different ways of shaping crochet by increasing and decreasing the number of working stitches. Adding or subtracting one or two stitches at intervals along a row of crochet is the easiest way and this process is known as working internal increases or decreases. When groups of stitches are added or subtracted at the beginning and end of specified rows, this is known as working external increases or decreases. The methods shown can be used with double, half treble, treble and double treble crochet stitches.

136

Working an internal increase

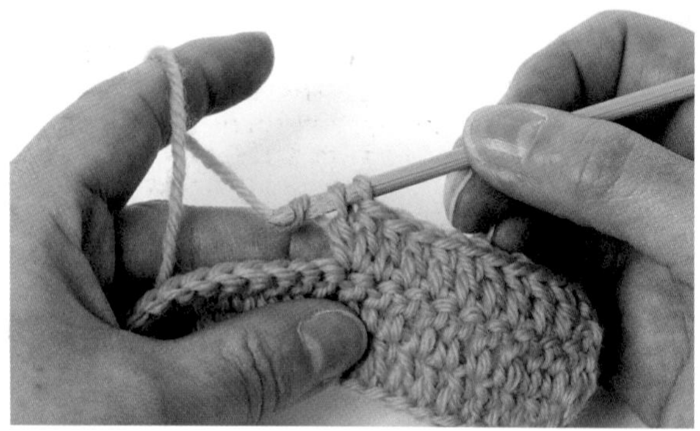

1 | The simplest method of working a single increase (adding a single stitch) at intervals along a row of crochet is by working two stitches into one stitch on the previous row.

2 | To work a double increase (adding two stitches) at intervals along the row, work three stitches into one on the previous row.

137

Working an external increase

1 | To increase several stitches at one time, you will need to add extra foundation chains at the appropriate end of the row. To add stitches at the beginning of a row, work the required number of extra chains at the end of the previous row. Do not forget to add the correct number of turning chains (page 54) for the stitch you are using.

2 | Turn and work back along the extra chains. Work the row in the usual way.

3 | To add stitches at the end of a row, leave the last few stitches of that row unworked. Remove the hook. Join a length of yarn to the last stitch of the row and work the required number of extra chains, then fasten off the yarn. Insert the hook back into the row and continue, working extra stitches across the chains. Turn and work the next row in the usual way.

138 Working an internal decrease

1 | Decrease one double crochet stitch by working two stitches together (known as dc2tog). Leave the first stitch incomplete so there are two loops on the hook and draw the yarn through the next stitch so you have three loops on the hook. Yarn over and pull through all three loops to finish the decrease. Two stitches can be decreased in the same way by working three stitches together (dc3tog).

2 | Decrease one treble crochet stitch by working two stitches together (known as tr2tog). Leave the first stitch incomplete so there are two loops on the hook and work another incomplete stitch so you have three loops on the hook. Yarn over and pull through all three loops to finish. Two stitches can be decreased in the same way by working three treble crochet stitches together (tr3tog).

139 Working an external decrease

1 | To decrease several stitches at one time at the beginning of a row, turn, work a slip stitch into each of the stitches to be decreased, then work the appropriate turning chain and continue along the row.

2 | At the end of the row, simply leave the stitches to be decreased unworked, turn, work the appropriate turning chain and continue along the row.

140 Shaping with groups of stitches

External increases and decreases are used to add or subtract groups of stitches at the beginning and end of rows. You can do this to make an unusually shaped edge (as shown) or work with larger groups of stitches such as when working sleeves all-in-one with the body on a simple 'T'-shaped garment.

141 Shaping to make a square

Working three stitches together at the centre of every row creates a neat square of double crochet. Begin by making a chain long enough to form two adjacent sides of your square (you will need an odd number) then work rows of double crochet with dc3tog across the three centre stitches of every row until three stitches remain. Work another dc3tog and fasten off the yarn.

142 Making a neat edge

Internal increases and decreases are often used at the beginning and end of rows to shape garment edges. To do this neatly at the start of a row, work the first stitch and then work the increase. At the end of the row, work until two stitches remain (the last stitch will probably be the turning chain from the previous row). Work the increase into the next to last stitch, then work the last stitch as usual.

Shaping filet crochet

Filet crochet is worked in rectangles or straight strips but there will be times when you may need to shape the edges of the fabric by keeping to the basic grid formation and increasing it by adding a block or space to the start and end of rows.

143

Working increases and decreases

Each increase and decrease is worked in a specific way, depending on whether you need to add or subtract a space or a block.

Increasing a space at the start of a row

Instead of turning after the usual five chains, work seven chains (counts as 2 ch, 1 tr, 2 ch) and work the first tr into the first tr on the previous row.

Increasing a space at the end of a row

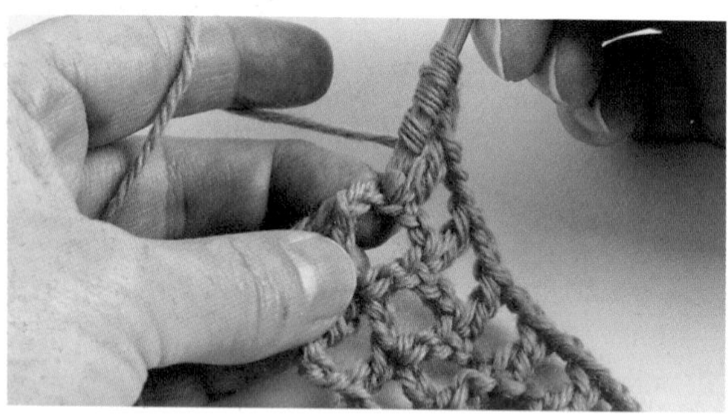

1 | Work two chains, wrapping the yarn three times over the hook. Insert it into the base of the last tr. Wrap the yarn over the hook and draw a loop through it to make five loops on the hook.

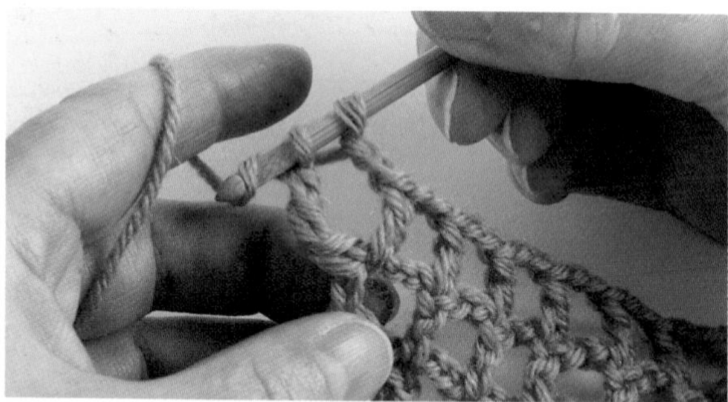

2 | *Wrap yarn over the hook and draw through two loops on the hook. Repeat from * three times to finish the increase and leave one loop on the hook.

Increasing a block at the start of a row

1 | Work five chains at the end of the previous row, turn and work a treble crochet into the second of the five chains.

2 | Work a treble crochet into the first of the five chains, then complete the block by working a treble crochet into the first dc of the previous row.

Increasing a block at the end of a row

1 | Work an extended treble crochet (page 53) into the same place as the last treble crochet on the row.

2 | *Work an extended treble crochet into the bottom section of the stitch just made. Repeat from * once again to complete the block.

Working a slanted increase at the start of a row

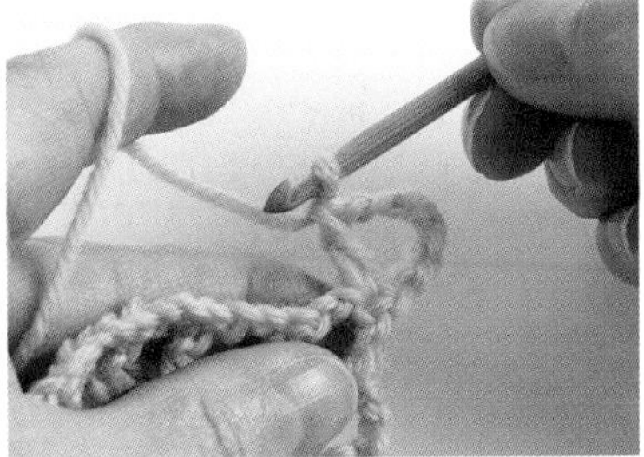

Work six chains (counts as 1 dtr, 2 ch) to turn, then a treble crochet into the same place as the base of the turning chain.

Working a slanted increase at the end of a row

Work two chains, then one double treble crochet into the appropriate stitch of the turning chain on the previous row.

Working a slanted decrease at the start of a row

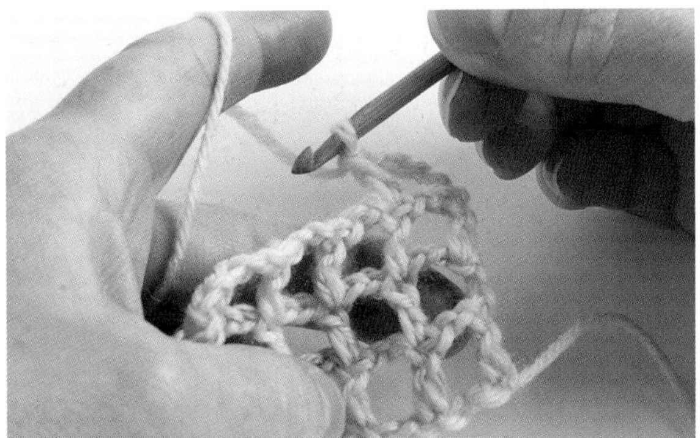

Work four turning chains (counts as 1 dtr), miss the next space or block, then work a treble crochet into the first stitch of the next space or block.

Working a slanted decrease at the end of a row

1 | Work an incomplete treble crochet into the first stitch of the last space or block of the row. Wrap the yarn twice over the hook and insert the hook into the appropriate stitch of the turning chain on the previous row. Wrap the yarn over the hook and draw a loop through the chain.

2 | *Wrap the yarn over the hook and draw it through the two loops on the hook. Repeat from *. Wrap the yarn over the hook. To finish, draw the loop through the three loops on the hook.

Pockets

Pockets come in different types, shapes and sizes. Stitched onto the outside of a garment or accessory, a patch pocket is a flat piece of crochet that can be both a functional feature and an embellishment. An inset pocket is more practical and less decorative – it may have a horizontal, vertical or diagonal opening. The opening leads to a pocket bag that is not visible from the outside of the garment. Seam pockets are similar to inset pockets but the opening always follows the line of a seam.

FIX IT

144 *Using a yarn that is too chunky for a patch pocket?*

Try working the pocket using a finer yarn in a colour that matches the main body of the garment. If you cannot find the exact shade, it is best to choose a contrasting colour over one that is a bad match.

145 *Want to avoid adding extra bulk to the front of a garment?*

Try adding patch pockets in strategic places. For example, why not group three or four tiny buttoned pockets down the length of a jacket sleeve or superimpose a smaller pocket over a larger one?

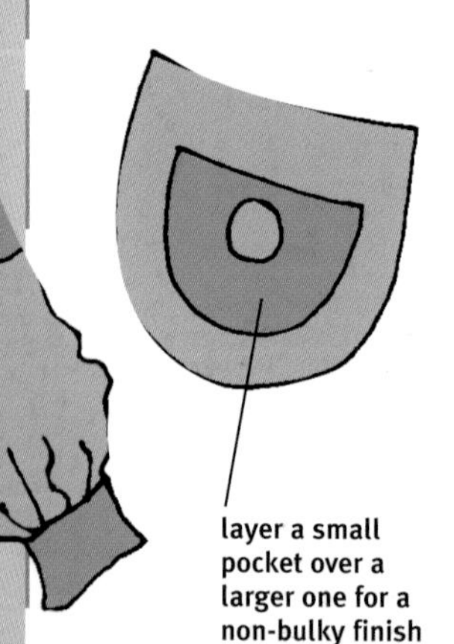
layer a small pocket over a larger one for a non-bulky finish

146 Patch pockets

A patch pocket is the simplest kind of pocket to make and apply to a garment. Use any of the shapes shown below and on page 87 or adapt one to suit your own style. Patch pockets can match a garment or provide an area of contrasting colour, texture and pattern.

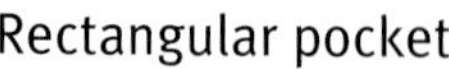

Rectangular pocket

This basic square or oblong pocket is worked in double crochet, treble crochet or using the same stitch pattern as your garment. Start at the lower edge and work it to the required shape, stopping about 1 cm (½ in.) short of the required depth and ending with a RS row. Add two rows of double crochet across the top of the pocket to make a firm, non-stretchy edge and finish with a row of reverse double crochet edging.

Round pocket

Make a round pocket with a neat edge by working a circular block in treble crochet. Stitch the pocket onto your garment with stitches going through the edge of each stitch on the last round. Leave the top one-third of the pocket unstitched.

Curved pocket with straight top

Starting at the top edge, work in double crochet for about two-thirds of the required depth without shaping. End with a WS row. To shape the bottom, repeat the decrease row (work the first stitch, then the next three stitches together) continue in dc to last 3 stitches, dc3tog, 1 dc, turn until the pocket is deep enough. End with a WS row. Work the final RS row (work the first stitch, miss the next, then work to the last two stitches, miss the next and work the last stitch). Fasten off the yarn.

Triangular pocket

Starting with an odd number of stitches, work about eight rows before shaping. To make the point, repeat the decrease row (work the first stitch, miss the next, then work to the end of the row) until you are left with three stitches. Work the first stitch, miss the centre stitch, work the last stitch, turn and work the two remaining stitches together. Fasten off the yarn.

Curved pocket with fancy edge

Make this pocket in the same way you would a plain curved pocket but ensure that the number of stitches is correct to work your chosen edging pattern. When you have finished, rejoin the yarn at the top edge and work a row of edging across the top. For a very neat finish, use a hook one size smaller for the edging.

Pocket with buttonhole

Make this pocket in the same way as a plain curved pocket but use an odd number of stitches and add a standard horizontal buttonhole (page 92) worked over three or more stitches. Position the buttonhole with care according to the size of your chosen button. For a small button, position the buttonhole about 1.5 cm (½ in.) from the top edge of the pocket but place it lower down for a larger button.

FIX IT

147 *Not sure exactly where to place the pockets?*

Pin or temporarily tack the pockets onto a jacket or coat, then try on the garment in front of a full-length mirror to check their positioning before you stitch them down permanently.

pin or tack a pocket to check its position on a garment

148 *Does the top of the pocket roll in on itself and refuse to lie flat?*

Simply unpick the pocket and work one of the stabilizing, non-rolling edge finishes on page 101 (such as reverse double crochet edging) along the top edge.

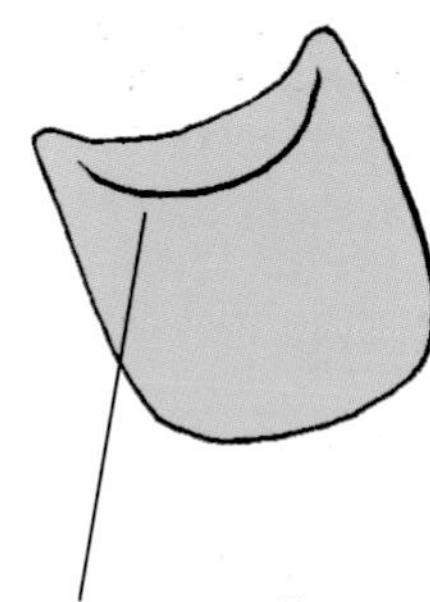

use a non-rolling edge finish for a neat, flat pocket

Making inset pockets

Inset pockets are functional rather than decorative unlike the pockets featured on pages 86–7. Pockets can be inset into the seams at the sides of a sweater, jacket or coat or inset directly into a piece of crochet fabric as it is being worked. This type of pocket is known as a welt pocket. The pocket bags for either type of inset pocket are best made from fabric as it is less bulky than crochet fabric. Choose a tightly woven cotton or cotton/synthetic blend: the fabric can be solid-colored or printed, whichever you prefer.

149

Types of pocket bag

Pocket bag for inserting into the seam

pocket opening

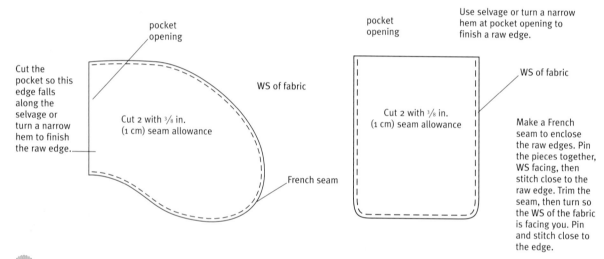

Cut the pocket so this edge falls along the selvage or turn a narrow hem to finish the raw edge.

Cut 2 with 3/8 in. (1 cm) seam allowance

WS of fabric

French seam

Pocket bag for a welt pocket

pocket opening

Use selvage or turn a narrow hem at pocket opening to finish a raw edge.

WS of fabric

Cut 2 with 3/8 in. (1 cm) seam allowance

Make a French seam to enclose the raw edges. Pin the pieces together, WS facing, then stitch close to the raw edge. Trim the seam, then turn so the WS of the fabric is facing you. Pin and stitch close to the edge.

150

Inserting a pocket into the seam

1 | Make a pocket bag like the one shown above. Pin the seam together, leaving an opening the same size as that on the pocket bag. Check the opening against the pocket bag, then stitch the seam.

2 | Using the same yarn as the garment, make facings down the pocket opening's front and back edges by working two rows of double crochet along each side. Join the short ends using the yarn tails.

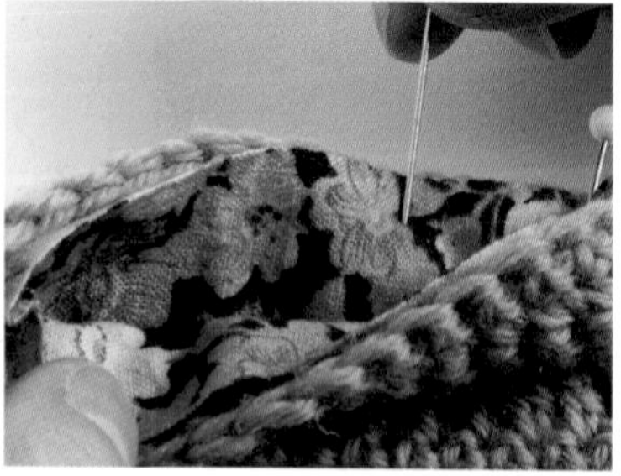

3 | With the garment's right sides facing, pin the pocket bag in place with the wrong sides facing and align the bag and garment seams. Carefully overcast the edge of the bag and the edge of the facings using matching thread. Tuck the facings through to the wrong side.

151 Making a basic welt pocket

2 | With right side of the piece facing, rejoin the yarn to the front edge of the opening. Work several rows of double crochet across the opening, ending with a right-side row. This strip of crochet is called a welt.

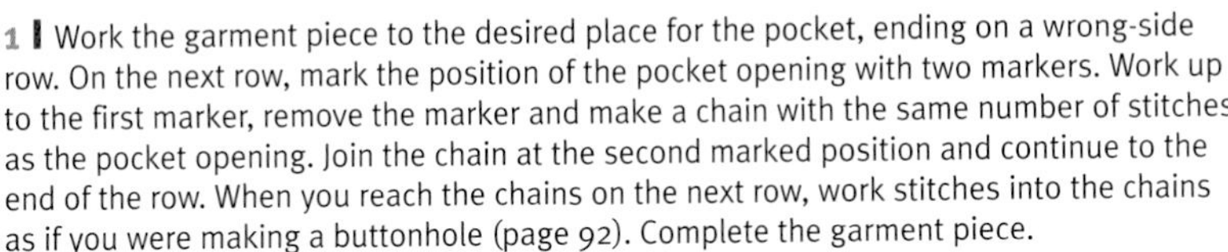

1 | Work the garment piece to the desired place for the pocket, ending on a wrong-side row. On the next row, mark the position of the pocket opening with two markers. Work up to the first marker, remove the marker and make a chain with the same number of stitches as the pocket opening. Join the chain at the second marked position and continue to the end of the row. When you reach the chains on the next row, work stitches into the chains as if you were making a buttonhole (page 92). Complete the garment piece.

3 | Working from the right side, stitch the short ends of the welt onto the garment. Use matching yarn and work the stitches as neatly as you can. Finish off the yarn ends on the wrong side.

4 | Working from the wrong side of the piece, pin and stitch the edge of the pocket bag to the bottom of the welt and the upper edge of the pocket opening using matching sewing thread.

Neckbands and collars

Crochet neckbands are much less stretchy than their knitted counterparts and it is a good idea to check that the finished neck will be large enough as you are working. You can leave one shoulder seam open, finish the edges with double crochet edging (page 100), buttons and button loops (page 93) or insert a short zip (page 98). Collars are best kept fairly small like the frilled example shown below.

152 Ruffled collar

This collar is worked in rounds, beginning with one round of evenly spaced double crochet edging worked into the right side of the neck edge. Round 1: 3 ch (counts as 1 tr), 1 tr into each dc, join with sl st into the third of 3 ch. Round 2: 3 ch (counts as 1 tr), 2 tr into same place as 3 ch, 3 tr into each tr, join with sl st into the third of 3 ch. Round 3: 1 ch, 1 dc into each tr, join with sl st into the first dc.

153 Neckband with picot edge

Finishing a neckband with a round of picots adds a dainty lace edging. To begin, work a round of evenly spaced double crochet edging into the RS of the neck edge using a size smaller hook than the size used for the garment – you will need to make a multiple of three stitches. On the next round, work picots as shown opposite, beginning and ending the round with 1 dc. Join the round with a slip stitch into the first dc.

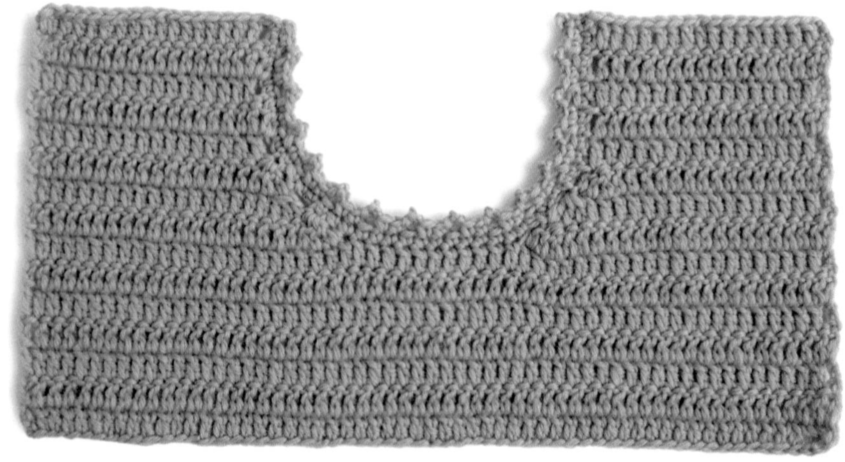

154 Double crochet neckband with slip stitch stripe

This neat and easy neckband can be worked in rounds or rows and also works well to edge armholes. Work a round of evenly spaced double crochet edging into the right side of the neck edge using a size smaller hook than that used for the garment. If you are working in rows, work the edging row into the wrong side not the right side. On the next round or row, work 1 dc into each st. You can leave the neckband plain, or add a stripe of colour by working a line of slip stitches between the two rounds or rows of dc.

155 Knitted ribbed neckband

This neckband stretches well and gives a good fit. Use a size smaller circular needle than the hook size used for the garment and pick up more stitches than if you were working a round of dc edging. As a guide, pick up five stitches to every two rows of treble crochet. To work K2, P2 rib as shown, pick up a multiple of four stitches. For K1, P1 rib, pick up a multiple of two stitches. Work the required number of rounds in rib, then cast off loosely in rib.

TRY IT

156 Working a picot edge

A picot edge finishes neckbands and armholes with a pretty lacy edge. You can work this edging in rows or rounds, but when working in rows, make sure that the right side of the garment is facing as you work the picot row.

1 | Work a double crochet into the first stitch on the first edging row or round. *Work three chains.

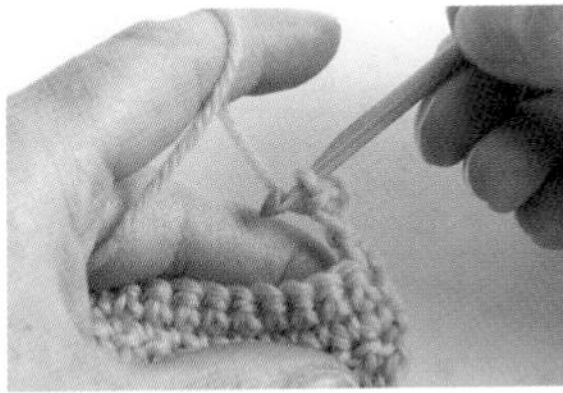

2 | Make the picot by working a slip stitch into the first of the three chains.

3 | Miss the next stitch, then work one double crochet into each of the next two stitches. Repeat from * to the last two stitches, work three chains, make the picot, miss the next stitch, and work one double crochet into the last stitch. If working in rounds, join the round by working a slip stitch into the first double crochet.

Button and buttonhole bands

Button bands and matching buttonhole bands are best when worked in double crochet for strength and neatness. Bands can be worked in vertical rows as an integral part of a garment or constructed separately and then stitched in place. Button loops are a decorative alternative to ordinary buttonholes. They look especially good on delicate, lacy garments, and can also be worked on jackets and coats in thick yarns to accommodate chunky toggles.

Making buttonhole bands

As a general rule, always make the button band first, mark the positions of the buttons on the band with safety pins, and then work the buttonhole (or button loop) band to match, making holes or loops opposite the safety pin markers. Only stitch the buttons in place once you have checked the original marked positions against the finished button band.

158 Basic buttonhole band

The basic band is worked in vertical rows directly onto the garment edge. With RS facing, work in dc until the band is half the width of the button band, ending with a WS row. To make each buttonhole on the next row, miss a few stitches to suit the button size, work the same number of chains over the missed stitches, and then work several dc after the missed stitches. Continue until all the holes have been worked. On the return (WS) row, work one dc into each stitch and the same number of dc into each chain loop as there are chains. Work further rows of dc until the buttonhole band is the same width as the button band.

band is 10 stitches wide

eight rows of dc between buttonholes

buttonhole over four stitches

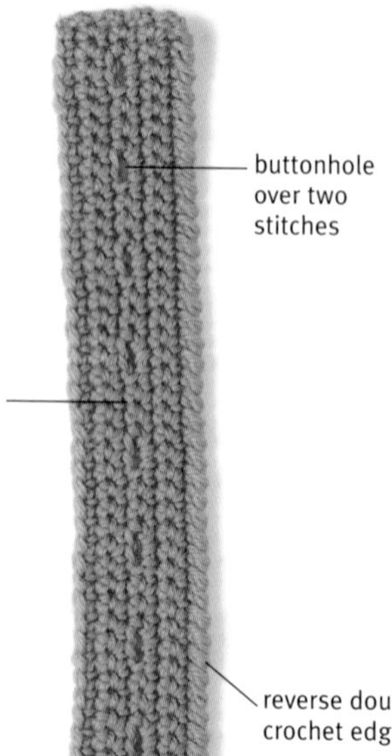

159 Narrow buttonhole band

Worked in vertical rows as above, this band is narrower and the small buttonholes are spaced closely together to accommodate tiny, delicate buttons. The outer edge of the band is finished with a row of reverse double crochet edging (page 100).

160 Band with horizontal buttonholes

Work this type of band in horizontal rows, and as a separate piece of crochet. Use a foundation chain of eight or more stitches, depending on the size of your buttons. On each buttonhole row, work an ordinary buttonhole as above, making sure that there are the same number of stitches before and after the hole. Work several rows of dc between the buttonholes, taking care to start each buttonhole on a RS row.

161 Button loops

A row of button loops is usually worked directly into the garment edge. Alternatively, depending on the amount of overlap required, work a few rows of dc on the edge first to make a narrow band, ending with a WS row. On the loop row, work in dc to the position of the first loop, then work several more stitches (the length of the gap between the buttonhole loop). Work several chains to suit the button size, and turn it back toward the point where you want the loop to begin. Slip the hook out of the chain and insert it back into the crochet at the point where you want the loop to start. Slip the loop of the last chain back onto the hook and join the loop to the band with a slip stitch.

To complete the loop, work dc into the loop until the chain is completely covered, then insert the hook into the last dc worked before making the chain and work a slip stitch. Continue along the row in double crochet, making loops as required.

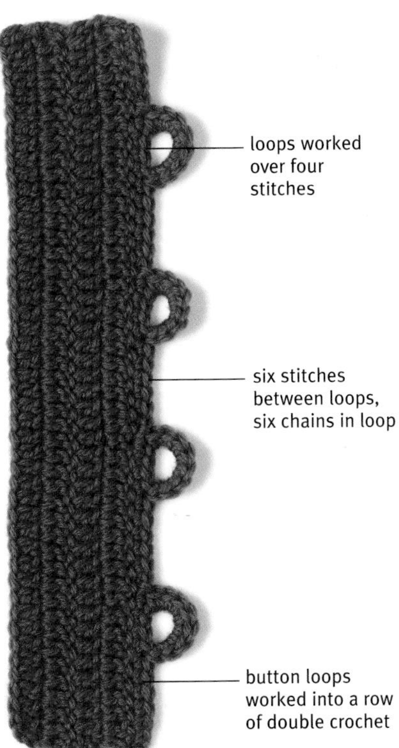

162 Button loops on textured fabric

When making a garment from textured or novelty yarns, it is a good idea to use a plain, smooth yarn in a toning colour to make a narrow button band and button-loop band. Work several rows of dc into the garment edge first, then proceed as above to make the button loops.

loops worked over six stitches

eight chains in loop

two rows of double crochet worked before the loop row

six stitches between loops

covered with 12 stitches

TRY IT

163 Strengthening buttonholes

When working with soft, easily abraded yarns, strengthen the buttonholes before you wear the garment. Choose a matching colour of thinner yarn and your stitches will be almost invisible, or be bold and use brightly coloured embroidery thread to add an eye-catching detail.

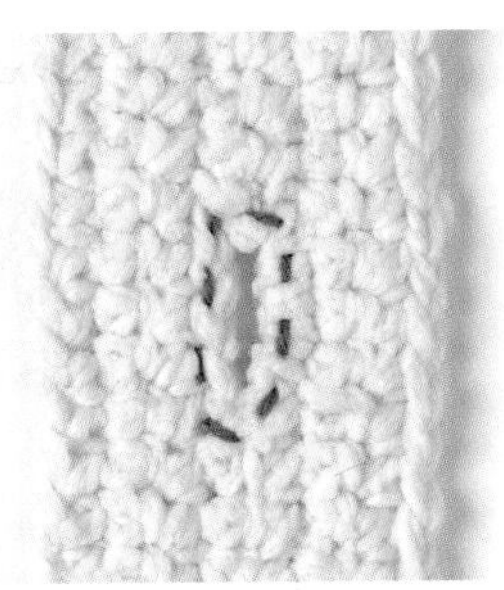

164 Running stitches

The easiest way to strengthen a buttonhole is to work a row of running stitches around the hole, close to the edge.

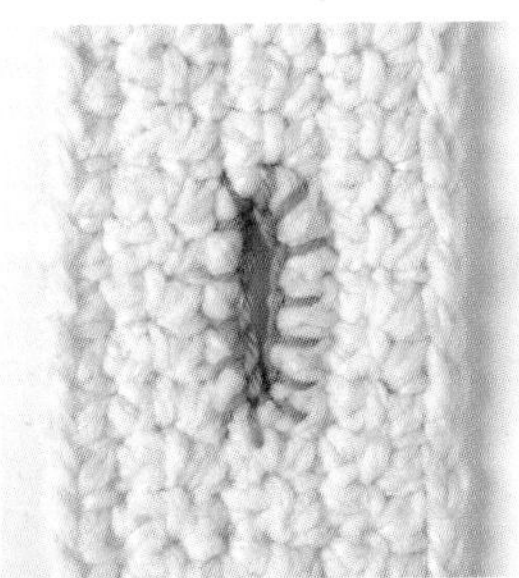

165 Blanket stitches

For a really hardwearing finish, choose blanket stitch and work a row all around the buttonhole. You could also oversew the edge of the buttonhole in the same way as you would oversew a seam (page 149).

Adding buttons

Buttons add style to any crochet garment. They may be purely functional or form one of the main design features. Choose buttons to emphasize the character of the yarn. For example, pair textured buttons with tweedy yarns, or choose a different colour of buttons to create a complete contrast.

Choosing buttons

Buttons come in a wide range of sizes, shapes and colours, and are made from all sorts of materials including plastic, resin, shell, wood, horn and metal. They are attached by stitching through a group of holes piercing the button or through a shank attached to the back. Use the same yarn to attach buttons if it is fine enough to fit through the holes on the button, or choose matching or contrasting thread, or suitable embroidery thread.

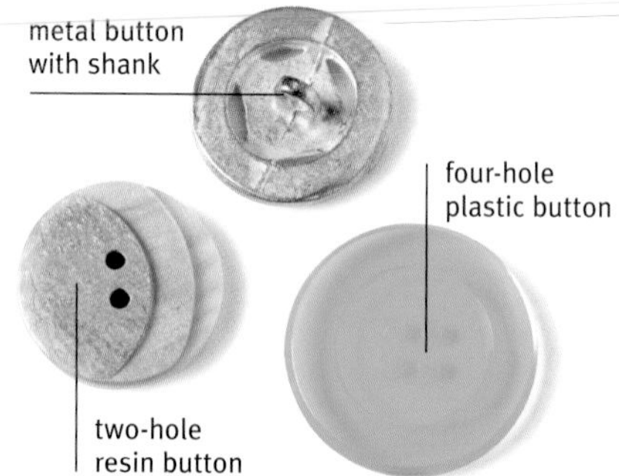

167

Attaching a shank button

1 | Double the thread on a needle and tie the ends in a knot. On the right side, take a stitch through the crochet, and slip the needle through the thread strands. Pull gently on the needle to lock the knot in place.

2 | Take several stitches through both the crochet fabric and the button shank, then take the thread through to the wrong side of the fabric and fasten off securely, working a few tiny stitches into the crochet.

Attaching a two-hole button

1 | Attach thread as for a shank button. Hold a cable needle, matchstick or bamboo skewer on top of the button. Stitch the button in place, stitching over the cable needle each time, and ending with the thread on the wrong side of the crochet. Do not fasten off.

2 | Carefully remove the cable needle from beneath the stitches. Ease the button upward until the thread loops are flush with the button top, creating a thread shank under the button.

3 | Bring the working thread through to the right side underneath the button, and wind the thread several times around the shank to strengthen it. Take the thread back to the wrong side of the fabric and fasten off securely.

169

Attaching a four-hole button

Attach with a thread shank in the same way as a two-hole button. To make plain buttons look more attractive, work the stitches to make a decorative feature of the holes.

170

Attaching toggles

Toggles made from wood, resin or horn make chunky fastenings for jackets and coats. One- or two-hole toggles are easy to attach using short lengths of crochet chain. Make an individual length of chain for each toggle and strengthen it with a row of slip stitch worked along each side of the chain. Thread the chain through the toggle, then thread the ends of the chain into a yarn needle and pull the ends through the crochet. Secure the ends with a few stitches.

171

Button materials

Buttons are made from many different materials, both natural and man-made. When choosing buttons, be aware that you will have to remove and replace some types every time you launder the garment.

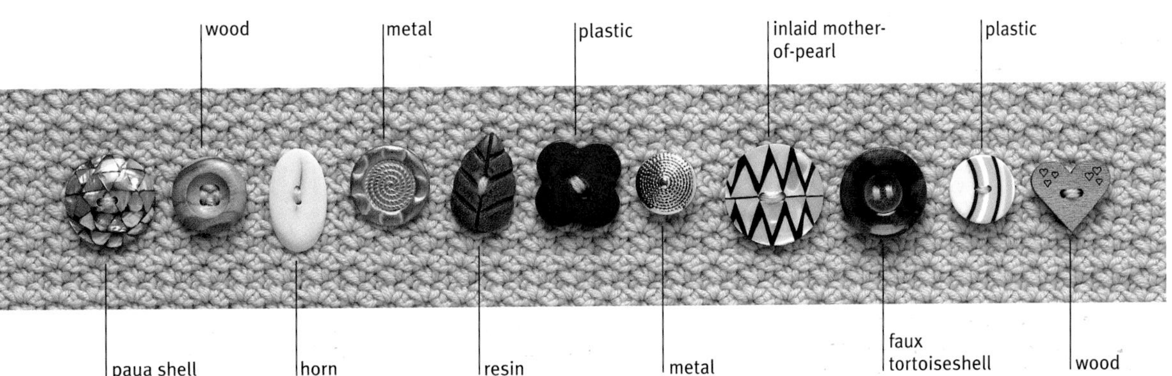

Making your own buttons

Handmade buttons add a certain something to crochet garments and they are very easy to make. Use a matching yarn colour or choose one that contrasts strongly to make a bolder statement. Remember to remove handmade buttons before cleaning a garment.

172 Covered bead

Worked in a spiral of double crochet using 4-ply (sportweight) yarn, using a 2.5 mm (size C) hook. The crochet covers a wooden bead 2 cm ($^{3}/_{4}$ in.) in diameter.

174 Multicolour button

Worked in a flat spiral of double crochet to cover the top of the foundation, then decreased to cover the back. Variegated sockweight yarn and a 2.5 mm (size C) hook were used to cover a 4.5 cm ($1^{3}/_{4}$ in.) flat button with shank.

176 Treble crochet rounds

Worked in rounds of treble crochet until large enough to cover the top of the foundation, then worked in decreasing rounds of double crochet to cover the back. DK yarn and a 3.5 mm (size E) hook were used to cover a 4.5 cm ($1^{3}/_{4}$ in.) flat button with shank.

173 Stretched-strip cover

Worked in a flat six-stitch wide strip of double crochet using DK yarn and a 3.5 mm (size E) hook to cover wooden bead 2 cm ($^{3}/_{4}$ in.) in diameter. Stretch the strip around the bead and secure by stitching the side edges together.

175 Domed button

Worked in a spiral of half treble crochet to cover the top of the foundation, then changed to double crochet and decreased to cover the back. 4-ply (sportweight) yarn and a 2.5 mm (size C) hook were used to cover a 3.5 cm ($1^{3}/_{8}$ in.) domed button with shank.

177 Metallic finish

Worked in a spiral of treble crochet until large enough to cover the top of the foundation, then changed to half treble crochet and decreased to cover the back. Metallic yarn with a 3.5 mm (size E) hook was used to cover a 4.5 cm ($1^{3}/_{4}$ in.) flat button with shank.

178

How to make a basic button

The instructions show you how to make a spherical button cover by working a spiral of increasing and then decreasing double crochet around a wooden bead. Use the same technique to cover domed and flat foundations shaping the cover as required by altering the amount of increases and decreases. See also working in rounds on page 106 and working a spiral block on page 116.

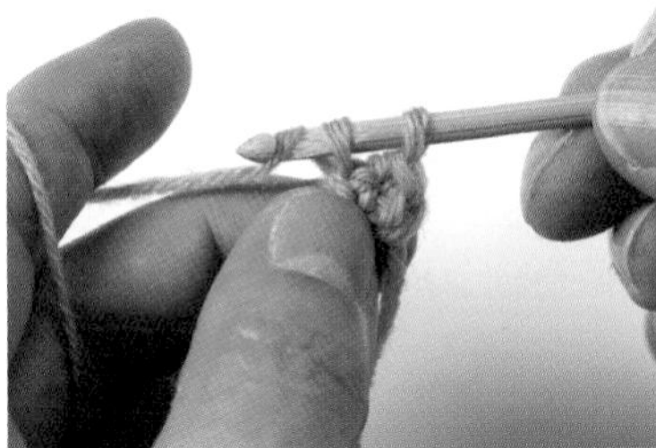

1 | To begin the spiral, make two chains, and then work four dc into the first chain. Without joining the round, work two dc into each of the four stitches made on the previous round.

2 | Continuing to work in spiralling rounds of dc (without joining rounds), shape the cover by working two dc into every alternate stitch until the piece is large enough to cover the foundation bead.

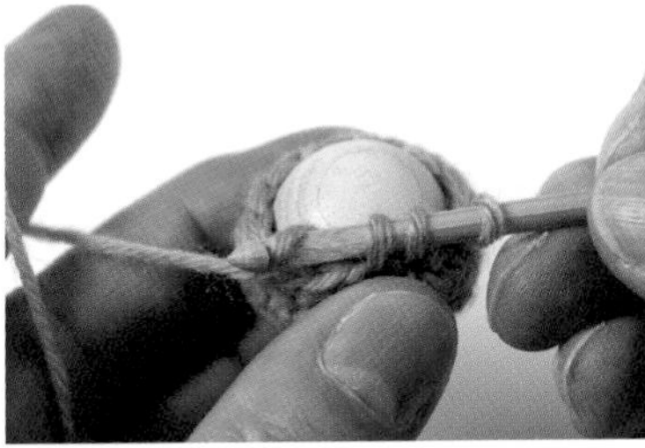

3 | Place the bead in the cover and start decreasing. Work one dc into the next stitch, then work the next two stitches together. Repeat until the bead is almost covered, then work every two stitches together until the cover is complete.

4 | Fasten off the yarn, leaving a 30 cm (12 in.) tail. Thread the yarn end onto a yarn needle and work a few stitches into the button cover to secure the end. Do not cut the end – you can use it to sew the button onto your garment.

179

Button foundations

Depending on the size and shape of the buttons you want to make, you can use different types of foundations and cover them with crochet. Dressmakers' cover buttons work well, as do ordinary wooden or plastic buttons, flat or domed buttons and buttons with or without shanks. For spherical buttons, choose chunky wooden or plastic beads.

TRY IT

180

Making decorative buttons

Make handmade buttons even more decorative by using novelty yarns, working in stripes and incorporating beads (see page 134 for how to add beads). Wool sock yarn with a percentage of nylon makes a good base for decorative buttons as it is both lightweight and durable. Try working with a 2.5 mm (size C) hook.

Novelty yarn

Worked in a lightweight novelty yarn over a domed plastic button with shank, 3.5 cm (1¼ in.) in diameter.

Two-tone beads

Worked in sock yarn with beads threaded onto the yarn in alternating colours and worked over a flat button, 2.5 cm (1 in.) in diameter.

Stripes

A square of striped double crochet worked in two colours of sock yarn, wrapped and stitched around a flat wooden button, 3.5 cm (1¼ in.) in diameter.

Random beads

A square of double crochet in sock yarn wrapped and stitched around a wooden button with shank, 2.5 cm (1 in.) square, and decorated with seed beads.

Zips

Zips can be inserted into the side or centre back seams for a little more ease getting in and out of a tight-fitting crochet garment. Short zips work well in a shoulder seam or at the centre back of a neckline while a separating zip makes a good alternative to buttons and buttonholes. Choose a zip to suit the weight of the crochet and one similar in colour to your yarn. Stitch in place with matching sewing thread.

182

Anatomy of a zip

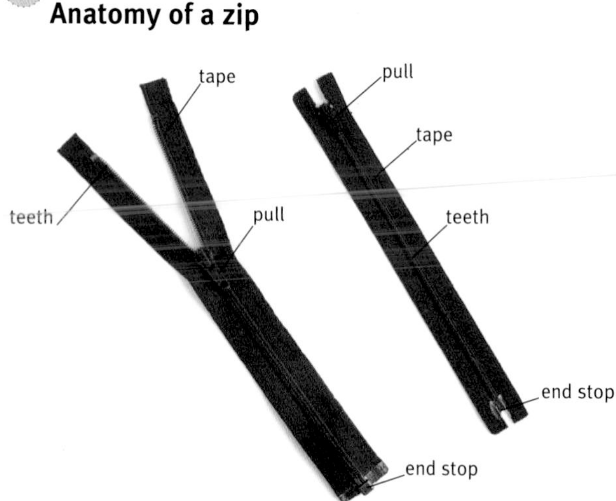

181

Inserting a zip into a seam

1 | Sew the seam, leaving an opening in the desired place long enough to accommodate the zip from the pull to just above the end stop. Press the seam open and check the opening against the zip.

2 | Pin the tapes of the zip into position, making sure that the crochet stitch pattern matches on either side of the zip.

3 | Using matching sewing thread in a sewing needle, stitch one tape of the zip in position using small, widely spaced back stitches. At the end of the zip, stitch across to the other side and then stitch the opposite tape in place.

4 | On the wrong side, carefully stitch the tape onto the back of the crochet fabric using small, evenly spaced stitches and taking care to stitch into the back of the crochet stitches, not right through the front of your work.

183

Inserting a separating zip

1 | Work a row of double crochet edging (pages 100–1) along each edge of the jacket. Pin the zip in place, turning under the tape ends at the top and bottom. The pull end of the zip should be flush with the top of the crochet. The end stop can be flush or a short distance above the lower edge of the garment.

2 | Try it on to check whether the edges fit and make sure the zip lies smoothly. Adjust any pins. With the zip separated, stitch down each side with matching sewing thread. Finish the wrong side by sewing the tape onto the crochet as for an ordinary zip.

FIX IT

184 *Unable to find the right length of zip?*

Choose one longer than you need and shorten it.

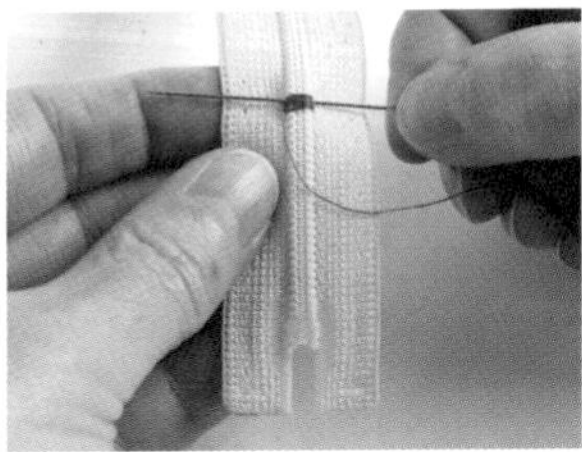

1 | Compare the zip with the length of the opening and shorten it at the bottom where the zip joins, not at the pull end. Using sewing cotton in a sewing needle, work stitches from side to side, taking them over the zip's teeth and into the tape at either side.

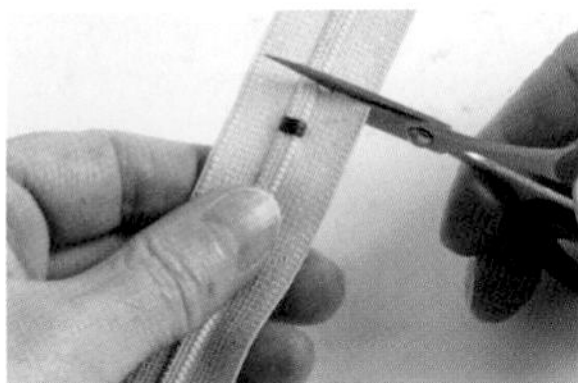

2 | Fasten off the thread end securely. Using a pair of scissors, cut off the end of the zip 1 cm (3/8 in.) below the stitching.

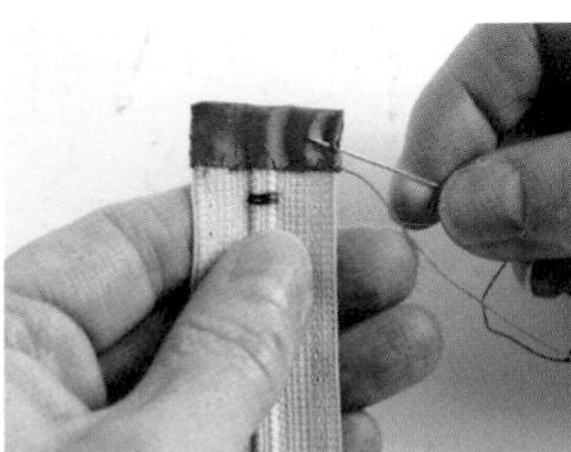

3 | To stop the end of the teeth from snagging, fold a piece of tape or scrap of lining fabric over the cut end of the zip to enclose both tape and teeth. Take care to fold in all the raw edges neatly. Stitch in place and fasten off the thread end.

Working edge treatments

Edge treatments differ from crochet edgings and borders (page 102) in the way that they are worked. An edge treatment is worked directly into the crochet fabric, whereas an edging or border is worked separately and then attached to the finished piece.

The simplest treatment is a row of double crochet stitches worked in a matching or contrasting colour. This can also be worked as a base for another more decorative treatment such as a ruffle edge. Reverse double crochet edging (also known as crab stitch) makes a knotted edge that is hardwearing. Ruffles in various widths add a pretty, feminine finish to garments, pillows and afghans.

185

Double crochet edging

1 | Working from right to left on the upper or lower edge of a piece of crochet, make a row of ordinary dc into the edge (page 48), working one dc into every stitch.

2 | When you reach a corner, work two or three extra stitches into the crochet to ensure that the corner will lie flat.

3 | When working this edge treatment into the row ends of a piece of double crochet, work one dc into every row end.

4 | When working this edge treatment into the row ends of a piece of treble crochet, work two dc into every row, taking care to space the stitches evenly.

5 | When working across the row ends of treble or double treble crochet fabric, double crochet stitches can be worked into the centre of stitches made at the beginning and end of every row of fabric (as shown) or they can be worked into the spaces between the first and second stitches.

186

Reverse double crochet edging

1 | Unlike most other crochet techniques, work this stitch from left to right along the row. Using the same or a contrasting yarn, work one chain then, keeping the yarn at the back of the work, insert the hook from front to back into the next stitch on the right.

2 | Wrap the yarn over the hook and draw a loop through from back to front, pulling the yarn through below the loop already on the hook. There are now two loops on the hook.

3 | Wrap the yarn over the hook, and draw the yarn through both loops to complete the stitch. Repeat along the row, continuing to work from left to right.

187

Working a basic ruffle

With right side of the work facing you, work a row of tr along the edge, working three tr into each stitch.

Double crochet edging

Use this edge treatment anywhere on a garment when you require a narrow, plain edge worked in a matching or contrast colour yarn.

Reverse double crochet edging

Use this edge treatment on front bands, cuffs, and hems where you require a durable finish on garment edges that need strengthening.

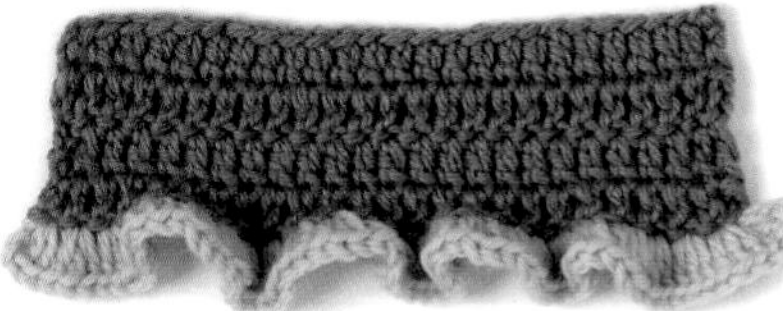

Basic ruffle

A narrow ruffle makes a pretty edging for cuffs and neckbands. This is the simplest type of ruffle and is worked in tr.

Deep ruffle

Wide ruffles add interest to a plain jacket. Work the first row like a basic ruffle (see above), then a row of tr, followed by a row working two tr into each stitch.

TRY IT

188 **Making ruffled scarves**

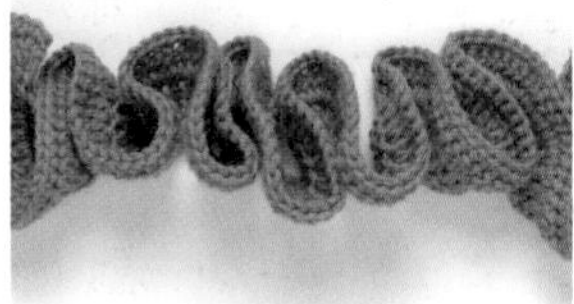

Fancy curly-whirly scarf

Work a long foundation chain, then a row of dc along the back of the chain. Work a deep ruffle (see left) into the row of dc, then edge the ruffle with a row of double crochet edging.

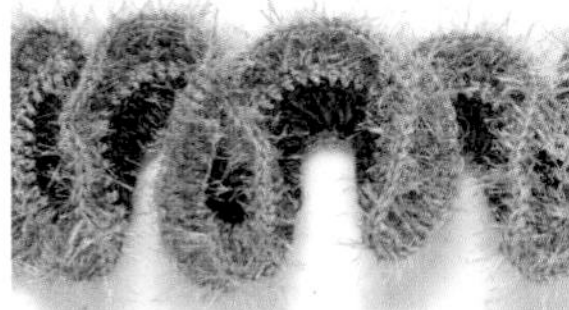

Fancy multi-yarn scarf

Using the same method as above, this time work a different yarn into each row. This scarf, edged with a row of eyelash yarn, combines cotton, wool, ribbon and metallic yarns.

Edgings and insertions

Edgings are strips of crochet used to decorate edges or that are stitched onto pieces of knitted and woven fabric. An edging usually has one straight and one fancy edge, although in some edging patterns both edges are shaped. Depending on the pattern, edgings are either worked widthwise over a small number of stitches, or lengthwise on a long foundation chain. Inserted between two pieces of fabric rather than added to edges, insertions, too, are strips of crochet but they have two straight edges.

Most edgings can be made deeper by working a straight band of crochet along the top edge. This is called a header and is usually worked in double crochet. On edgings worked lengthwise, the header is worked into the foundation chain before the pattern commences. On edgings worked widthwise, the header is added after the decorative part of the edging has been completed. Headers are usually plain but a regular band of holes to accommodate a narrow piece of ribbon can be incorporated.

189 Narrow shaped edging

Worked lengthwise over a multiple of four chains plus one, this edging begins with two rows of double crochet. On the last row, work 3 ch, miss next 2 tr, 1 tr into next dc, *3 ch, 4 tr into sp made by tr just worked, miss next 3 dc, 1 tr into next dc. Repeat from * to end.

a header can be made deeper by adding extra rows of double crochet before working the fancy edge

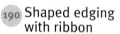

190 Shaped edging with ribbon

Worked as above but with a variation to the header. Work one row of dc, and one row of holes thus: *1 dc into next dc, 2 ch, miss next 2 dc, 1 dc into next dc; repeat from * to end, turn. On the next row, work 1 ch, 1 dc into each dc and 2 dc into each 2 ch sp, to end, turn. Work one row of dc, then the last row (as given above) and thread the ribbon through the holes.

191 Shaped edging worked widthwise

This classic edging with shamrock motifs is worked across the width on a narrow foundation chain. With this type of edging, continue repeating the pattern rows until the strip is the required length.

192 Fringed chain edging

Make the required length of foundation chain, then work two rows of sc. On the fringe row, work 1 ch, 1 dc into first dc, *1 dc into next dc, 16 ch, sl st into same place as dc just worked. Repeat from * to end. Try increasing the length of the chain loops to make a deeper fringe.

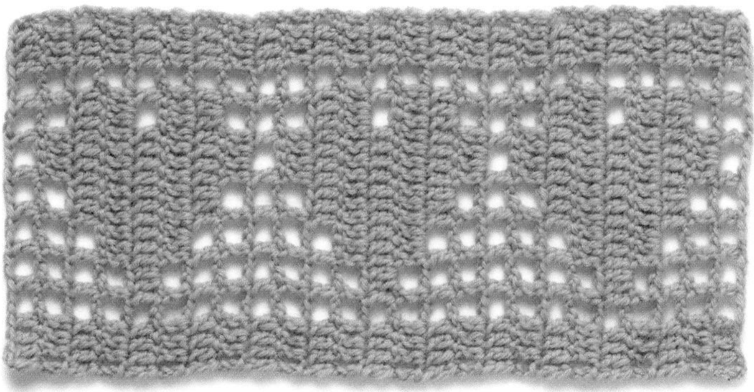

193 Filet crochet insertion

Small filet crochet motifs look good when repeated in a strip to form an insertion. Work widthwise and repeat the pattern until the strip is the desired length, remembering to finish working at the end of a repeat so that both ends of the strip match. Turn to pages 62–5 for more on filet crochet.

194 Crochet braid

This edging looks like a narrow upholstery braid and works well both as an edging or surface trim. Begin with a 7 ch ring, then work 3 ch, 3 tr into ring, 3 ch, 1 dc into ring, turn. On the next and subsequent rows, work 3 ch, 3 tr into 3 ch sp, 3 ch, 1 dc into same 3 ch sp, turn.

TRY IT

195 Edging variations

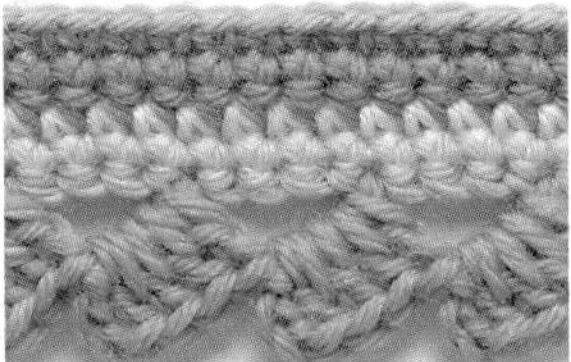

Add interest and colour to a plain edging by introducing stripes. Work four rows of double crochet using a different colour for each row, then work the pattern row in a fifth colour.

Add beads to the last row to trim the shaped edge. Turn to page 134 to find out how to apply individual beads using a small-gauge crochet hook.

Handspun yarn in a mix of colours makes an attractively rustic edging that contrasts well against a piece of smooth crochet fabric.

Combine different yarn textures to make a fun edging. Here, smooth cotton/viscose yarn is paired up with eyelash yarn in variegated colours.

Jazzy trims and fringes

An oversized tassel makes a fun decoration for a quirky hat or the points of a triangular shawl. Whether plain, striped or beaded, spirals are quick to make and add a finishing touch to all sorts of items. Trim a key ring or the tab on a zip using a crochet spiral or make several to sew onto the ends of a scarf.

As a novel alternative to a tassel, you can make a large cluster of spirals to decorate each corner of a crochet throw. Corkscrew fringe, as is the felted flower brooch on the opposite page, is closely related in technique to a spiral. Braided chains make good ties for fastening jackets and bags and can be worked on a small scale to make bracelets and chokers. Take the trims and fringes shown here as sources of inspiration and be bold with different sizes, yarns, colours and beads.

198 Oversized tassel

Begin by working a strip of dc. The strip can be as long or wide as you like, depending on the size of tassel you want to make. For the last row, work fringed chain edging (page 103) with at least 50 chains per loop. Roll the strip tightly and sew the ends in place with yarn tail. Take both tails up through the centre and use to attach the tassel.

196 Striped spiral

Work a loose foundation chain of 30 ch, then work 2 tr into the fourth ch from hook and 4 tr into each rem ch. Fasten off the yarn, leaving a yarn end of about 30 cm (12 in.) to attach the spiral. Join the contrasting yarn to the top of the outer edge, work 1 dc into each st along edge, then fasten off the yarn.

197 Beaded spiral

Use thin, durable yarn (wool/nylon or cotton is good) and thread 50 beads onto yarn before starting to crochet, work the foundation chain of 25 ch, then work 2 tr into 4th ch from hook, 3 tr into each ch to end. On the tr row, add one bead (page 135) to the final stage of each tr.

add the beads with a tiny hook
choose a bead size that complements your yarn weight

199 Corkscrew fringe

Make a foundation chain of the length required, then work four rows of dc. On the fringe row, work 1 ch, 1 dc into first dc, *10 ch, working back down chain 2 dc into 2nd ch from hook, 2 dc into each rem ch, sl st into st just worked, 1 dc into each of next 2 dc. Rep from * along row, ending by working 1 dc into last st.

200 Beaded fringe

Work as above, but change yarn colour to work the fringe row. On the fringe row, 15 ch instead of 10 to make a longer corkscrew. Add beads using a small-gauge hook (page 135) before turning to work back down the chain.

201 Braided chain

Work several lengths of chain using different colours of yarn and braid them together. The braid shown here is made from two lengths of braided chain in three colours.

202 Felted flower brooch

Finished with a brooch back, a felted flower makes a great accessory to liven up any jacket or coat collar. Sew on sequins, ceramic or gemstone embellishments (page 135), or decorate the centre with vintage buttons.

TRY IT

203 Making a felted flower

You will need yarn that felts (page 132), a brooch back and two buttons.

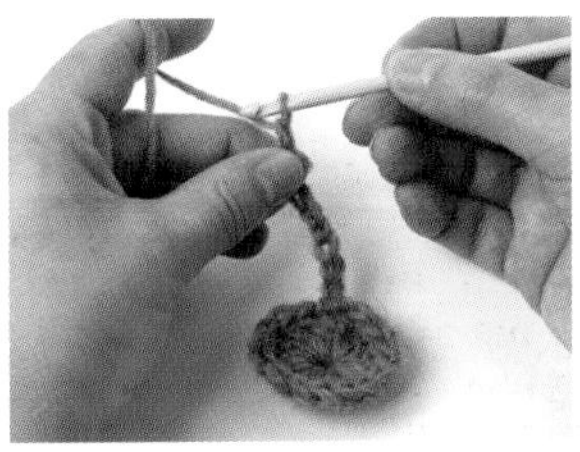

1 | Work a finger wrap, then 3 ch, 15 tr into the ring, and join with a slip stitch (pages 107 and 108). After joining the round, work 10 ch to begin the first petal.

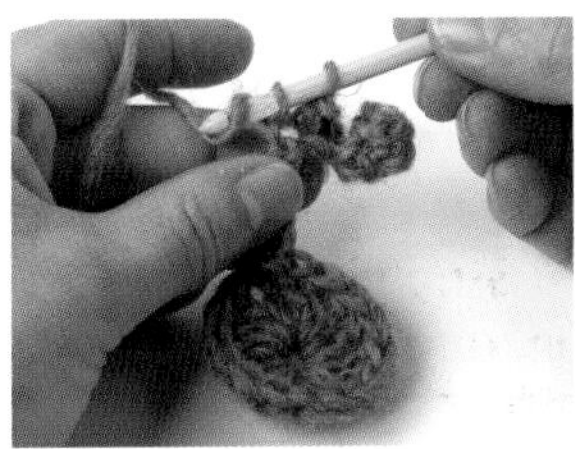

2 | Working back down ch, 2 dc into the second ch from hook, 2 dc into each rem ch. Finish the first petal by working a slip stitch into where the chain began.

3 | Work *dc into the next st, 10 ch, 2 dc into second ch from hook, 2 dc into each rem ch, sl st into dc just worked. Rep from * until you have made 15 more petals. Join the round with sl st, break off yarn, and darn in the ends. To finish, felt the flower by hand or machine (page 132). Allow to dry. Using matching thread, sew the buttons at the centre of the right side and sew on the brooch back securely to the wrong side.

WORKING IN THE ROUND

Working crochet in flat rounds rather than backwards and forwards in straight rows offers a new range of possibilities that make colourful and intricate pieces of crochet called blocks or medallions. Crochet blocks are worked outwards from a central ring and the number of stitches on each round increases.

Working out from the centre

Evenly spaced increases result in a flat, circular block, but when the increases are grouped together to make corners, the resulting block can be a square, hexagon, triangle, or any other flat shape. Blocks can be solid, textured or lacy in appearance. Joined together using a variety of techniques, they make afghans, shawls and wraps as well as simply shaped garments.

204

Making a ring of chains

The usual way to start working on a block is to make a short length of chain and join it into a ring. The ring can be made any size, depending on the pattern instructions, and leaves a small or large hole at the centre of the block.

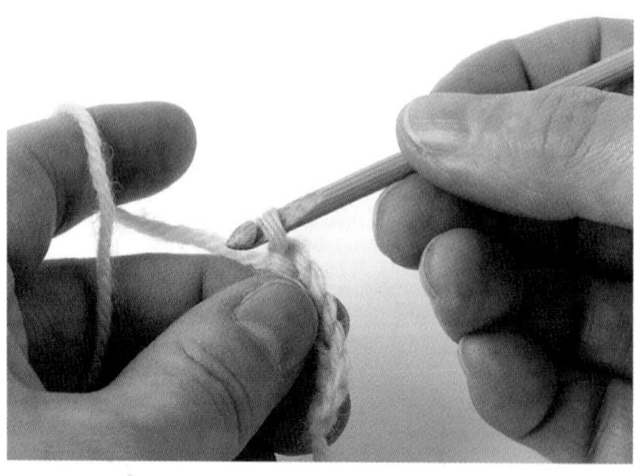

1 | Make the foundation ring by working a short length of chain (page 47). Work the number of chains in the pattern.

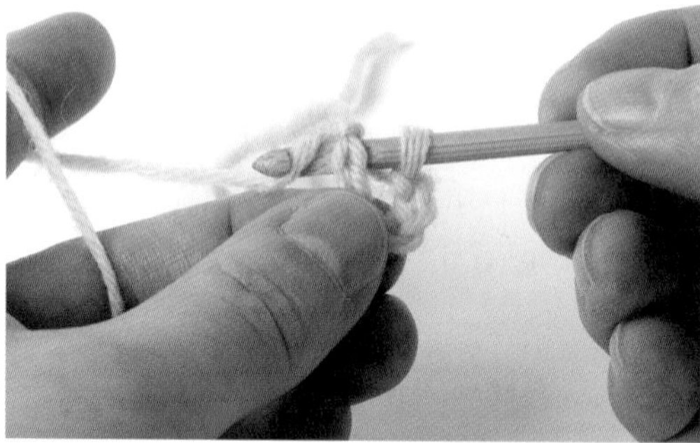

2 | Join the chains into a ring by working a slip stitch (page 48) into the first stitch of the foundation chain.

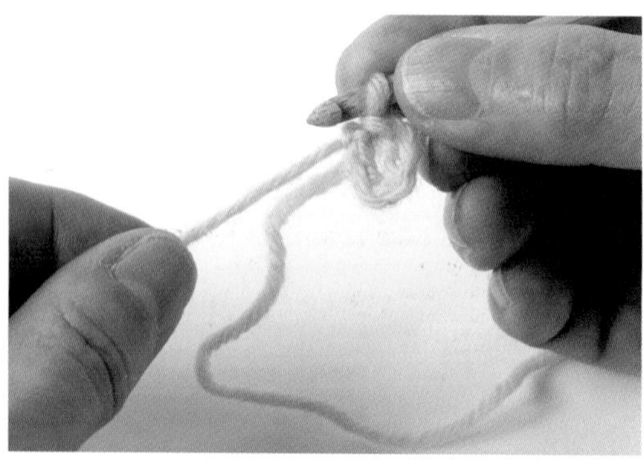

3 | Tighten the first stitch by pulling the loose yarn end with your left hand. The foundation ring is now complete and you are ready to work the first round of stitches.

205

Making a finger wrap

This alternative method of making a foundation ring is useful as the yarn end is enclosed within the first round of stitches and will not need darning in later but it should not be used with slippery yarns such as mercerised cotton or silk blends because the yarn ends may work loose.

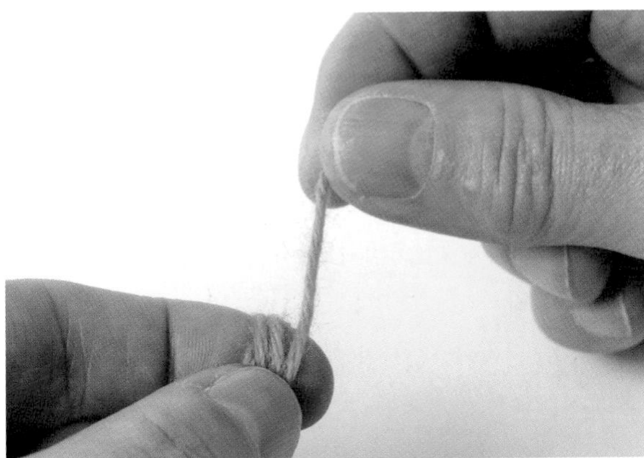

1 | Hold the yarn end between the thumb and first finger of your left hand and wind the yarn several times around your fingertip.

2 | Carefully slip the yarn ring off your finger. Insert the hook into the ring, pull through a loop of yarn, and work a double crochet stitch to secure the ring ready to work the first round of stitches.

206

Making a magic circle

This method of starting a block has advantages over the two previous methods. As you work, the ring can easily be made smaller or larger and tightened to eliminate the hole in the centre after the first round is completed. However, the ring is less durable than making a ring of chains or beginning with a finger wrap.

1 | Make a slipknot (page 46) in the yarn, ensuring that the short end is on the left and the yarn from the ball on the right. Pull the loop into a circle.

2 | Work the exact number of chains for the stitch you are using (page 54). Begin to work the required number of stitches into the circle made by the slipknot.

3 | At the end of the round, gently pull the short end of the yarn to close off the circle's centre. Join the round.

Working a basic round block

Now you have made the foundation ring using one of the methods on pages 106–7, it is time to work the round block, the simplest of the block shapes. Carefully positioned increases on each round make the block a nice round shape as well as keeping it flat.

207 **Colour variations**

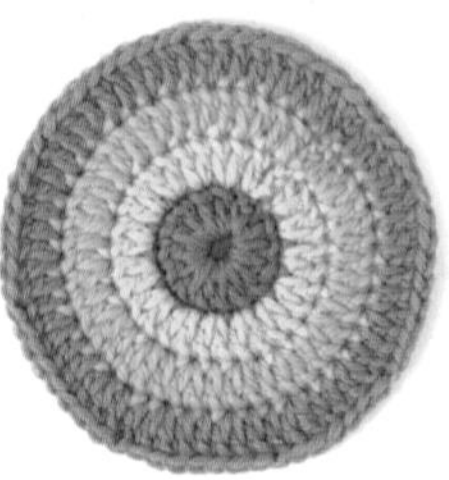

Round blocks look great worked in more than one colour. Try working each round in a different colour, taking care to change the yarns neatly at each join (page 59).

Try working the central circle in one colour (light) and the rest of the block in a second colour (dark).

For another effect, work all but the last round in one colour (dark) finishing the last round in another colour (light).

208 **Round blocks are versatile**

Round blocks can be worked in a variety of yarns and sizes to make items such as coasters and tablemats. Although easy to work, they join less easily than blocks with straight sides because of their curved shape and look best arranged in rows and sewn together with a few stitches where the curves touch.

Working the first round

The usual way of starting to work a block is to make a short length of chain and join it into a ring. The ring can be made any size, depending on the pattern instructions, and leaves a small or large hole at the centre of the block.

1 | Begin the first round by working the number of starting chains (page 54) stated in the pattern (three chains are shown here and will count as a treble crochet stitch). Work the first stitch into the ring.

2 | Inserting the hook into the space at the centre of the ring each time, work the correct number of stitches into the ring as stated in the pattern. Count the stitches at the end of the round to make sure you have worked the correct number.

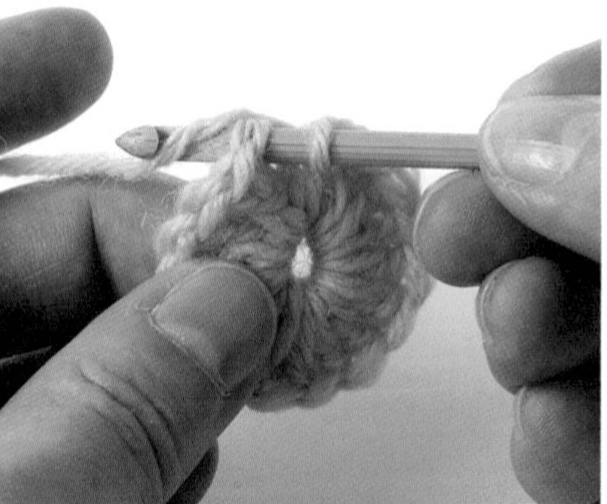

3 | Join the first and last stitch of the round by working a slip stitch into the top of the starting chain.

Working the second round

1 | Work three chains to count as the first treble crochet of the next round, then work a treble crochet into the same place as the three chains.

2 | Work two treble crochet stitches into each stitch of the previous round. Join the round by working a slip stitch into the third of three chains beginning the round.

Working the third round

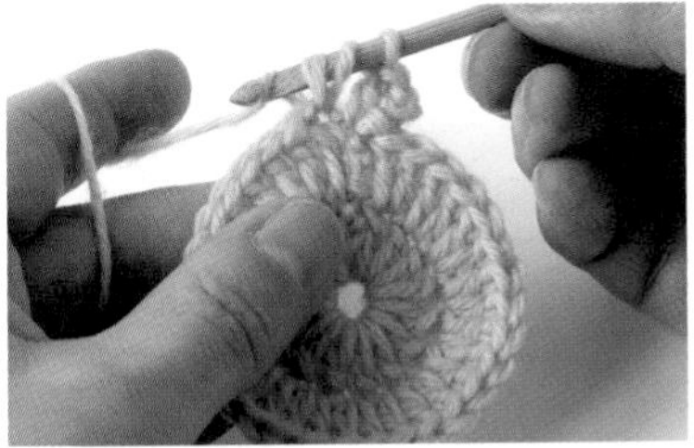

1 | Start the round by working three chains and one treble crochet into the same place, then work one treble crochet into the next stitch.

2 | *Work two treble crochet into the next stitch, then one treble crochet into the stitch after that. Repeat from * to the end of the round. Join the round as before.

Working the fourth round

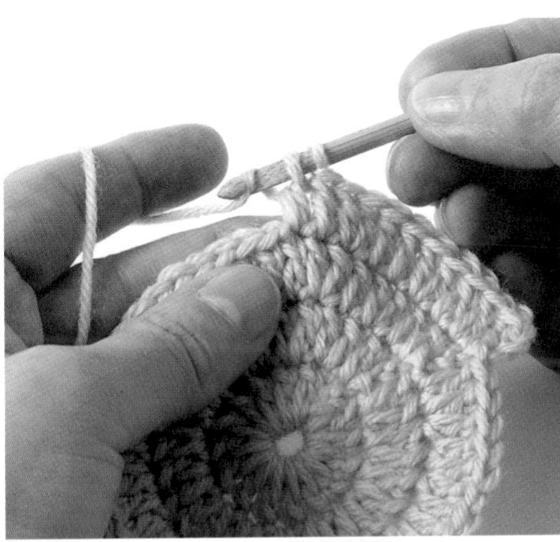

Work in the same way as the third round but work one more treble crochet between increases. To make a bigger block, work one or two more rounds in the same way.

FIX IT

209 *Messy join on the last round?*

Joining the last round with a slip stitch gives a less-than-perfect finish.

1 | After working the last stitch of the final round, cut the yarn to about 10 cm (4 in.) and pull it through.

2 | Thread the end into a yarn needle. With the right side facing, take it under both loops of the stitch next to the turning chain. Pull the needle through.

3 | Insert it into the centre of the last stitch of the round. On the wrong side, pull the yarn through to complete the stitch, adjust the length of the stitch to close the round, and darn in the end on the wrong side in the usual way.

Fitting blocks together

Crochet blocks can be made in different geometric shapes. Round, square, triangular, hexagonal or octagonal, most will happily fit together with other blocks of the same size and shape to make larger pieces of crochet. The one exception are the octagonal blocks which will need tiny squares added when joined together.

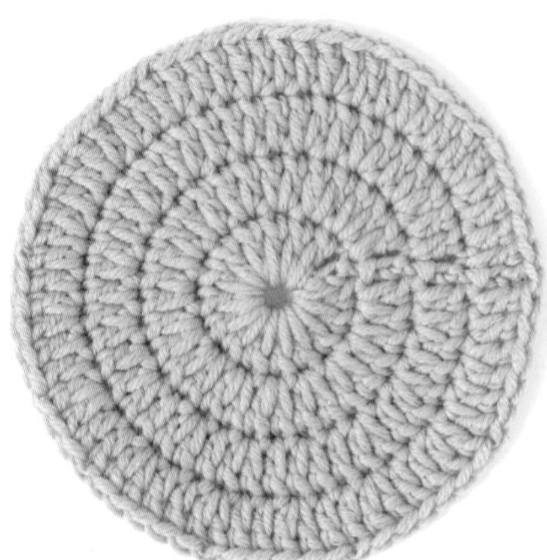

210 Round block

Round blocks work best when arranged in rows and sewn together with a few stitches where the curves touch.

211 Triangular block

Triangular blocks are best joined into horizontal strips. When joining the strips together, pay particular attention to the points where the corners meet. When triangles are fairly small, leave the side edges wavy (as shown). For large triangles, you may prefer to work half blocks to fill the spaces at the sides.

212 Square block

Classic square blocks join easily to make blankets, throws and afghans. When making a large piece, it is best to join the squares into horizontal or vertical strips first, then join the strips together.

213 Octagonal block

Octagonal blocks need tiny square blocks added when joined together. You can omit the squares when working on a small scale by leaving tiny holes in between the octagons. This shape of block is best joined individually rather than in strips.

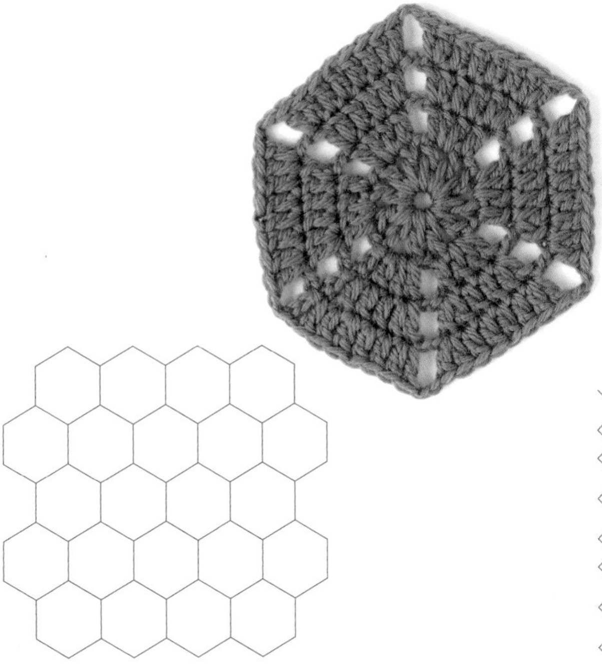

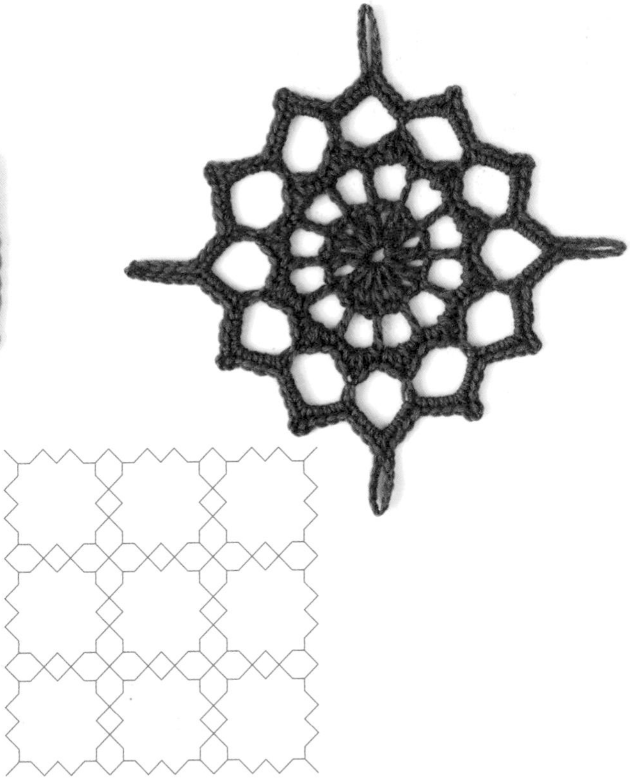

214 Hexagonal block

Hexagonal blocks fit together beautifully. You can join them in strips using the same method as square blocks, or use a less rigid approach and add them individually. When making a large piece, it is usual to work half blocks to fill the spaces at the sides.

215 Lace block

Lace blocks with chain loops at the corners and chain spaces at regular intervals along the sides are usually joined together as the last round of crochet is worked (page 118). Lace blocks can be any of the shapes shown here and this type of join is usually detailed in the pattern instructions.

Turning corners on shaped blocks

Shaped blocks are worked in a similar way to round blocks but with the addition of three or more corners. Shaped blocks may begin with a circle of stitches or the block shape may be formed on the very first round.

Whether you are working a triangular, square, hexagonal or octagonal block, pay particular attention to turning the corners. After every round, also check that you have made the correct number of stitches or blocks along each side.

216

Turning corners on a square block

1 | Some blocks start with a square shape, formed on the first round after the centre ring is made. On the classic granny square, four blocks of stitches are separated by 3 ch spaces to form corners.

2 | On the second round, two blocks of stitches separated by a 3 ch space are worked into each 3 ch space of the previous round to make the corners. The corner blocks are separated along each side by a single chain.

3 | On the third and subsequent rounds, work the corners as step 2. Work blocks of stitches separated by single chains into each 1 ch space along the sides.

4 | Other block designs start with a circle of stitches worked over one or more rounds. Corners start to be formed after these rounds are finished. Three circular rounds are worked in this pattern.

5 | On the next round, a series of chain spaces are worked around the block. The smaller chain spaces form the block sides and the larger spaces form the corners.

6 | On the next round, work small groups of stitches into the chain spaces along the block sides and larger blocks into the corner spaces.

217

Turning corners on other blocks

1 | When working hexagonal and octagonal blocks that begin with any shape other than a circle, start with a larger ring than if making a round and square block. This will create space for the extra number of sides and corners you need to make. On the classic granny hexagon, work groups of stitches separated by chain spaces. Take care to make the correct number of sides and corner spaces.

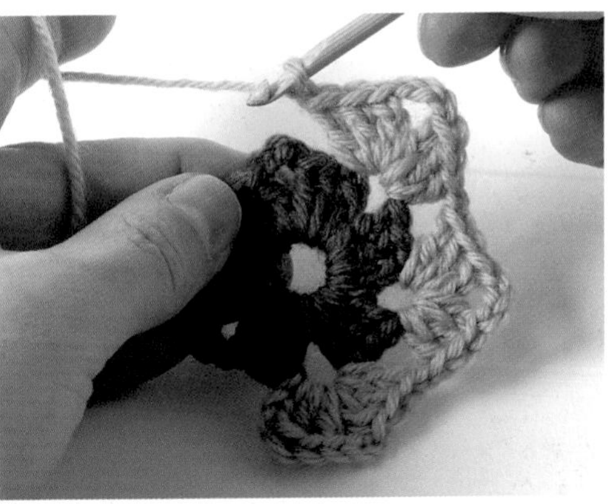

2 | On the next round, work two groups of stitches separated by a chain space into each chain space to form the corners. The corner blocks are separated along each side by a single chain. On the next and subsequent rows, work corners and blocks as in a granny square.

3 | When working a shaped block starting with a circle, work one or more rounds of stitches before you begin to form the corners.

Working in layers

These techniques allow you to work several rounds of stitches arranged one on top of another rather like flower petals. Working outwards from the centre, each layer is made successively wider so they can all be seen from the top. Each round of petals is worked into a series of chain loops that are hidden from view by the previous round. When working the chain loop rounds, it is easier to use a smaller size hook but switch back to the usual size when working the petal rounds.

218

Simple layered flower in two colours

1 | Using the first colour, make the centre as in your pattern instructions. A round of 1 tr, 3 chwas worked into a foundation ring for a total of eight spaced tr (as shown here). Join the round with a sl st, break off the yarn, and darn in the end.

2 | Join the second colour into any 3 ch space and work the first petal of [1 dc, 2 ch, 3 tr, 2 ch, 1 dc] into it. Make a petal into each of the seven remaining spaces for a total of eight petals. Do not join at the end of the round.

3 | Change to a smaller size hook, *5 ch, working behind the petals made on the previous round; 1 dc into the top of the next tr on the first round. Repeat from *, making eight 5 ch loops. Do not join at the end of the round.

4 | Change back to the usual hook size. Work the second round of [1 dc, 2 ch, 5 tr, 2 ch, 1 dc] into each 5 ch loop. Do not join at the end of the round.

5 | Working behind the petals in the same way as step 3, *7 ch, miss 1 petal, 1 dc into next dc of round 3. Repeat from * to end. On the next round, work a petal of [1 dc, 2 ch, 7 tr, 2 ch, 1 dc] into each chain loop. Continue, working two more ch and two more tr each time and ending with a petal round. Join the last round with a slip stitch into the first dc.

6 | Use one yarn colour for the flower centre and a contrasting colour for the petals. Dark or light solid colours are good for the centre and you can experiment with colourful handpainted yarns (page 140) for the petals.

219

Multicoloured layered flower

1 | Make the centre using the first colour, as indicated in your pattern instructions. Work a round of 1 tr, 2 ch into a foundation ring for a total of eight spaced tr (as shown here). Join the round with a sl st, then work a petal of [1 dc, 1 ch, 2 tr, 1 ch, 1 dc] into each ch sp. Join with sl st. Break off the yarn. Darn in the end.

2 | Turn the flower over and working from the wrong side, join the second colour with a sl st to a spoke of the first colour. Ch 6 (counts as 1 tr, 3 ch), *work 1 tr round post of next spoke, 3 ch. Repeat from * to the end. Join the round with a sl st into the third of 3 ch.

3 | Turn the flower over. Working from the right side, 1 ch, work a petal of [1 dc, 1 ch, 3 tr, 1 ch, 1 dc] into each chain loop. Join the round with a sl st into the first dc. Break off the yarn. Darn in the end.

4 | Repeat step 2 to join the third colour to a spoke of the second colour. Make a round of chain loops as above but work 7 ch (counts as 1 tr, 4 ch) to begin and 4 ch to make each loop. Repeat step 3 to make petals but work [1 dc, 1 ch, 4 tr, 1 ch, 1 dc] into each chain loop. Continue, working one more ch and one more tr each time and ending with a petal round.

5 | This type of layered flower works best when using three or more shades of the same colour. Begin with the lightest shade at the centre (as shown here) or use the darkest shade and work the next and subsequent rounds in lighter shades.

Making a spiral

Spiral shapes are worked in a similar way to round blocks (page 108). The rounds are not joined and restarted but worked continuously so the lines of stitches spiral outwards from the shape's centre. The secret to working a successful spiral is to mark the start of each round as you work, taking care to remove and replace the marker on every round. Spirals can be plain or worked in two colours. Plain spirals are often worked in treble crochet while two-colour spirals work best in double crochet.

TRY IT

220 **A stepped end spiral**

If you want the shape to have a stepped end (shown below), finish the round like this:

When you reach the marker on your last round, fasten off the yarn by breaking it off. Pull the end through the last loop and darn it in on the wrong side.

221 **A tapered end spiral**

If you prefer the shape to have a tapering end (shown below), finish the round like this:

When you reach the marker on your last round, remove the marker and work 2 (or 3, depending on the size of the spiral and the length of taper required) htr, then 2 or 3 dc. Finish with a sl st. Fasten off.

222

Basic spiral in treble crochet

1 | Begin by making two chains. Into the second chain from the hook, work two double crochet, two half treble crochet and eight treble crochet (12 stitches). Pull the yarn end gently to tighten the hole at the centre. Do not join the round.

2 | Work two treble crochet into the first double crochet. Mark the first of these two stitches with a marker to indicate the beginning of the second round.

3 | Work two treble crochet into each of the remaining 11 stitches of the first round (24 stitches). The next stitch (and the beginning of the third round) will be the marked stitch.

4 | Remove the marker, work two treble crochet into this stitch, then replace the marker into the first of the two stitches to indicate the start of the third round.

5 I Work 1 tr into the next stitch, then *2 tr into next st, 1 tr into next st. Repeat from * 10 more times to complete the round and reach the marker (36 stitches).

6 I Removing and replacing the marker in the first stitch of the new round, work 2 tr into next st, 1 tr into each of next 2 sts 12 times (48 stitches).

7 I Repeat step 6, removing and replacing the marker and working 2 tr into next st, 1 tr into each of the next 3 sts 12 times (60 stitches).

TRY IT

223 Working a spiral in double crochet

1 I Begin by working the first round as for the treble crochet spiral. Work further rounds in double crochet, following a similar pattern of increases to the treble crochet spiral. To make a nice flat spiral, you need to alternate plain rounds with increase rounds to compensate for the shorter stitch used here.

2 I Work the double crochet spiral in two yarn colours. Begin as for the plain spiral (step 1) using the first colour. Work half of the stitches in the second round in the first colour, elongate the loop on the hook and remove the hook. Join the second colour to the first dc, work 2 dc into the same stitch, and mark the first of the two stitches.

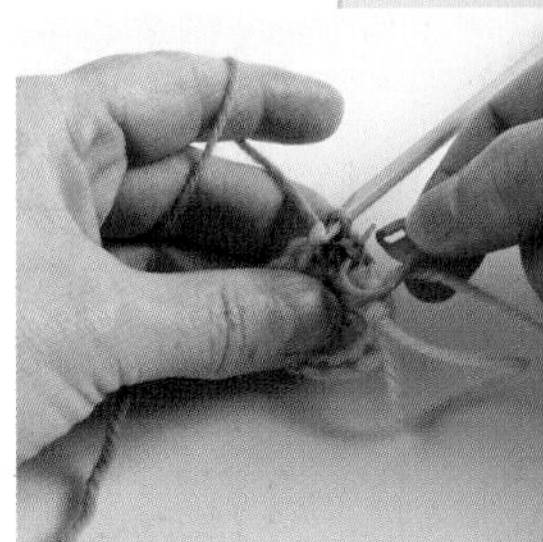

3 I Work half the round in the second colour, stopping opposite the marker. Remove the hook. Insert it in the loop of the first colour and work the half round, removing and replacing the marker in the first stitch of the new round and stopping one stitch before the end of the second colour half round. Change to the second colour and complete the round.

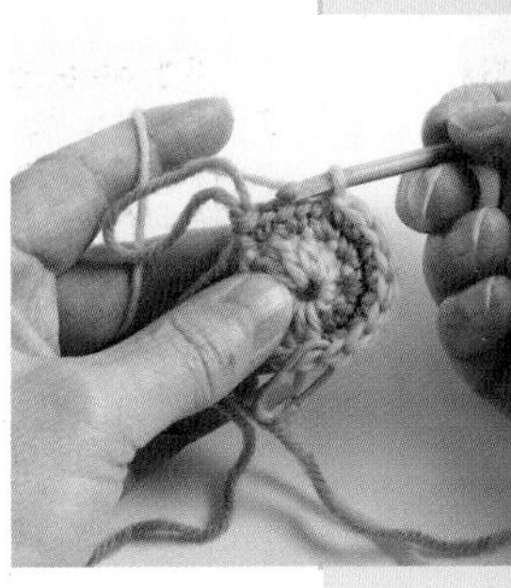

4 I Change to the first colour and complete the round. Continue in the same way, working half of the stitches in every round alternately with each colour. Remember to increase as you did for the plain spiral, taking care to remove and replace the marker in the first stitch of every new round.

Joining lace blocks

Perfect for making shawls and wraps, lace blocks come in different shapes and sizes. These kinds of blocks can be easily joined together as you go without needing any sewing.

Joined together as the last pattern round is worked, it is best to start by joining several blocks in a strip. Add further blocks along one edge until you have two strips joined together. Keep adding blocks in strip formation as you work until your crochet piece is the required size. The only disadvantage of this method is that you cannot block individual pieces before joining them. However, you can block your finished piece using the method on pages 146–7 which is compatible with the yarn you have used.

224

Joining as you go

1 | Complete the first block as stated in the pattern instructions and darn in the yarn ends.

2 | Work the second block up to the last round, then the first side of the last round, finishing at the point where you will work the first join. In this instance, it is halfway along the chain loop at the corner of the block.

3 | With the first and second blocks together, wrong sides facing, join the half-worked loop of the second block to the corner loop of the first block with a double crochet stitch. Continue along the side of the second block, joining the chain loops of both blocks together in the same way.

4 | Join the next corner of the two blocks together as before and complete the last round of the second block in the usual way. Join further blocks in the same way to make a strip.

5 | Work the first block of the second strip, stopping when you reach the joining point of the last round. Place the block with wrong sides together against the first block in the previous strip and join the chain loops as before. When you reach the point where three corner loops meet, work the double crochet into the stitch to join the two existing blocks.

6 | Work the second block of the strip, again stopping when you reach the joining point. Place against the side of the previous block, wrong sides together, and join the chain loops as before. When you reach the point where all four corner loops meet, work the double crochet into the stitch joining the first two blocks.

7 | After joining the second corner, join the next block to the adjacent side of the previous strip, working double crochet stitches into the chain loops as before.

8 | Complete the remainder of the round. Continue adding blocks in this strip formation until the piece is the desired size.

TRY IT

225 **Blocking lace**

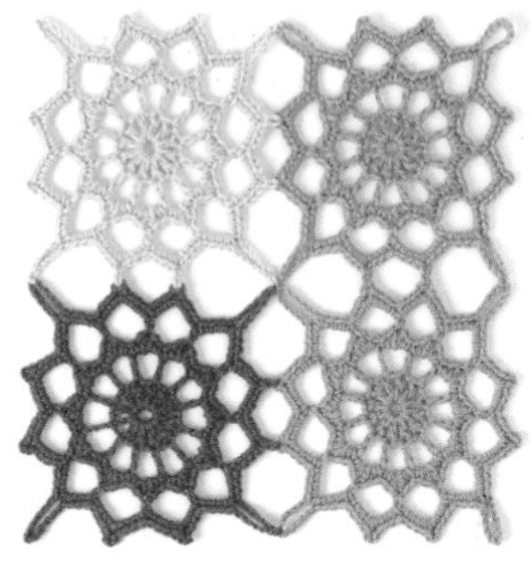

Block your finished piece in order to open out the pattern and show off the intricate stitches. This type of block looks equally good worked in medium-weight woollen yarn (as shown) or in finer weights of wool, cotton or silk.

Tubes and cylinders

Crochet tubes and cylinders are worked in the round using ordinary crochet hooks. Although the rounds are worked and joined in a similar way to making round blocks (page 108), the end result is very different.

Unlike flat, disc-shaped blocks, this type of crochet forms a cylindrical shape and can be as wide or narrow as you wish. Cylinders have many uses and their construction allows you to make an item, such as a hat, in one piece without a seam. Cylinders are often combined with flat pieces of crochet to make garments and accessories. For example, you can work a round block (page 108) to make the base of a bag, then work a wide cylinder to form the body of the bag.

Tubes and cylinders can be worked in three different ways but each one begins with a length of chain joined into a ring. You can work rounds of double crochet stitches into a spiral shape without making a single join. When using taller stitches, make a seam running up the cylinder. If you turn the work at the end of each round, you will have a straight seam. If you continue working in the same direction on every round, the seam will gradually spiral round the cylinder.

226

Working a spiral cylinder in double crochet

1 | Make the required length of chain and join with a slip stitch into a ring without twisting. Work one round of double crochet into the chain (this is easier if you insert the hook into the top loop of each chain rather than into the bumps on the back). Join the round by working a double crochet into the first stitch.

2 | Insert a marker into the double crochet just worked to mark the start of a new round. Continue the new round, working a double crochet into each stitch of the previous round.

3 | When you reach the marker, do not join the round. Instead remove the marker, work the marked stitch, and replace the marker in the new stitch to mark the start of a new round. Continue working round and round, moving the marker each time you reach it, until the cylinder is the required length. Fasten off the yarn.

227

Working a treble crochet cylinder without turns

1 | Make and join the required length of chain as shown for the double crochet cylinder. Work three chains (or the correct number of starting chains for the stitch you are using) to start the next round.

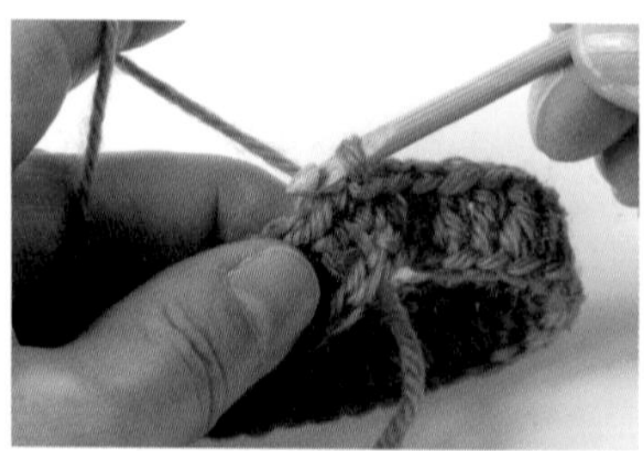

2 | Work one treble crochet stitch into each chain until you reach the end of the round. You can insert the hook through one or two loops of each chain, depending on your preference. Join the first round by working a slip stitch into the third of the three turning chains.

3 | Continue to work the next and subsequent rounds in treble crochet, starting each round with three chains and joining the round with a slip stitch as before. When all the rounds have been worked, fasten off the yarn.

228

Working a treble crochet cylinder with turns

1 | Work the foundation chain and first round of stitches as for step 1 (below left). Join with a slip stitch and *work three chains to begin the next round. Turn the cylinder to reverse the direction of your work. Work this and every alternate round from inside the cylinder.

2 | Work one treble crochet stitch into each stitch. At the end of the round, work a slip stitch into the third of the three chains to join and work three chains to begin the next round.

3 | Turn the cylinder, working the next and every alternate round from outside of it. Repeat from *, making sure that you turn the work at the start of each round.

Double crochet cylinder worked in a spiral

Treble crochet cylinder worked without turns

Treble crochet cylinder worked with turns

229

Joining the ring

1 If you are having problems joining the chain into a ring without getting it twisted, work the first round of stitches flat without joining the chain. Join with a slip stitch, then work the next and subsequent rounds in the usual way.

2 | After you have worked the first few rounds, thread the yarn tail into a yarn needle and use it to sew up the gap in the first round.

TRY IT

230

Working a striped crochet cylinder

Do not break the yarn at the end of each round but loosely carry the colour not in use inside the cylinder so it is ready to work the next round.

Socks

Socks are a little more tricky to make than mittens. A good fit is everything so remember to take accurate foot measurements before you start to compare against those given in the pattern. A tension swatch is vital. Choose sock yarns spun from machine-washable wool or from machine-washable wool plus a small percentage of nylon for added durability. You can also buy cotton sock yarns which are best knitted as they have very little stretch but are harder to work with.

231 Cuff methods

Sock cuffs can be worked sideways in rows of double crochet (page 125), worked in post stitches (page 78), or knitted in rib (as shown on page 123) on a circular needle or set of double-pointed needles for a snug fit. You can also omit the cuff and work a rolled edge in the same way as a mitten.

232 Working direction

Socks can be worked from the toe to the cuff (toe up) or from the cuff down to the toe (cuff down). Choose the toe-up method if you are not sure you have sufficient yarn. Most patterns give one way of working; a few may offer both.

233 Heel shaping

There are different ways of shaping the heel of a crochet sock. The short-rowed heel is shown here but the heel flap-and-gusset method fits large feet and high insteps better and also offers a little more room at the ankle.

234 Stitch patterns

When choosing a fancy stitch pattern for your sock, remember that lace patterns offer more stretch than solidly worked stitch patterns. Use them for the leg when you need more stretch, but work the heel and foot in a smooth stitch such as double crochet as this will be more comfortable to wear.

235 Stitch markers

When working socks, use stitch markers (page 15) to help you position the increases and decreases or mark the start of different crochet rounds.

236 Sock blockers

When you have finished making a pair of socks, give them a really professional finish by stretching them over a pair of sock blockers. Wash the socks, roll them in a towel to get rid of excess moisture, insert a blocker in each sock and allow to dry. Sock blockers come in different sizes, so choose a size to suit your socks.

237

Anatomy of a sock

Familiarize yourself with the names of the different parts of a sock before you start to work the pattern. Each sock part will have its own set of pattern instructions.

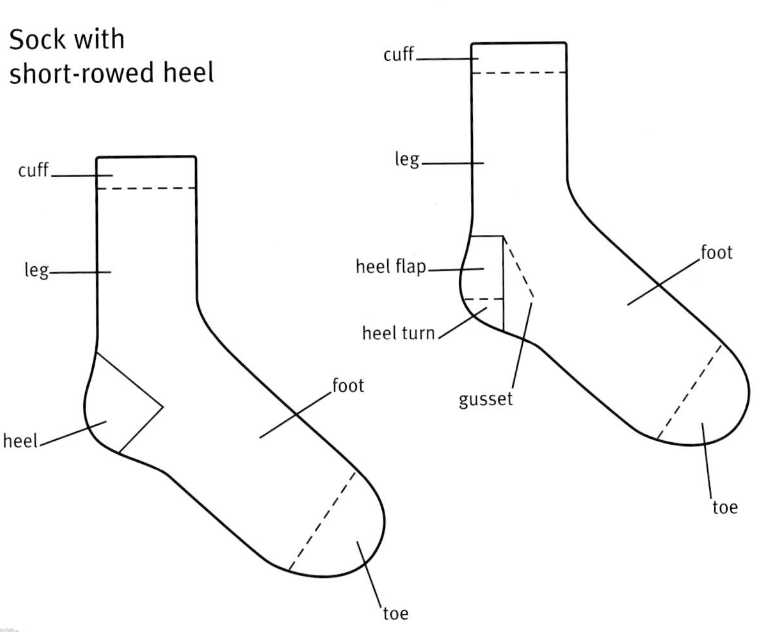

238

Measuring your foot

Measure accurately, keeping a careful note of the measurements. Measure foot length by standing on a ruler and a tape measure to take circumference and leg measurements.

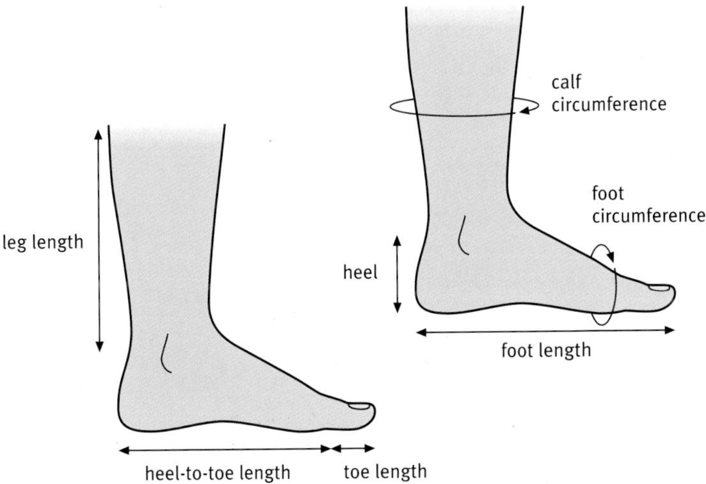

TRY IT

239 Working a knitted cuff

Work a knitted cuff first, then crochet into the last row of stitches and work your sock as usual. You can use K2, P2 rib (as shown) or another rib formation providing you have the right number of stitches to work the pattern.

1 | Work the cuff to the required depth on a circular needle (or set of double-pointed needles) a size smaller than the hook you will be using to crochet the sock. To work a crochet stitch into a knitted stitch, begin by slipping the first stitch from needle to hook. One loop on the hook. *Insert the hook into the next stitch and slip it onto the hook. Two loops on the hook.

2 | Working behind the point of the knitting needle, wrap the yarn over the hook and draw it through both loops on the hook to work a double crochet stitch. Repeat from * until all the stitches have been worked, then join the round with a slip stitch into the first double crochet.

Mittens

Crochet mittens are warm and comforting to wear in cold weather. Easy to make once you have mastered crocheting in rows and rounds, they are a good way of using up odd balls of leftover yarn from larger projects. If you are always losing mittens, join them together with a long crochet chain so they dangle below your sleeves and never get lost.

240 Thumb

The thumb is worked in rounds. When the thumb reaches the right length (try the mitten on to check this), decrease on the next round by working pairs of stitches together. Thread the yarn end through these remaining stitches and draw them together to close the top of the thumb. Finish off the yarn end securely inside the thumb.

242 Fibre composition

You can choose yarn of almost any fibre composition to make mittens, although a pure wool yarn will be the warmest to use. If you have leftover yarn that is too thin to make mittens, try using two or three fine yarns held together to give a chunkier result.

244 Yarn quality

Handspun and hand-dyed yarn makes an attractive crochet fabric with a slightly uneven surface. Although this type of yarn tends to be fairly expensive, mittens require much less yarn than a scarf or whole garment. You will need to handwash this type of yarn.

241 Thumb gusset

The thumb gusset is shaped to accommodate the base of the thumb after the first few unshaped rounds are worked. It is a good idea to keep trying on the mitten you are making to check the fit. The top of the thumb gusset is usually left while the rest of the mitten body is made, then the thumb is added.

243 Cuff methods

Cuffs can be worked sideways in rows of double crochet (opposite), worked in post stitches (page 78), or knitted in rib (page 123) on a circular needle or set of double-pointed needles for a really snug fit.

245 Edges

Another way of finishing mitten edges is to omit the cuff and make a rolled edge. To do this, work the first few rounds fairly loosely in double crochet, then continue with the body of the mitten – the double crochet rounds will curl naturally over on to the front of the fabric.

246 Working a sideways cuff in double crochet

1 Leaving a long yarn tail, chain the number of stitches given in the pattern. Work a double crochet into the back loop of the second chain from the hook and into the back loop of each chain to the end, turn. Next row: 1 dc into the back loop of each st on the previous row, turn. Repeat this row until the cuff is the desired length.

2 Turn the cuff and begin to work into the long edge of the cuff. Work a row of evenly spaced double crochet stitches (1 dc into each row end) along the edge.

3 Join the row of double crochet into a round by working a slip stitch into the first double crochet. Continue working in rounds as directed by your pattern. When the mitten is complete, use the beginning yarn tail to stitch the cuff seam.

TRY IT

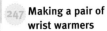

247 Making a pair of wrist warmers

Fun to make and great to wear, wrist warmers require less yarn than a pair of mittens. Both right and left wrist warmer are identical. Choose your yarn and a suitably sized hook.

1 Make a tube (page 120) wide enough to fit over your hand and wrist. Start with a round of double crochet, then continue in rounds of treble crochet. Make the tube long enough to stretch from above your wrist to the base of your thumb.

2 Stop working in rounds and begin working in rows of double crochet. Work even until the side edges of double crochet are long enough to accommodate the base of your thumb, ending ready to work a right-side row.

3 With right side facing, join into a round and work rounds of double crochet until the tube is halfway down your fingers. Fasten off. Darn in the end on the wrong side. Make a second wrist warmer to match the first.

FUN WITH COLOUR

Choosing and using colour can be an exciting experience. Try out some of the colour hints and combinations suggested here to assemble a palette of colours that is right for you instead of reaching for the yarn colour shown in the pattern photograph.

Grouping colours

It is often helpful to begin by dividing colours into a few basic groups or palettes. You may find yourself naturally drawn to those from one palette (say neutrals or pastels) or definitely prefer warmer or cooler tones. Avoid restricting your choice just to colours that you like but try combining a colour from an unfamiliar palette. Often a colour scheme can spring to life this way. If you automatically tend to choose shades of purples, magenta and deep pinks, try adding contrasts of acid lime green or yellow to the mix. You probably only need a tiny amount of contrast, perhaps a single stripe or an edging.

248 Neutral, warm, cool, pastel and accent colours

As a general rule, neutral colours (beiges, greys, light browns, black and white) are 'safe' in that they usually look good when worn but can be a little boring unless spiced up with a brighter or darker colour. Warm colours (yellow, peach, coral, orange, tan, yellow-green) tend to advance while cool colours (blue, turquoise, purple, clover pink, blue-green) tend to recede. The same is true of a colour's light and dark tones: darker tones tend to advance and lighter tones to recede. Pastel colours (powder blue, baby pink, lemon, pale green, lavender) can be warm or cold but are very pale. Accent colours (also known as 'brights' or 'jewel' colours) are clear and strong – sunshine yellow, raspberry, asparagus, royal blue, emerald green. They look overwhelming when combined with each other but are fantastic if used in small amounts to jazz up other colours.

Yarn palettes

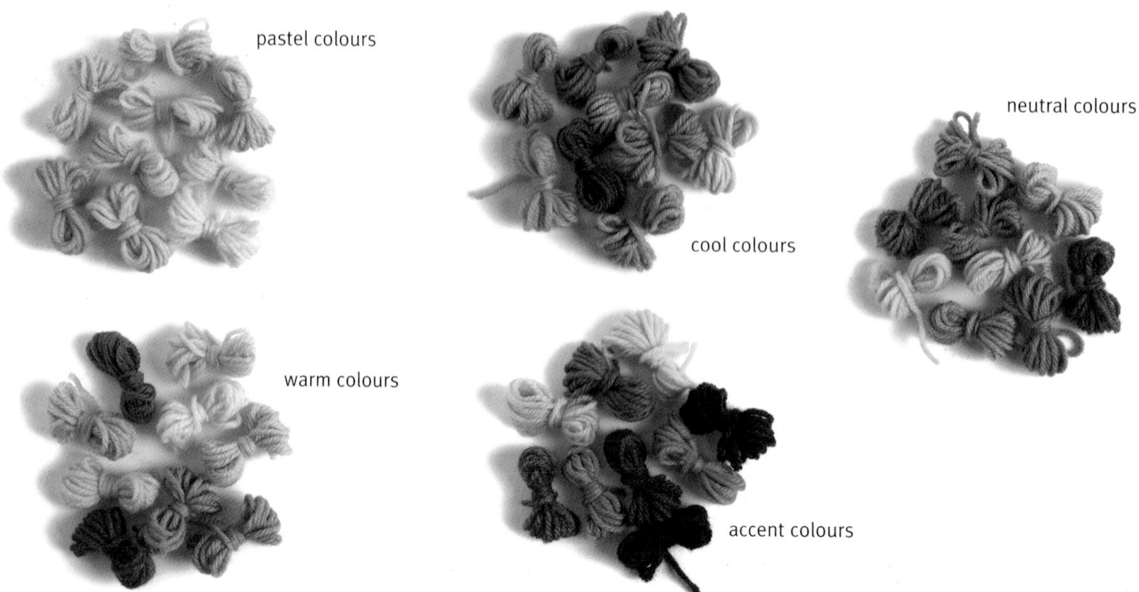

249

Accent colours

A simple design can really be lifted out of the ordinary with the use of accent colours. The traditional granny square looks pleasant enough worked in a neutral palette of creams, camel, mushroom and shades of grey but consider how much the design changes when you choose shades of grey plus two accent colours (asparagus green and bright fuchsia pink). The central part of this block really stands out and the colour scheme demands attention.

250

Work the same pattern in different colour palettes

Working the same stitch pattern swatch in different colours is a good crocheting exercise. The three swatches below are worked in a ripple stitch pattern that repeats the same striped sequence using cool colours (left), warm colours (middle) and pastel colours (right).

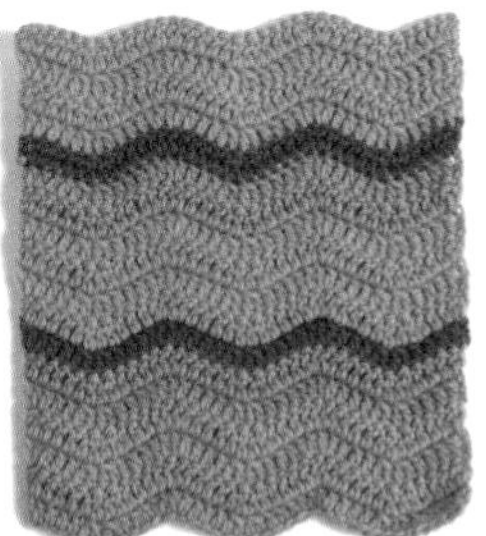

cool colours

warm colours

pastel colours

251

Colour tools

Quilter's colour palette

Originally designed to help quilters choose fabric combinations, this tool consists of numbered colour swatches arranged in a handy fan shape. Each swatch contains strips of the same colour: one strip shows the pure colour; the other strips show gradual variations of the pure colour mixed with white to give tints, black to give shades, and grey to give tones. On the back of the swatch are colour plans for other colours. Also included are rectangles of red and green transparent plastic. Look through either piece to remove colour but not value from your chosen scheme. If some colours appear lighter or darker, you will have a more interesting colour scheme than if all colour values were the same.

Artist's colour wheel

When choosing colours, colour wheels and books for artists and designers can be a great help. A colour wheel can be a printed picture or come with a series of removable discs that fit over the coloured star (shown here). The star consists of 12 bands of pure colour, each one accompanied by two light and two dark variations. The discs – black on one side and white on the other – are rotated, removed, and replaced to give a wide variety of colour combinations.

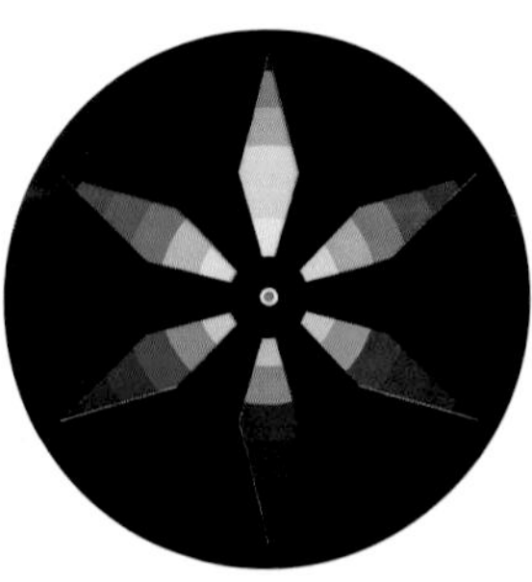

TRY IT

252 **Colour tips**

- Neutral colours get a new lease on life when combined with small amounts of colours from another palette.
- Colours that go with almost anything include black, dark loden green, very dark purple, navy and chocolate brown.
- Turquoise and aqua look good against most skin tones.
- When working intarsia and Jacquard patterns, small areas of colour will look more lively set against a darker background.
- Baby garments can be worked in colours other than pastels so long as the yarn is suitable for delicate skin.
- When you have narrowed down your choices, place a skein of each colour in natural daylight to see how well they blend together.
- When in doubt, swatch, swatch, swatch.
- Colours can change when placed next to each other in a piece of crochet. A blue-green, for example, will appear greener when placed next to blue yarn and bluer when placed next to green yarn.

Stripe patterns

Working colour stripes is the easiest way to add interest to a crochet piece and also uses up small balls of leftover yarn. You can stripe one of the basic crochet fabrics (pages 48–51) or add bands of colour to a fancy stitch pattern. The bands can represent a strong colour contrast or the effect can be more subtle using a restricted palette of shades in one colour, or one basic colour plus one or more coordinating colours.

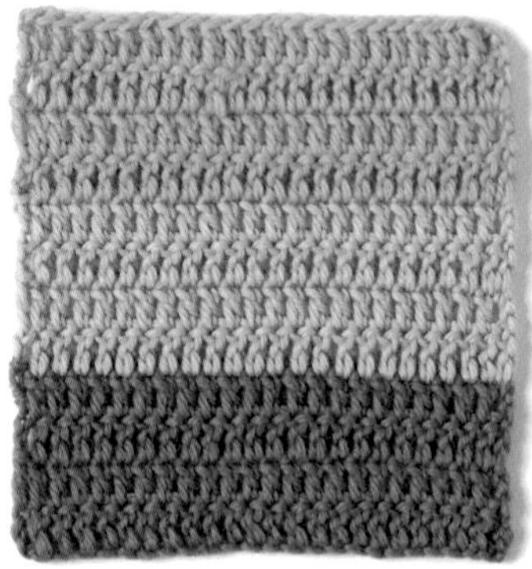

253 Wide stripes

Wide horizontal stripes worked in treble crochet are a quick, easy way of adding colour to garments and home furnishings. Repeat several bands of colour or add different colours as you go.

255 Vertical stripes

Colourful vertical stripes are easy to work using the intarsia technique (page 131). Choose similar weights of yarn for each stripe to make nice, neat joins.

257 Sequenced stripes

Worked in rows of treble and double crochet stitches, the stripes are different widths and arranged in a repeating pattern. Work and repeat the four-colour sequence to the desired length.

254 Random stripes

Worked in rows of treble and double crochet stitches, these stripes are worked in different widths and arranged in a random colour sequence. Experiment using a variety of yarn textures when working this type of stripe pattern.

256 Chevron stripes

Chevrons and wave patterns (page 72) look great when worked in stripes that enhance the stitch pattern formation. Choose two or three toning colours or use an exciting palette of strong, rich colours for added emphasis.

258 Stitch pattern stripes

Many lace and textured stitch patterns achieve a new look with the addition of contrasting colour bands. Use the main yarn colour for the background and add narrow bands of contrast.

259 Diagonal stripes

Starting at one corner and working in stripes of double crochet, increase at each end of every second and third row until the piece is the right width. Work a row without shaping and decrease at the end of every second and third row until three stitches remain. Work dc3tog to finish.

261 'L'-shaped stripes

Worked outward along two adjacent sides of a group of four treble crochet stitches, 'L'-shaped stripes make a bold colour statement. Work several blocks and join them together to make a larger piece or simply keep working outward until the piece is the required size.

263 Contrasting stripes

Match a colour from a handpainted yarn with a solid same-weight yarn and work alternate narrow colour bands. Striping makes an expensive handpainted yarn go further and will help prevent colours from pooling.

260 Tri-colour stripes

Worked in three yarn colours, the stripes break up the textured surface of the stitch to make an attractive pattern. Alternating three yarn colours eliminates most of the yarn ends usually associated with stripe patterns.

262 Magic crochet

Wind short yarn lengths into balls, knotting the ends together about 1.5 cm (½ in.) from the end and mixing colours at random. Work the stitch pattern as usual, pushing the knots through to the wrong side as you reach them.

264 Themed magic crochet

This magic stripe variation is worked in alternate rows of treble and double crochet in a range of green yarns. When making an item in magic crochet, you can use either side of the crochet fabric as your right side.

Working Jacquard and intarsia patterns

Worked from a chart using two or more yarn colours, Jacquard and intarsia patterns create colourful double crochet. The main difference between the two techniques is that with intarsia the colour areas are larger, may be irregularly shaped and each colour area is worked using a separate ball of yarn. For information about how to work from a chart with a key, turn to page 28.

265

Two-colour Jacquard pattern

1 | Make the required length of foundation chain in yarn A, turn, and begin to work the first row of the chart. When you reach the last stitch worked in yarn A, omit the last stage of the double crochet stitch, leaving two loops on the hook.

2 | Join yarn B by drawing a loop of the new colour through the two loops on the hook. This completes the last double crochet stitch worked in yarn A. Don't break off yarn A.

3 | Continue to work across the chart in yarn B. When you reach the last stitch worked in yarn B, change back to yarn A by carrying it loosely behind the work. Draw a loop of it through to complete the colour change and finish the last stitch worked in yarn B. Continue changing yarns in the same way across the row, repeating the pattern as indicated on the chart.

4 | At the end of the row, turn and work the chart in the opposite direction, from left to right. At each colour change, bring the old colour forward and take the new one to the back ready to complete the stitch partially worked in the old colour. Carry the colour not in use loosely along the wrong side of the work.

Jacquard patterns

Each row of a Jacquard pattern is usually worked using two yarn colours. When changing yarns, carry the yarn not in use loosely across the back of the work and pick it up again when it is needed. This is called stranding and it works well when the areas of colour are narrow.

266

Multicoloured intarsia pattern

1 I Make the required length of foundation chain in yarn A, turn, and work any plain rows at the bottom of the chart in double crochet. Work the first multicoloured row, beginning with yarn A. At the colour changes, omit the last stage of the stitch before the change, leaving two loops on the hook. Join the next yarn by drawing a loop of the new colour through the two loops. This completes the last stitch worked in the first yarn. Continue in this way along the row.

2 I When you reach the last colour change in the row, where the chart indicates a change back to yarn A, work with another ball of the same yarn, not the one you used to begin the row.

3 I At the end of the row, turn and work the chart in the opposite direction, from left to right. At each colour change, bring the old colour forward and take the new one to the back ready to complete the stitch partially worked in the old colour, making sure that you loop the new yarn around the old one on the wrong side of the work to prevent holes from forming.

4 I At the end of wrong side rows, check that all the yarns are back in the right place on the wrong side of the work. When you reach new areas of colour further up the chart, join in the yarns as before, making sure that you work each colour change into the last stitch of the previous colour.

Intarsia patterns

Each colour area of an intarsia pattern is worked using a separate small ball of yarn without stranding. When darning in the yarn ends, take care to darn each end into the back of an area of the same colour so it is not visible on the right side.

Felting crochet

Crochet fabric made from suitable yarn felts beautifully, shrinking and thickening to give a sturdy yet pliable fabric. Choose a pure wool yarn, avoiding those that have been treated to prevent shrinkage (usually labelled 'superwash' or 'machine washable') as most will not felt.

Begin by making several swatches using different hook sizes. For each swatch, make a note of the number of stitches and rows plus the hook size used (essential information for calculating the size of your finished piece). The amount of shrinkage varies depending on the yarn used, water temperature, amount of friction, and how loosely the swatch has been crocheted. The aim is to shrink the fabric until the stitch definition begins to disappear: some yarns will felt quickly, others may require several washes to do so.

One way to felt crochet is to machine wash in hot water, adding an old pair of jeans or towels to the wash for added friction. This method, though less controllable than rubbing the pieces between your hands while soaking in hot, soapy water, is useful for larger pieces. Whichever method you choose, remember that felting is an inexact science and you may need to crochet and felt several swatches until you are satisfied with the result. Finally pull the wet pieces into shape and dry flat.

267 Handfelting a crochet flower

1 | Prepare a bowl of hot, soapy water. Washing up liquid works well for felting. Immerse the crochet flower in water and leave to soak for a few minutes until wet right through.

2 | Hold the wet flower between your hands and rub hard to create friction. Dip it in water every few minutes and continue rubbing until the crochet begins to thicken and shrink and the stitch definition disappears.

3 | When you are happy with the result, remove the flower from the bowl and rinse in several changes of clean water to remove the washing up liquid. Squeeze out as much moisture as you can, pull the felt into shape and dry flat.

Felted flower

The felted flower on the right is smaller and thicker than the unfelted one on the left. Both were crocheted from untwisted Icelandic wool which loses most stitch definition once felted. Turn to page 105 for instructions on how to make a crochet flower.

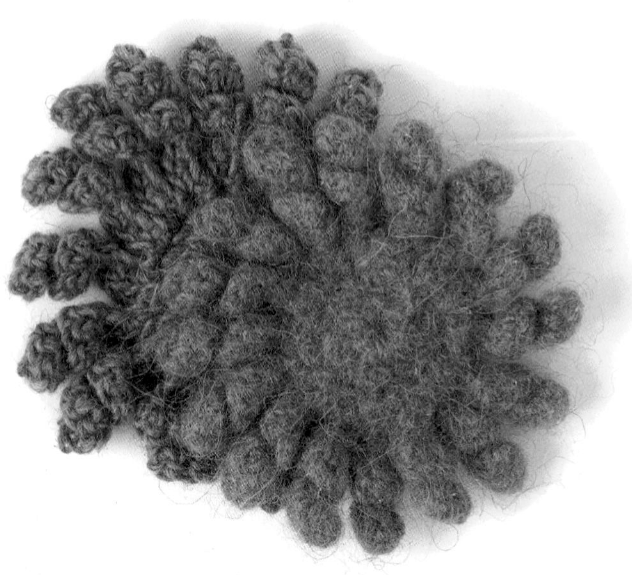

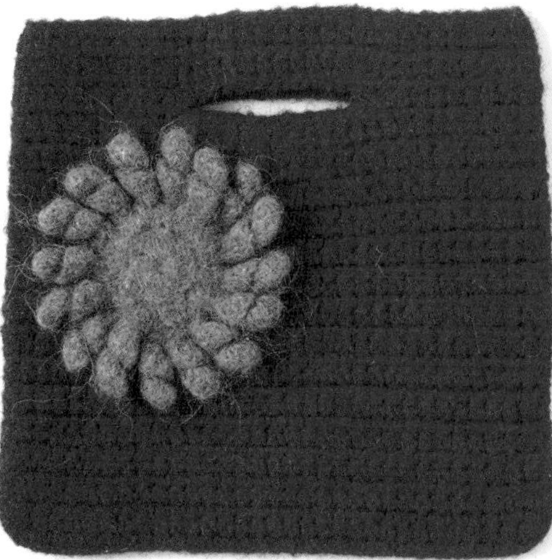

Lightly felted

The finished felted flower decorates a lightly felted crochet bag made from pure, chunky-weight wool. Front and back bag pieces were felted separately by hand, then stitched together once dry.

Felt, then assemble

Made from a folded and stitched piece of magic crochet (page 129), this bag was felted separately by machine from the long strip of crochet forming the handle. The handle was stitched firmly in place once the pieces were dry.

Felt, then assemble

Another bag but this time showing the felted components before assembly. Both the bag body and handles were worked in double crochet using the magic crochet technique (page 129) to join leftover lengths of tapestry wool.

More felting experiences

This piece of felted crochet started life as a pile of hexagonal blocks worked in pure, light DK wool. The hexagons were randomly joined together and the piece was felted by machine.

FIX IT

268 *Having trouble finding a needle size to suit both bead and yarn?*

Thread the beads onto a loop of strong thread (buttonhole thread is ideal). Slot the end of the yarn through the thread loop and slide the beads from the thread onto the yarn.

The beads in both swatches were applied using the threading method. When working with different bead colours arranged in a pattern, string different colours onto the yarn in reverse order so the pattern will work out correctly as you crochet.

Applying beads

Beads can be applied to crochet as stitches are being worked. There are two methods and each one is straightforward to work.

269

Threading beads onto yarn with a needle

Beads applied after being threaded onto yarn look most effective against a double crochet background and add touches of colour, glitz and sparkle. When choosing beads for this method, match the size of the holes in the beads to the thickness of your yarn: small beads are best on fine yarns and large beads on chunky yarns.

1 | Before starting to crochet, thread all the beads onto your yarn. If you are using several balls of yarn to make a garment, the pattern instructions will tell you how many beads to thread onto each ball. Thread the beads onto the yarn using a needle that will accommodate the yarn weight and still pass through the holes in the beads.

2 | Slide the beads along the yarn as you work to the position of the first bead (on a wrong-side row). Slide it down the yarn so it rests against the right side of the work.

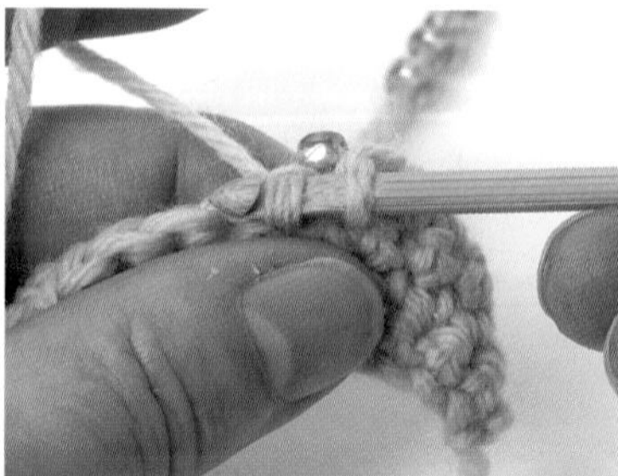

3 | Keeping the bead in position, insert the hook in the next stitch and work a double crochet stitch to secure. Continue adding beads in the same way across the row, following the pattern instructions.

270

Threading beads with a hook

Applying beads individually on right-side rows with a second, smaller hook is useful for 'spot' beading where small clusters or individual beads are scattered here and there on the crochet fabric. It is also good when beads are too small to run along your yarn easily and can be used with any crochet stitch. Use a small metal thread hook (page 11) to apply the beads. Choose one to fit the chosen size of bead. The tip of the hook should be small enough to pass right through the bead and emerge on the other side.

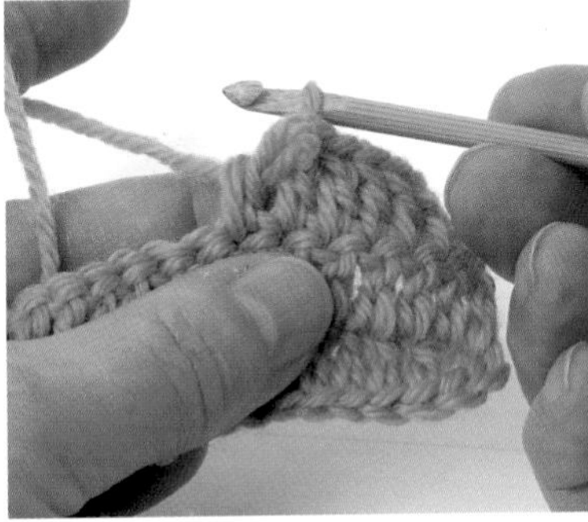

1 | Work to the position of the first bead on a right-side row. Leave the stitch to be beaded incomplete and slip the hook out of the new stitch, leaving the loop from the previous stitch still on the hook.

2 | Slot a bead onto the tiny hook, slip it through the loose loop of the incomplete stitch and carefully draw the loop through the bead with the hook.

3 | Replace the yarn loop on the main hook and complete the stitch. Continue adding beads as required.

TRY IT

271 **Adding decorations**

In addition to beads, you can also sew on embellishments, such as sequins and charms, to a piece of crochet. Choose a durable thread to match the colour of the fabric not the embellishment. Stranded cotton is ideal as it can be split into strands and recombined to suit both fabric and embellishment.

a. Resin shapes

b. Metal charms

c. Decorated ceramics

d. Semi-precious gemstones

e. Sequins

f. Paillettes

277

Dyeing with acid dyes

You will need:
Wool or other animal fibre yarn, skeined and tied
Acid dyes
White vinegar
Detergent
Plastic washing-up bowl
Jug, a small plastic container and metal spoon for measuring and mixing
Large pan (or bottom portion of steamer)
Wooden spoon or short length of dowel

Acid dye formula

For dyeing 200 g (8 oz) yarn, use 4 litres (4 quarts) of water, 250 ml (8 fl oz) white vinegar to fix the colour. Use 1 tsp dye for a standard shade, ½ tsp dye for a lighter shade, 1½ tsp for a darker shade.

1 | Soak the yarn for about 20 minutes in a bowl of warm water with a little detergent. Keep the yarn saturated and submerged by placing a plate on top.

2 | Mix the required amount of dye into a paste with warm water in a plastic container. Add a little boiling water and stir until the dye is dissolved. Fill the pan with water and put on the stove to heat. Pour the dye into the pan, add vinegar and stir well.

3 | When the mixture is warm, carefully lower the yarn into the dye bath. Continue heating until the liquid simmers. The odd bubble rising to the surface is fine but do not let the water boil as the yarn may begin to felt.

4 | Stir frequently for the first 10 minutes to ensure an even spread of colour. Do this slowly and gently to avoid felting. Time from the point when the liquid simmers and dye for 20–30 minutes. The yarn should have soaked up all the dye, leaving clear liquid in the pan (some dyes, particularly magenta and turquoise, leave a dye residue in the pan). Rinse once in hot water, then gradually lower the temperature of the rinses until the water runs clear. Squeeze out. Hang to dry.

278

Dyeing with Procion dyes

You will need:
Cotton yarn, skeined and tied
Procion dyes
Salt
Washing soda
Detergent
Plastic washing-up bowl
Plastic jugs, a small plastic container and plastic spoon for measuring and mixing
Bamboo tongs or wooden spoon

Procion dye formula

Salt solution: 200 g (8 oz) salt dissolved in 1 litre (1 quart) of hot water. The salt helps drive the dye into the fibres.

Washing soda solution: 200 g (8 oz) soda dissolved in 1 litre (1 quart) of hot water. The soda helps fix the colour.

For dyeing 200 g (8 oz) yarn, use 1 quantity salt mix, 1 quantity soda mix, plus dye dissolved in a small amount of warm (not hot) water. Use 1/2 tsp dye for a standard shade, 1/4 tsp dye for a lighter shade, 1 tsp for a darker shade.

1 | Soak the yarn in warm, soapy water for 20 minutes as for acid dyeing. Pour the salt and soda solutions into the bowl and allow to cool to below 60°C (140°F). Mix the dye with warm not hot water as this will kill the dye and stop it from working. Pour it into the bowl.

2 | Stir the dye bath vigorously with tongs or a wooden spoon to make sure the dye is completely dissolved and the solutions are well blended.

3 | Lower the yarn into the dye bath. Stir frequently for 10 minutes, then at intervals for the rest of the dyeing period.

4 | Leave the yarn in the dye bath for two hours, making sure that the yarn stays submerged in the liquid. You can put a lid or piece of plastic over the yarn to keep it under the surface. Rinse in several changes of water and hang to dry.

Handpainting yarn with acid dyes

This technique is a way of creating unique yarns with bands of different colours running along the yarn. You can use any combinations you like, choosing from two, three or more colours or shades of the same colour on the same skein. Acid dyes are ideal for this technique as the colours can be easily fixed on wool yarn by steaming. As with ordinary dyeing, wear old clothes and protective gloves when painting yarn.

Each skein will be slightly different as the bands of colour are applied by hand. If you have dyed several skeins of yarn to use in the same piece of crochet, it is a good idea to crochet with two skeins at once, working two alternate rows from each one. This will help to prevent a noticeable line appearing across the work where the two skeins meet.

279

Handpainting yarn

You will need:

Wool or other animal fibre yarn, skeined and tied
Acid dyes
White vinegar
Detergent
Plastic washing-up bowl
Foam brushes
Jug, a small plastic container and metal spoon for measuring and mixing
Steamer
Roll of clingfilm
Sheet of polythene to cover the work surface

Acid dye formula for handpainting

For soaking the yarn, use 250 ml (8 fl oz) white vinegar to 5 litres (5 quarts) of water. To make the painting solution, dissolve the dye in warm water at the rate of 1 tsp dye to 500 ml (16 fl oz) of water. Mix the dye into a paste with a little water first, then add the remaining water and stir until the dye is dissolved.

1 | Soak the yarn for about 20 minutes in a bowl of warm water and vinegar. Cover the work surface with polyethylene and place a length of clingfilm on top. Squeeze most of the water out of the skein and lay it on the clingfilm. Mix the first colour and paint it across the yarn in stripes using a foam brush. Make sure you apply enough dye to colour the skein right through. Turn the skein and apply more dye if necessary.

2 | Mix the second colour and apply it to the skein using another foam brush. Position the stripes of the second colour close to the first colour so the two dyes blend into each other.

3 | Repeat with the third colour, painting until there are no undyed spots left. Fold the clingfilm edges over the painted skein, squeeze the ends together and fold them over. If you intend to paint more than one skein using the same colour sequence, mark the plastic at the sides of the wrapped skein to show the position of each colour.

4 | Coil the wrapped skein in the steamer basket. You will probably be able to fit in two or three skeins in a single layer. Pour about 5 cm (2 in.) of water into the base and bring to the boil. Fit the basket and lid on top and start timing from when the food wrap puffs up. Steam for 30 minutes and allow to cool before rinsing in several changes of water. Hang to dry.

Earth colourway

Double knitting weight merino wool yarn handpainted in green, blue, yellow and brown.

Fire colourway

Double knitting weight merino wool yarn handpainted in yellow, orange, rust and magenta.

Swatch worked in handpainted yarn

Crocheted in alternate rows of double and treble crochet, the colours spread fairly evenly across the swatch and make a nicely coloured fabric.

FIX IT

280 *Do the colours in your handpainted yarn have a patchy finish?*

Crocheted in alternate rows of double and treble crochet, this swatch shows how concentrations of the same colour running down together gives a patchy effect. This so-called 'pooling' can be avoided by working over a larger or smaller number of stitches or changing to a different stitch pattern.

ASSEMBLING AND FINISHING

Pressing and blocking, finishing off yarn ends neatly and choosing suitable seams are important elements for helping you achieve a professional finish on your crochet garments and home furnishings. Although some processes appear rather time-consuming, taking the extra time to ensure a good result is well worth the effort.

Dealing with yarn ends

It is important to fasten off the yarn ends securely so that they do not unravel during wear or laundering. Try to fasten off as neatly as possible so the darned yarn ends do not show through the front of the work.

281 Finishing a yarn end on the top edge

To finish a yarn end at the top edge of a piece of crochet, thread the end into a large-eyed yarn needle. Take the yarn through several stitches on the wrong side of the crochet, working stitch by stitch across the top row of stitches. Trim the remaining yarn.

282 Darning into the side edges of double crochet

To finish a yarn end by darning it into a side edge of double crochet, thread the yarn end into a yarn needle. Take the yarn through several row ends on the wrong side of the crochet. Trim the remaining yarn.

283 Finishing a yarn end on the lower edge

To finish a yarn end along the lower edge of a piece of crochet, thread the end into a yarn needle. Draw the needle through the backs of several stitches on the wrong side of the fabric and trim the remaining yarn.

284 Darning into the side edges of treble crochet

To finish a yarn end by darning it into a side edge of treble crochet, thread the end into a large-eyed yarn needle. Take the yarn through two or three end stitches on the wrong side of the crochet, working stitch by stitch, and two or three stitches into each row end. Trim the remaining yarn.

285 Finishing yarn ends on a stripe pattern

When darning yarn ends using more than one colour of yarn, it pays to take a little more care and avoid the colours showing through on the right side. Undo the knot securing the two yarn ends, thread the needle with one colour, and darn the end into the wrong side of the same colour stripe. Repeat with the second colour.

286 Finishing multiple ends

When working with several strands of yarn, use any of the methods above but treat each yarn end separately and darn them in one at a time. Trim the ends.

287 Finishing the ends of slippery yarn

Use any of the methods shown left but, instead of sliding the needle through several stitches or row ends in one movement, make a series of tiny back stitches (pages 148–9) on the wrong side to anchor the yarn securely. Trim the remaining yarn.

288 Finishing the ends of ribbon yarn

When working with a wide ribbon yarn, pin the yarn end down the edge of the crochet and use a matching sewing thread to stitch the first 2.5 cm (1 in.) securely in place. Trim the remaining yarn.

FIX IT

289 *Yarn too thick?*

When working with a chunky yarn too bulky to darn in neatly without creating unsightly lumps and bumps on the front of the fabric, carefully divide the yarn into separate strands. Darn each strand in one at a time, taking the needle into the crochet at a slightly different point for each strand.

290 *Using novelty yarn?*

When working with a novelty yarn that incorporates tiny flags of fabric or tufts of yarn, trim these off close to the yarn core before attempting to darn in the end. Cut these away carefully with a small, sharp pair of scissors but take care not to snip into the core itself. Thread the core into a needle and finish in the usual way.

Blocking and pressing

The process of blocking involves easing and pinning the crocheted pieces into the correct shape on a fabric-covered board, then either steaming with an iron or moistening with cold water, depending on the fibre content of the yarn. A light press on the wrong side with a cool iron is often all the treatment crochet needs before being stitched together, although some pieces, such as garment sections and crocheted blocks, will require more attention.

291 Blocking

Yarns made from most natural fibres (cotton, linen, wool but not silk which is more delicate) can be blocked with warm steam. Always be guided by the information given on the ball band of your yarn as most man-made fibres are easily damaged by heat. When in doubt, choose the cold-water blocking method.

It is a good idea to make your own blocking board to block garment pieces and separate blocks. You can do this inexpensively by covering a 60 cm x 90 cm (24 in. x 36 in.) piece of flat board (a lightweight bulletin board made from cork is ideal) with one or two layers of quilter's wadding. Secure the wadding on the back of the board with staples or drawing pins, then cover with a layer of fabric and secure in the same way. Choose a cotton fabric to withstand the heat of the iron. A check pattern is useful so the lines help you pin out the straight edges. Use plenty of rustproof pins to pin out the pieces. If you are using ordinary dressmaking pins rather than special blocking pins (page 14), make sure they have glass rather than plastic heads as these will melt when heat is applied.

293 Pressing large items

Avoid using steam or a hot iron on a crochet piece made from man-made nylon or acrylic. You will flatten it and make the yarn limp and lifeless. Instead use a cool iron on the wrong side or the cold-blocking method on page 147.

A large item, such as a shawl, blanket or throw, made in one piece or from blocks joined together as you go can be carefully pressed from the wrong side over a well-padded ironing board using a light touch to avoid crushing the stitches. Lay a couple of old towels on the board if the surface is very flat.

292 Blocking long pieces

When pinning out long pieces, such as edgings or borders, work in sections and allow each section to dry completely before moving onto the next section. Block before attaching to an item, taking care to ease out and pin any loops along the edge.

294 Block before joining

Crochet blocks benefit from being blocked before they are joined. When pinning out a square block, pay special attention to pinning the corners out neatly.

295 Blocking pieces made from wool, cotton or linen yarn

1 | Pin out the piece, inserting the pins through the fabric and wadding layers. Be generous with the amount of pins that you use around the edges and gently ease the crochet into shape before inserting each pin. Unless the piece is heavily textured and needs blocking face upward, you can block the crochet piece either with the right or wrong side facing up.

2 | Hold a steam iron set at the correct temperature for yarn about 2 cm (¾ in.) above the surface of the crochet and allow the steam to penetrate for several seconds. Work in sections but avoid the iron coming into contact with the crochet surface. Pat the crochet lightly with the flat of your hand to help the moisture from the steam penetrate the yarn. Lay the board flat and allow the crochet to dry before removing the pins.

296 Blocking pieces made from acrylic and other synthetic fibres

Pin out the pieces as above, then use a spray bottle to mist the crochet with clean, cold water until it is evenly moist all over but not saturated. When blocking heavyweight yarns, gently pat the crochet with your hand to help the moisture penetrate more easily. Lay the board flat and allow the crochet to dry before removing the pins.

FIX IT

297 *Blocks look distorted when finished?*

Whether square, hexagonal or triangular, blocks pull out of shape as they are worked. The shape of most blocks, even a slightly distorted one (below right), will be much improved after blocking (below left).

298

Wet blocking

This is the best method of blocking a piece, such as a lacy shawl, to show off the stitch pattern. Use this method for colourfast yarns made from natural fibres and do not trim off the yarn ends after darning them in. Do this once the blocked item is dry. You will need a large, flat surface on which to spread out the crochet. A carpeted floor or the top of a bed work well but you will need to cover the area with an old, clean sheet.

1 | Soak the item in water until the yarn is thoroughly wet. This will take about 20 minutes for fine yarns but heavy yarns will need longer and are best left overnight. Before soaking, wash the item using special wool wash or baby shampoo.

Intricate lace patterns look best after blocking. This piece of lace is part of a wrap worked in lace-weight Shetland wool. The pattern is made from rows of lacy blocks joined together (page 118).

2 | Carefully squeeze the crochet to remove most of the water. Avoid wringing it as this can cause felting; just squeeze it between your hands. Place between two towels and press to get rid of any excess moisture. Large pieces can be spun dry on a slow spin but protect delicate fabrics by placing them in a mesh washing bag or an old pillowcase.

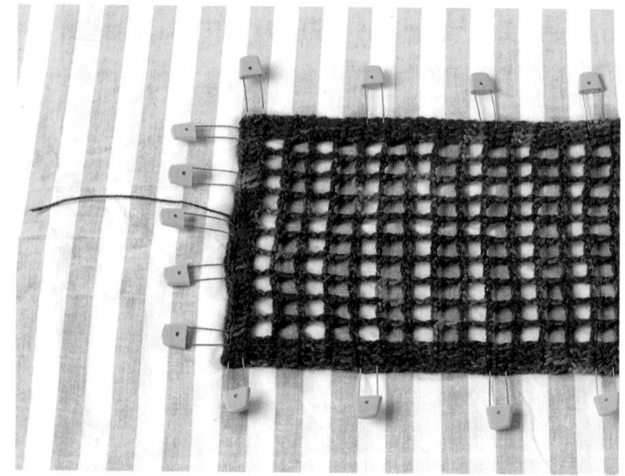

3 | Lay out the damp piece on your flat, fabric-covered surface and gently ease into shape. Checking the measurements with a tape measure as you work, pin in position, paying special attention to points, corners and fancy edgings. Leave the pins in place until the crochet is dry.

299

Wet blocking using blocking wires

Particularly useful for pinning out items with long, straight edges, blocking wires are lengths of special stainless-steel wire threaded through the edges of a piece of crochet, then pinned in place at intervals with T-pins until the fabric is dry.

1 | Repeat steps 1 and 2 for wet blocking (opposite). Thread blocking wires through the straight edges of the damp piece and move onto your fabric-covered surface.

2 | Use a tape measure to check measurements as you work and gently ease the piece into shape. Secure the blocking wires with T-pins. Leave the pins and wires in place until the crochet is dry.

300

Cold blocking

Not as drastic as wet blocking, cold blocking is extremely useful for pieces that have not distorted badly while working or those made from acrylic yarns or yarns with a high synthetic content.

Pin out the dry item on a flat surface (see wet blocking) and cover with a damp cloth. Press down on the cloth to moisten the crochet. Allow to dry overnight before removing cloth and pins. Use either a clean cotton pillowcase or a linen dishcloth, wringing out most of the water before applying.

Seams

There are several methods of joining pieces of crochet, either by sewing or using a crochet hook. Use the same yarn for both crochet and seams unless your yarn is too thick or textured, in which case use a finer yarn of matching colour.

FIX IT

301 *Messy blocks?*

Take great care to match corner stitches accurately when stitching blocks together and make sure all the seams are of identical length. Stitch evenly without pulling the yarn too tightly, and take care to stitch through either both loops of each stitch or only the outer loops of each block.

302 *Puckered seam?*

When working crochet seams, it is important to insert the hook at regular intervals along the edge in order to space your stitches evenly and avoid unsightly puckering. Line up pairs of stitches along the top and bottom edges of fabric, and match up the rows accurately when working across row ends.

Stitched seams

A back stitch or chain stitch seam is durable, and a good way to join irregular edges but can be bulky. These methods are best for seaming loose-fitting garments such as winter sweaters and jackets. A woven seam gives a flatter finish; the straight edges are joined edge to edge. This method works best when making up fine work and baby garments. An oversewn seam works well for joining blocks and for seaming lace.

303

Back stitch seam

1 | Place the pieces to be joined together with the right sides facing. Pin them together, inserting the pins at right angles to the edge. Thread a yarn needle with a matching yarn. Secure the yarn end then make two or three stitches at the beginning of the seam, taking the yarn through both layers of crochet and over the edge.

2 | Working one or two stitches away from the edge, make a row of back stitches from right to left. For each stitch, bring the needle through a short distance in front of the previous stitch, taking it back through where the previous stitch emerged. Finish off the thread end securely.

304

Chain stitch seam

This is the stitched version of the slip stitch seam shown on page 150. Place the pieces to be joined together with the right sides facing. Pin together, inserting the pins at right angles to the edge. Thread a yarn needle with matching yarn and work a row of chain stitches as shown, positioning the stitches close to the edge.

305

Woven seam

1 | Place the pieces to be joined side by side on a flat surface with the right sides facing upwards and the row ends touching. Thread a yarn needle with matching yarn. Work a vertical row of evenly spaced stitches in a loose zigzag pattern from edge to edge in the following manner. Work one stitch through the right-hand piece of fabric and pull the yarn through.

2 | Work the next stitch through the left-hand piece of fabric and pull the yarn through, carefully tightening the tension of the yarn every two or three stitches as you work so that the edges pull together neatly. For double crochet, pick up one stitch at a time. For treble crochet, pick up half a stitch.

306

Woven seam across upper edges

Place the pieces to be joined side by side on a flat surface with the wrong sides facing upward and the top edges touching. Thread a yarn needle with matching yarn and work a horizontal row of evenly spaced stitches through the chains. Work from edge to edge in the same way as the woven seam above, carefully tightening the tension of the stitches as you work so the edges pull together.

307

Oversewn seam

1 | Place the pieces to be joined together with the right sides facing but do not pin. Secure the yarn end as for back stitch seam (opposite). Hold the pieces together, placing your left index finger between the layers. Make a series of small stitches over the edges, picking up one stitch at each side.

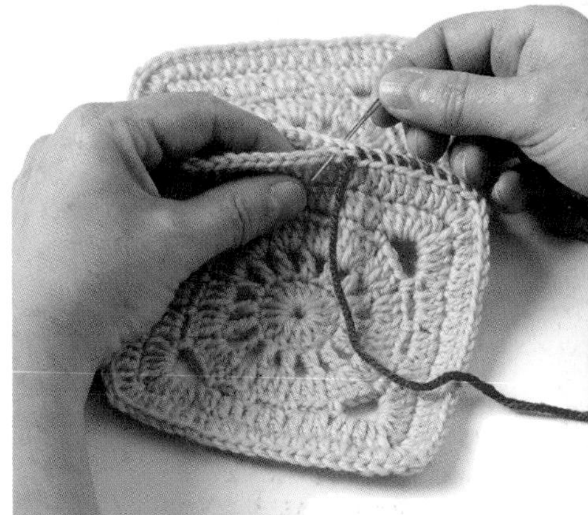

2 | When oversewing blocks together, match the corner stitches at the beginning and end of the seam. Work the stitches through both loops of the crochet stitches or through the outer loops only. For more information about joining blocks in sequence, see page 110.

Crochet seams

A slip stitch seam is the crochet equivalent of a chain stitch seam (page 148). A double crochet seam is good for joining straight edges and makes a less bulky seam than the slip stitch method. Double crochet seams can also be used on the right side of a garment. Work the seams in contrast yarn to make a decorative statement. The final method, a double crochet and chain seam, gives a flatter effect than the crochet methods mentioned above and has the advantage of being slightly stretchy. Slip stitch and double crochet can also be used to join blocks together in a similar way to the oversewing (page 149).

308

Slip stitch seam

Place the pieces to be joined together with the right sides facing and pin together, inserting the pins at right angles to the edge. Holding the yarn behind the work, insert the hook through both layers of fabric, and draw a loop of yarn through both the fabric and the loop on the hook. Repeat, working from right to left. Take care to secure the yarn ends carefully as slip stitch seams unravel easily.

310

Double crochet seam across upper edges

Place the pieces to be joined together with the right sides facing for a concealed seam, or wrong sides facing for a decorative seam. Pin the layers together with the top edges aligning, inserting the pins at right angles to the edge. Holding the yarn behind the work, insert the hook through corresponding chains on both pieces and work a row of double crochet stitches, one dc into each pair of chains.

309

Double crochet seam across row ends

Pin the pieces to be joined together. Holding the yarn behind the work, insert the hook through both layers of fabric and work a row of double crochet stitches close to the edge. For double crochet fabric, work one stitch into every row end. For treble crochet fabric, work two or three stitches per row, depending on the yarn weight. For other stitch patterns, space the seam stitches evenly to ensure the work remains flat without stretching or puckering.

311

Double crochet and chain seam

1 | Place the pieces to be joined together with the right sides facing and pin together, inserting the pins at right angles to the edge. Holding the yarn behind the work, insert the hook through both layers of fabric and work a double crochet stitch at the beginning of the seam. Work a chain, then another double crochet stitch a short distance away from the first.

2 | Repeat along the edge, alternating double crochet stitches and chains. Finish the row with a double crochet stitch. Space the stitches as evenly as possible to make sure the fabric lies flat and does not pucker.

Working guidelines

Following a few simple guidelines as you work will keep your pieces of crochet looking fresh and clean. Wash your hands before starting to crochet and avoid using handcream as the oils contained will make your hands feel sticky and may transfer onto the yarn. When crocheting with light-coloured yarns, avoid wearing dark-coloured garments that shed while you are working. Angora or mohair sweaters are the worst as they shed tiny hairs that get trapped in your work. Getting cat and dog hairs on your crochet is also best avoided as they are difficult to remove.

312

Laundering crochet

Follow the washing and pressing instructions given on the ball band (page 18). If the yarn you have used is machine washable, put the item into a zipped mesh laundry bag to prevent it from stretching and snagging during the wash cycle. If you do not have a mesh bag, use an old, clean white pillowcase instead. Secure the open end with an elastic ponytail band or work a row of running stitches across the opening to close the pillowcase. If you have household items, such as tablecloths or crochet-trimmed tray cloths, treat spills and stains as soon as they occur and repair any damage to the crochet before washing the item.

Washing crochet

For crochet pieces made from yarns that are not machine washable, handwash in hot water with a mild, detergent-free cleaning agent. Most purpose-made wool or fabric shampoos are ideal but check that the one you choose does not contain optical brighteners which will cause yarn colours to fade. Rinse the piece thoroughly in several changes of water at the same temperature as the washing water to avoid felting. Without wringing, squeeze out as much surplus water as you can, roll the damp item in a towel and press to remove any moisture. Gently ease the item into shape and dry it flat out of direct sunlight. For very lacy items, such as shawls, you will probably need to block (page 146) every time they are washed.

313

Making a note of project details

When you have finished making a crochet project, store a small amount of leftover yarn from each project in case you need to make future repairs. Punch a hole in a piece of cardboard and knot several lengths of yarn through the hole. Make a note of the type of yarn and colour, as well as details of the project, and attach one of the ball bands to remind you of the yarn composition and any special pressing or washing instructions. File the cards away in a closed box with a lid and store in a cool, dry place.

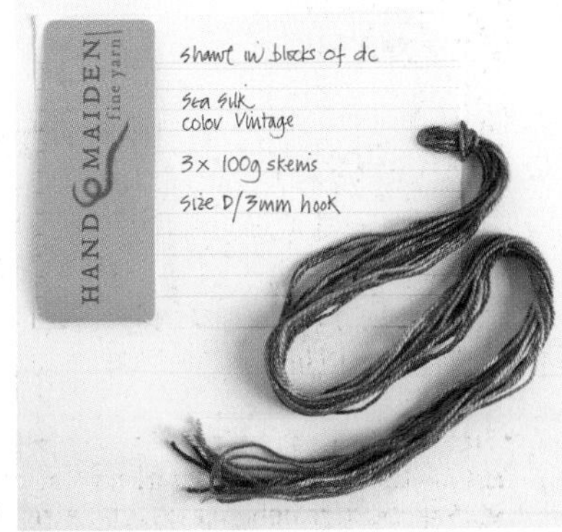

314

Storing crochet

Apart from dust and dirt, the main enemy of crochet fabrics is direct sunlight which can cause yarn colours to fade and fibres to weaken. Excessive heat, too, makes yarn dry and brittle, damp rots fibres, and moths can damage woollen yarns.

Avoid storing yarns or finished crochet items in polyethylene as it attracts dirt and dust particles that will transfer readily to your work. Polyethylene bags prevent yarns with natural fibres, such as cotton and linen, from breathing, which can result in mildew attacks that will eventually weaken or rot the fibres. Store small items wrapped in white, acid-free tissue paper or an old cotton pillowcase. Large, heavy items, such as winter jackets and sweaters, will probably drop and stretch out of shape if stored on coat hangers so fold them loosely between layers of white tissue paper, making sure that each fold is padded.

Store all items in a drawer, closet or other dark, dry and moth-free place. Check them regularly, refolding the larger garments. It is also a good idea to make small cloth sachets filled with dried lavender flowers to tuck into your drawer or cupboard along with your crochet as the smell deters moths.

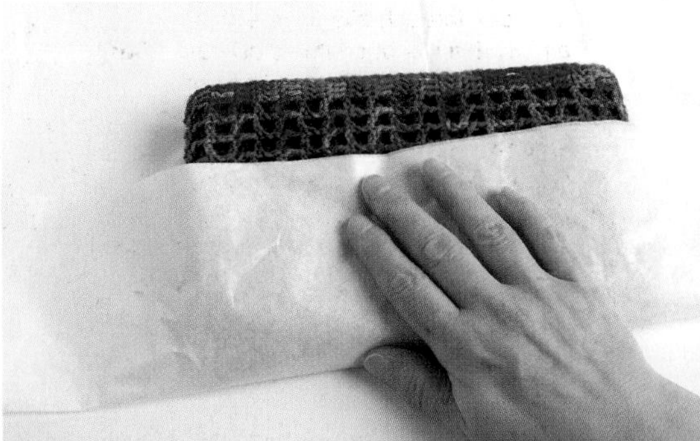

Size charts

Most crochet pattern instructions will provide written sizing information or a schematic with specific garment measurements. Check this information before you begin. The charts below give guidance on body measurements and corresponding garment sizes for babies, children, women and men. The length charts show average measurements and changes can be made in body and sleeve lengths to suit the individual.

Body length measurements for children

Waist length: actual body measurement

Hip length: 5 cm (2.5 in.) down from waist

Tunic length: 15 cm (6 in.) down from waist

Body length measurements for women

Waist length: actual body measurement

Hip length: 15 cm (6 in.) down from the waist

Tunic length: 28 cm (11 in.) down from the waist

Body length measurements for men

Men's length usually varies only 2.5–5 cm (1–2 in.) from the actual 'back hip length' measurement (see chart on page 154).

Standard body measurements and sizes

Baby	3 months	6 months	12 months	18 months	24 months
1. Chest (in.)	16	17	18	19	20
(cm)	40.5	43	45.5	48	50.5
2. Centre Back Neck-to-Cuff	10½	11½	12½	14	18
	26.5	29	31.5	35.5	45.5
3. Back Waist Length	6	7	7½	8	8½
	15.5	17.5	19	20.5	21.5
4. Cross Back (Shoulder to shoulder)	7¼	7¾	8¼	8½	8¾
	18.5	19.5	21	21.5	22
5. Sleeve Length to Underarm	6	6½	7½	8	8½
	15.5	16.5	19	20.5	21.5

Child	2	4	6	8	10	12	14	16
1. Chest (in.)	21	23	25	26½	28	30	31½	32½
(cm)	53	58.5	63.5	67	71	76	80	82.5
2. Centre Back Neck-to-Cuff	18	19½	20½	22	24	26	27	28
	45.5	49.5	52	56	61	66	68.5	71
3. Back Waist Length	8½	9½	10½	12½	14	15	15½	16
	21.5	24	26.5	31.5	35.5	38	39.5	40.5
4. Cross Back (Shoulder to shoulder)	9¼	9¾	10¼	10¾	11¼	12	12¼	13
	23.5	25	26	27	28.5	30.5	31	33
5. Sleeve Length to Underarm	8½	10½	11½	12½	13½	15	16	16½
	21.5	26.5	29	31.5	34.5	38	40.5	42

Woman	X-Small	Small	Medium	Large	1X	2X	3X	4X	5X
1. Bust (in.)	28–30	32–34	36–38	40–42	44–46	48–50	52–54	56–58	60–62
(cm)	71–76	81–86	91.5–96.5	101.5–106.5	111.5–117	122–127	132–137	142–147	152–158
2. Centre Back Neck-to-Cuff	27–27½	28–28½	29–29½	30–30½	31–31½	31½–32	32½–33	32½–33	33–33½
	68.5–70	71–72.5	73.5–75	76–77.5	78.5–80	80–81.5	82.5–84	82.5–84	84–85
3. Back Waist Length	16½	17	17¼	17½	17¾	18	18	18½	18½
	42	43	43.5	44.5	45	45.5	45.5	47	47
4. Cross Back (Shoulder to shoulder)	14–14½	14½–15	16–16½	17–17½	17½	18	18	18½	18½
	35.5–37	37–38	40.5–42	43–44.5	44.5	45.5	45.5	47	47
5. Sleeve Length to Underarm	16½	17	17	17½	17½	18	18	18½	18½
	42	43	43	44.5	44.5	45.5	45.5	47	47

Man		Small	Medium	Large	X-Large	XX-Large
1. Chest	(in.)	34–36	38–40	42–44	46–48	50–52
	(cm)	86–91.5	96.5–101.5	106.5–111.5	116.5–122	127–132
2. Centre Back Neck-to-Cuff	(in.)	32–32½	33–33½	34–34½	35–35½	36–36½
	(cm)	81–82.5	83.5–85	86.5–87.5	89–90	91.5–92.5
3. Back Hip Length	(in.)	25–25½	26½–26¾	27–27¼	27½–27¾	28–28½
	(cm)	63.5–64.5	67.5–68	68.5–69	69.5–70.5	71–72.5
4. Cross Back (Shoulder to shoulder)	(in.)	15½–16	16½–17	17½–18	18–18½	18½–19
	(cm)	39.5–40.5	42–43	44.5–45.5	45.5–47	47–48
5. Sleeve Length to Underarm	(in.)	18	18½	19½	20	20½
	(cm)	45.5	47	49.5	50.5	52

		Infant/Child				Adult	
		Small baby	Average baby	Toddler	Child	Woman	Man
6. Head circumference	(in.)	12	14	16	18	20	22
	(cm)	30.5	35.5	40.5	45.5	50.5	56

Stitch symbols

Bobble

Chain

Cluster

Treble crochet

Treble crochet in back loop

Treble crochet in front loop

Half treble crochet

Popcorn

Puff stitch

Change colour

Direction of working

Back post treble crochet

Front post treble crochet

Shell

Double crochet

Double crochet in back loop

Double crochet in front loop

Slip stitch

Spike stitch

Double treble crochet

Join in new colour

Fasten off

English/ American terminology

The patterns in this book use English terminology. Patterns published using American terminology can be very confusing because some American terms differ from the English system as shown below:

English	**American**
double crochet (dc)	single crochet (dc)
extended double (exdc)	extended single crochet (exsc)
half treble crochet (htc)	half double crochet (htr)
treble crochet (tr)	double crochet (dc)
double treble crochet (dtr)	treble crochet (tr)
triple treble crochet (trtr or ttr)	double treble crochet (dtr)

Arrangements of symbols

Description	Symbol	Explanation
symbols joined at the top	 	A group of symbols may be joined at the top, indicating that these stitches should be worked together as a cluster
symbols joined at the base		Symbols joined at the base should all be worked into the same stitch below.
symbols joined at the top and bottom		Sometimes a group of stitches is joined both at the top and the bottom, making a puff, bobble, or popcorn.
symbols on a curve		Sometimes symbols are drawn along a curve, depending on the construction of the stitch pattern.
distorted symbols		Some symbols may be lengthened, curved, or spiked to indicate where the hook is inserted below, as for spike stitches.

Standard laundering symbols

Hand Washing

Do not wash by hand or machine

Hand washable in warm water at the stated temperature

Machine Washing

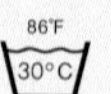

Machine washable in warm water at the stated temperature

Machine washable in warm water at the stated temperature, cool rinse, and short spin

104°F 40°C

Machine washable in warm water at the stated temperature, short spin

Bleaching

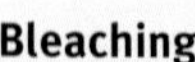

Bleaching not permitted

Bleaching permitted (with chlorine)

Pressing

Do not press

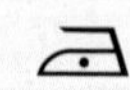

Press with a cool iron

Press with a warm iron

Press with a hot iron

Dry Cleaning

Do not dry clean

May be dry cleaned with all solutions

May be dry cleaned with perchlorethylene or fluorocarbon or petroleum-based solvents

May be dry cleaned with fluorocarbon or petroleum-based solvents only

Categories of yarn, gauge ranges, and recommended hook sizes

Yarn weight category	Super fine 1 SUPER FINE	Fine 2 FINE	Light 3 LIGHT	Medium 4 MEDIUM	Bulky 5 BULKY	Super bulky 6 SUPER BULKY
Type of yarns in category	Sock, fingering, baby	Sport, baby	DK, light worsted	Worsted, afghan, Aran	Chunky, craft, rug	Bulky, roving
Crochet tension ranges in double crochet to 10 cm (4 in.)	23–32 sts	16–20 sts	12–17 sts	11–14 sts	8–11 sts	5–9 sts
Recommended hook in metric size range	2.25–3.5 mm	3.5–4.5 mm	4.5–5.5 mm	5.5–6.5 mm	6.5–9 mm	9 mm and larger
Recommended hook US size range	B–1 to E–4	E–4 to 7	7 to I–9	I–9 to K–10½	K–10½ to M–13	M–13 and larger

The above reflect the most commonly used tensions and needle or hook sizes for specific yarn categories.

Conversions

Centimetres x 0.394 = inches

Grams x 0.035 = ounces

Inches x 2.54 = centimetres

Ounces x 28.6 = grams

Metres x 1.1 = yards

Yards x 0.91 = metres

Equivalent weights

20 g = ¾ oz

28 g = 1 oz

40 g = 1½ oz

50 g = 1¾ oz

60 g = 2 oz

100 g = 3½ oz

Index